Car Company

ouis, Mo.

f the Safety Car"

St. Louis Car Company

For most of its life, the St. Louis Car Co. was universally known as the *Quality Shops*. That name was one of the company's greatest assets, and helped assure the successful promotion of products not normally thought to be a part of the Car Company's range. This is the first of 105 motor bus bodies on Kelly-Springfield chassis, built in 1915 for the Pacific Motor Coach Co. of Los Angeles. It is shown being demonstrated at a convention later in the year.

The History of the

St. Louis Car Company

"Quality Shops"

by ANDREW D. YOUNG and
EUGENE F. PROVENZO, JR.

BERKELEY Howell-North Books CALIFORNIA

Printed and bound in the United States of America

Library of Congress Catalog Card No. 78-52511

ISBN 0-8310-7114-1

Published by Howell-North Books

1050 Parker Street, Berkeley, California 94710

Contents

A 1919 St. Louis Car Co. Birney car demonstrator. These one-man lightweight safety cars had a reputation for being cheaply built, and the *Quality Shops* slogan seen in the car's destination indicator must have been reassuring to those customers who had doubts about the vehicle's durability.

Acknowledgments

WE WOULD LIKE to acknowledge our appreciation to the many people who have assisted us with this book. Of greatest importance was the initial gift of the St. Louis Car Co.'s surviving business records and photographic files to Washington University Archives, St. Louis, by Mr. Edwin B. Meissner Jr., on behalf of General Steel Industries. Without access to these materials, this study would have been most difficult to complete. Mrs. Beryl Manne, Washington University's Archivist, encouraged us both throughout the research, as did several former Car Company officers, who were very generous of their time in granting us interviews. These gentlemen were (in alphabetical order) Richard Ashby, William F. Kamman, William Fitzgerald and Severin Merz. Mrs. Edwin B. Meissner too was of great help to us and consented to a lengthy interview.

We are especially indebted to Mr. Edwin B. Meissner Jr., whose interest and enthusiasm for this project has been constant and unwavering. He has continually made himself available to answer questions of detail, as well as check innumerable facts and introduce us to others who could further help us.

We are obliged to Mr. Richard Kobusch of St. Louis, grandson of George J. Kobusch, for talking to us, and to Mr. E. I. Robinson of Mt. Vernon, Illinois for providing the letters that form a part of Chapter Six. Encouragement and critical comment on the draft manuscript was provided by Mr. John H. White Jr., Curator of Land Transportation at the National Museum of History and Technology, Smithsonian Institution, Washington, D.C., and by Dr. Harold E. Cox of Wilkes College, Wilkes-Barre, Pa. We are grateful to both.

Dr. Glen Holt of Washington University's History Department, initiated the original negotiations which led to the University accepting the materials which now form part of the University Archive's St. Louis Car Company collection. Dr. Raymond Callahan of Washington University's Graduate Institute of Education encouraged Mr. Provenzo to work with Mr. Young on this book, while at the same time completing his doctorate. We are obliged to them both.

Early photographs were made available to us by Mr. William J. Clouser, Mrs. Mary Roberts and Mr. Bill Hoss of the National Museum of Transport, St. Louis, by Mr. Edwin J. Klasky of St. Louis, and by Mr. Kevin T. Farrell of Boston, and their efforts on our behalf are greatly appreciated. Mr. J. H. Price, Historical Features Editor of *Modern Tramway*, London, England, and Mr. Sigurd Hilkenbach of Berlin, Germany, helped unravel several knotty problems, while Mr. Berl Katz, also of the National Museum of Transport, St. Louis, indicated the existence and whereabouts of a vital piece of research material now incorporated in Chapter 3. Mr. Walter F. Robinson Jr., of Bellevue, Washington, provided many articles from the automobile press concerning the American Mors and the Standard Six. Mr. F. Travers Burgess, patent attorney of St. Louis, provided a copy of the Robertson patent from which the description in this book is drawn, and also compiled the list of Car Company patents reproduced in the Appendix. The serials department staff of the St. Louis Public Library allowed us access to their collection of early magazines and newspapers, from which much of the Car Company's early history was drawn. Our thanks to all of them.

All photographs not otherwise acknowledged, are from the St. Louis Car Company collection, Washington University Archives, St. Louis, and we are grateful to both Washington University and their Archives for allowing us to use them. When the St. Louis Car Co.'s plant at Baden was opened in 1899, the company began to maintain a record of the contracts received. This record was strictly for internal use, but it was maintained without a break until the company closed in 1973. This record, known as the "job order book," was of major importance in our research, but we have reluctantly decided not to reproduce it in this book. We have done so because we found a great number of inconsistencies, inaccuracies and gaps. Publication of the job order book in its present state would put those faults in permanent form. Accurate surveys of the St. Louis Car Co.'s production are currently being made, and the authors will be glad to refer any interested reader to those in charge of the project. Finally, our thanks to our wives, Evelyn Young and Asterie Provenzo, for their patience, forebearance and encouragement given throughout the long period during which this book was researched and written.

Andrew D. Young, *St. Louis, Missouri*

Dr. Eugene F. Provenzo, Jr.,
School of Education, University of Miami,
Coral Gables, Florida

May, 1977

Introduction

St. Louis was not much more than a frontier town when Missouri was admitted to the Union in 1820, and its subsequent growth was largely based on its unique position in the American lumber trade. Rafts of timber from Wisconsin's great forests were floated down the Mississippi to St. Louis, and once there, a variety of factories, yards and shops were waiting to process the wood and distribute it throughout the nation.

By 1845 St. Louis had grown sufficiently to warrant a horse bus service. This in turn led to the provision of a streetcar line in 1859, and from that time on, the convenience offered by reliable urban transit was reflected both in the continued outward growth of the city, and the astonishing proliferation of transit companies catering to that need. By 1875, over 17 companies had franchises to operate horse buses or streetcars within the city. While this tremendous growth in transit facilities was a phenomenon common enough elsewhere, St. Louis had by far the largest number of independent companies competing for business of any city in the nation. Their incessant demands for new and better vehicles, the distance from the established builders in the East, and the increased nationwide demand for ready-made cars, prompted St. Louis capital into the financing of streetcar manufacturers.

In the 19th century wood was the universal car building material, a commodity which St. Louis had in abundance, as well as men skilled in the working of it. Thus it is not surprising that St. Louis had one of the very first street railway car building firms in the country, established in 1858 by Andrew White. While his business was not at first confined wholly to streetcars, by the 1870s his firm was building virtually nothing else, so great was the demand, and by the beginning of 1891, the St. Louis area could boast at least five establishments primarily or exclusively devoted to streetcar manufacture.

The presence of these companies in or near the city led to the location of many other businesses in the area devoted to ancillary supplies for street railways. Firms in this trade included the Heine Boiler Co., the John O'Brien Boiler Works, the Scarritt Seat Co., and the St. Louis Car Wheel Co. Other major firms in the area included street railway parts distributors and contractors such as the Wagner Electric Co. and Arthur S. Partridge Co. Initially the business of these firms had been confined to the Midwest, but later their markets expanded to take in the southern and western regions of the country, and in some cases national distribution was achieved.

With the acquisition of the lucrative eastern market in the 1890s, St. Louis came to dominate the streetcar manufacturing industry of the U.S.A., and maintained that position for many years. The city's natural geographic advantages were the most obvious reasons for this dominance, but its central location as a national distribution center, and the presence of a large immigrant population from South Germany, skilled in foundry and woodworking techniques were other factors which contributed to the city's leadership in the industry.

By 1900 over $5 million was invested in St. Louis streetcar manufacturing companies, over $10 million worth of cars were built, and more than 2500 men were employed, with salaries exceeding $500,000 each year.[1] Not only did the city supply cars to the domestic market, but there was also a large international trade, with cars being sent to Argentina, Australia, Canada, Cuba, England, France, Germany, Hawaii, Ireland, Mexico, Portugal, Puerto Rico, Russia, South Africa and Trinidad.[2]

How had all this happened? In the case of St. Louis, there was no completely clear-cut answer, but much of the industry's expansion in the city had to do with the character and personality of one Frederick Brownell.

Brownell had joined Andrew White in the late 1860s as a hired hand, a man of great ability and considerable ambition. By 1875, Brownell was not only in partnership with White, but had managed to change the name of the firm to Brownell and White, a sure indication of where the money and brains of the business now lay. Frederick Brownell was a fine craftsman, but as he got older he became a highly conservative individual who resisted change wherever he could. He was notorious in the trade for refusing to fill orders on the grounds that they were unsuited to his designs, which he was not prepared to modify, being perfectly satisfied as to their excellence and quality. It is to his credit as a builder that so many of his customers were prepared to tolerate this attitude, for his staff certainly couldn't. In his refusal to change his designs to more closely match the needs of the 1880s, and in his unwillingness to delegate any authority within his firm, he was continually in conflict with his staff. More than once these conflicts led to rupture, and in turn these ruptures led to the proliferation of new car building establishments in St. Louis. The Laclede Car Co. was formed in the aftermath of just such a rupture in 1883 by ex-Brownell men, who felt that in neglecting his own opportunities, he was opening up the chance of profit for them, a chance which they readily seized. And the St. Louis Car Co., the subject of this book, was established during 1887 in the wake of yet another of these Brownell conflicts.

J. H. KOBUSCH

FOUNDER OF THE ST. LOUIS CAR COMPANY

CHAPTER 1

By 1887, St. Louis could already boast of two major streetcar manufacturers within the city limits. Was there really room for a third? There was indeed, said a faction in the Brownell Co. Once again, a number of Brownell's men were beginning to feel that the personal idiosyncrasies of their chief were leading him to neglect his market, and that their opportunity lay before them. J. H. Kobusch, one of Brownell's financial backers, and Peter Kling, Brownell's plant superintendent, decided to sever their connection with him and form their own company, to be plentifully stocked with men who would accompany them from Brownell.

Shortly after the withdrawal of Kobusch and Kling from Brownell, the St. Louis Car Co. was formed. It was organized as a joint stock company

> to manufacture and sell all kinds of vehicles, street cars and all other kinds of rolling stock of street and steam railways.[1]

The company was officially incorporated on April 4, 1887. On that date $25,000 in capital was subscribed for, and paid. The money was divided into 250 shares of $100 par value and distributed among the seven St. Louis stockholders, each of whom was also elected to the Board of Directors of the new company. Daniel McAllister held 20 shares, Henry Maune 10, Julius Lefmann and Henry Schroeder each had 30 shares, Charles Ernst had five, Peter Kling 75 and William Lefmann 80 shares.

The first company meeting was held a few days later in their offices at 913 North Market Street, and at that meeting the bylaws were adopted and the officers elected. Daniel McAllister was elected president, Julius Lefmann secretary, and Peter Kling treasurer. Nothing is known of Lefmann and McAllister, and it is assumed they came with Kling from Brownell.

Kling indeed was the new company's pivotal man. It was upon his shoulders that the new company's future rested. Kling had started his professional life as a self-taught wagon builder but quickly became a skilled mechanic. By the mid-1880s he had developed ideas on streetcar design which he believed to be far superior to those used in other plants, or indeed at Brownell. Without a chance to experiment with them at Brownell, it is hardly surprising he was ready to join Kobusch in establishing a new company, and while his new ideas had not yet been tested commercially, the St. Louis Car Co's. backers obviously believed they would work.

By July 1887, the new company was beginning to take shape.

> St. Louis Car Co. . . . has let the contract for building their new shops, which are to be specially adapted for the manufacture of streetcars. The shops are to be entirely of brick and will contain an area of 48,370 square feet.[2]

The buildings were to cost $20,000, a considerable sum for the period and 80% of the new company's capitalization. Power for the machinery was to come from a 60-hp engine and by July 30, 1887, the plant would be ready to open. July also saw the placing of the first advertisements, which misleadingly suggested that the company already possessed a plant which was the "largest and best equipped in the country," and further stated that on receipt of orders, which were currently being sought, manufacture would begin on August 1.[3]

Business did not in fact start on that date, but by the end of the month the buildings were complete, a stock of dry lumber had been acquired and ten pattern makers hired. The activity of the preceding months, however, had totally depleted the company's reserves of capital, and on August 12 capital was increased from $25,000 to $50,000. The financial statement filed in connection with the capital increase showed the company's assets as being $159,503, and its liabilities as $104,210.[4] With this new money, the company was ready to start work in September.

The plant was located at 3023 North Broadway, an ideal location for a business that needed lumber in great amounts, for it was in this part of

THE

ST. LOUIS CAR CO.,

St. Louis, Mo.,

BUILDERS OF

Street Cars

OF EVERY DESCRIPTION.

Works among the most complete in this country.
Ready for business about August 1st.

Announcement of company's formation, June, 1887. *(Street Railway Journal)*

the city that the log rafts from Wisconsin ended their long Mississippi journey. The main building was 150′ long and three stories high. The first floor contained the mill, where the wood was dressed, and other basic procedures dealt with. The second floor contained the erecting shop, while the third floor housed the machine shop, paint shop and blacksmith's shop.[5] All three floors were connected by elevators, large enough to move complete streetcars.

Apart from those documents compulsorily registered with the State of Missouri, no company records survive from this period, but in October, the *Street Railway Journal* did note that there was sufficient work on hand in the new plant "to keep them busy for months to come," further noting that the St. Louis Car Co. could finish work within four to six weeks of receiving the order. Among the first cars completed were two 34′ cars for Memphis, Tennessee, four 12′ cars for Ashland, Wisconsin, and four cars for "an electric railway in Lafayette, Indiana." There were also orders from campanies in Wichita and Kingman, Kansas, Butte, Montana, Pine Bluff, Arkansas, Shreveport, Louisiana, a number of California operators, and the local Benton-Bellefontaine line in St. Louis. The first completed cars were shipped from the plant during October 1887.[6]

The presence of this new and aggressive company created a highly charged competitive atmosphere in St. Louis. Brownell in retaliation announced its intention to build sufficient plant immediately to double its output and thus put the new company out of business, while Laclede was so intimidated that it managed to solve the financial problems which had kept it out of business since January 1887, and resumed production in September, seemingly in self-defense!

In spite of its full order books, the end of 1887 saw the new company still chronically short of cash. The $50,000 of working capital had to suffice to finance work in hand, pay suppliers' bills, and meet their 250-man-strong payroll. Production capacity was already estimated at over 400 cars per year, and not surprisingly then, the St. Louis Car Co. experienced its second financial crisis at the end of 1887, after only a few months in business. Orders continued to arrive with undiminished rapidity, and new capital again had to be quickly found.[7]

It was at this juncture that the Kobusch family decided to take a more active interest in the Car Co. Though no Kobusch appears in the documents relating to the increase of capital from $50,000 to $150,000 in 1888, it was in that year that George J. Kobusch was appointed, and took up his duties, as company secretary.

This infusion of fresh money aided the company greatly, and its benefits were quickly to be seen. By the end of 1888 St. Louis Car Co. had become a major business, and one of the industry's largest manufacturers. This though was a situation as much due to good luck as it was to good management, for the application of mechanical traction to street railway cars had invigorated a hitherto stagnant business. The market for new streetcars had suddenly begun to grow, and the Car Company was alive to the possibilities, so that its earliest years were busy and output of cars was high. The *Street Railway Journal* noted that the plant had been full of orders in 1888, many being for California operators.[8] Major car orders of 1888 included 30 open cars for the Cass Ave. and Fairground Railway of St. Louis, 35 forty passenger open cars for the Citizens' Railway of Indianapolis, and a number of 34′ long double deck cars for San Diego. There were many repeat orders, but the year's most interesting job was the

Car Company plant in 1887.

Car Company plant in 1889.

Car Company plant in 1890.

completion of an 1887 order from the Topeka Rapid Transit Co. for 30 electric cars.

During 1888 it was decided to diversify the company's activities, and ancillary supply production was decided upon. The company bought the rights to the Tom Johnson farebox in May 1888, and began its manufacture shortly thereafter.[9] A little later in the year the company contracted with Short Co. to produce cars and motor parts, for the Short "series" electrical system, designed to run a number of streetcars simultaneously on one electric line independently of each other, in the days before series-parallel control was proven to be workable. It is unfortunate that the agreement between the Car Co. and Short has been lost for it seems to have committed St. Louis Car Co. to make gears for the Short series motor.

> St. Louis Car Co. report they are very busy, and the outlook seems to be favorable . . . They are making gears for the Short Electric System which they have adopted as their standard and have on hand work amounting to $80,000, which will all be complete within four months. They state Sidney H. Short will have their road ready in St. Louis by December 5 (1888) and it will no doubt be a success.[10]

The Short series system proved a technical failure, but the Short Co. had other activities in which it engaged. Indeed its reputation was largely based on its being a very successful early manufacturer of electrical apparatus for street railways until its sale to the Thomson-Houston Co. in mid-1892, a company which shortly thereafter became one of the constituent parts of the newly-created giant General Electric. Consequently the relationship between St. Louis Car Co. and Short was healthy and profitable in spite of the debacle with the "series" system.

1889 was another good year for the Car Company. In September it was announced that a new building was to be erected, and large quantities of extra machinery purchased, in view of the great number of orders already on hand.[11] The expansion was certainly justified, for orders in 1889 exceeded the 400 car per year capacity of the plant. These were not just repeat orders, but orders from new customers throughout the entire country including, Seattle, Los Angeles, Denver, Peoria, Cincinatti and Wheeling. And there were the almost inevitable local orders which grew ever larger.

An extensive account of the St. Louis Car Co's. plant and production methods was published in 1890, and it is apparent that manufacturing technique had not changed radically in the two and a half years of the Car Company's life, despite the ever-larger order books.

> The buildings are located well out on Broadway . . . only the office however fronts on this street. The main buildings are hidden from view by the houses which flank the offices on either side. Entering and passing through the offices . . . is a large open yard . . . Beyond, and on the next block are the extensive lumber yards . . . said to contain a stock worth $40,000.
>
> The buildings are of brick. The main building is 60′ x 150′, three stories and a basement. The paint shop and the blacksmith shop occupy a two-story building, while the boiler house and machine shop are only one story. The entire plant is heated by steam and lighted with . . . electric lights. The paint shop is warmed by direct radiation, and the other rooms by Smith's hot air blast system. The woodworking department occupies the entire first floor of the building and has first class equipment . . . The shafting is all placed under the floor, and every machine has a pipe connecting it with the Smith dust collecting system. Over the boilers and opening into this room is the kiln for drying the lumber . . . An elevator 40′ long and 12′ wide carries the cars to and from the various floors, and there is also a small elevator for lifting the material.
>
> The set-up room is on the second floor and it is kept at a uniform temperature of 60°F. This is claimed to be a great advantage for the stock, being kept perfectly dry, is not liable to shrink or crack after being put into service. "Build to last" is a motto with this firm and it is impressed on every workman. All the joints are covered with whitelead before being put together, and the side panels are lined with canvas glued on, and the sills

Car Company advertisement of 1890. *(Street Railway Journal)*

are all painted on the top before the floors of the car or the platform are put down. The side panels before being put on are warped to their proper shape by being laid over a series of steam pipes arranged in the form of an arch. The cabinet work, including the varnishing, is done on the third floor. A close room is partitioned off, free from dust, in which the polished surfaces are finished. The inside work receives three coats of the best English varnish, that made by Noble and Hall. We are told that two cars of the same size may be built, that differ $300 in price, the difference depending on the character of the inside finish. There are two paintshops, one 70′ x 180′ the other 70′ x 80′. The blacksmith shop is 75′ x 100′ and among the tools we note one 25-ton press, two lathes, one boring mill, a furnace for heavy forging, one steam hammer and six forges. The company turn and fit their own wheels[12]. . .

Obviously the company had been established with the very best of equipment, and with the most modern woodworking techniques. With so many experienced men in charge of the company's affairs, it was hardly surprising that the high quality of their work was evident from the beginning. Normally St. Louis Car Co. cars were panelled with birds-eye maple ceilings, fitted with solid mahogany door frames, and sported carved panels at the seat ends. Many early cable and electric cars were vestibuled, since it was felt that their increased speed made it necessary to shield the driver against the cold. Some cars had window curtains, usually of Russian leather trimmed with silk and mounted on roller lock fixtures.

By 1890 the success of the St. Louis Car Co. was no longer in doubt, and J. H. Kobusch, possibly on his son's insistence, ousted the incumbent president and treasurer of the Car Company and himself assumed their offices. Kling, the ex-treasurer did not however leave the company, as he was instead promoted by Kobusch to company vice-president and general manager, but from this time on, the St. Louis Car Co. was owned by the Kobusch family.

For some reason now lost to us, J. H. Kobusch soon gave up the post of treasurer in favor of his son George, and while remaining company president, preferred to remain largely in the background, devoting his attention to his other successful business affairs. Thus in all day-to-day matters, the company became the prime interest and concern of George J. Kobusch.

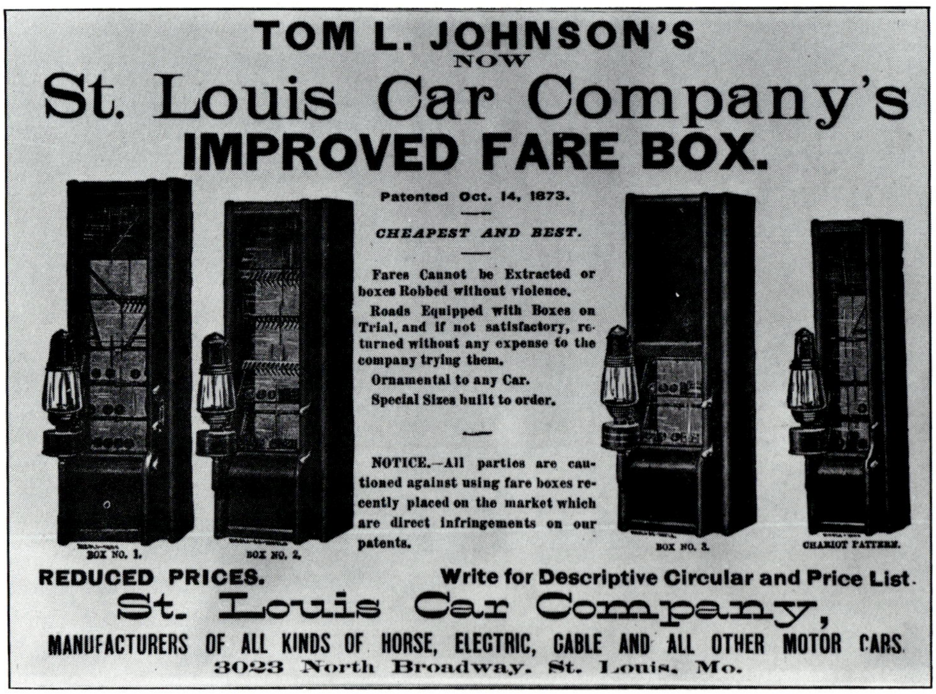

Advertisement for the Johnson farebox, 1888. *(Street Railway Journal)*

CHAPTER 2

Crowned by the placing of the first export orders, 1890 was an excellent year. Thirty cars were ordered by Mexico City, and two by the town of Victoria, British Columbia, though it is thought all the vehicles were horse cars.[1] This was a good omen for the year to follow as 1891 turned out to be the Car Company's first boom year. By May over 300 cars were on order, as yet unbuilt, among them the largest single order to date: 120 closed trailer cars for the St. Louis and Suburban Railway's cable lines. Under construction then were 25 very large electric cars for St. Louis' Union Depot Railway, with a seating capacity in excess of eighty, while eight similar cars were also being built for the Put-In Bay Electric Railway of Ohio.[2] At the same time Vice President Kling was in Mexico, ostensibly to supervise the shipment of cars ordered earlier, but in fact negotiating another sale, with which he returned a little later.[3]

The success of the Johnson fare box, and the work done for Short had firmly established the need to stay in the ancillary supply business, but with Short products no longer available for distribution, a new line had to be found. Kling was equal to the task, and with the inadequacy of horse-car trucks to stand up to service in an electrically powered car now almost a scandal in the industry, his design ingenuity was throughout most of 1891 devoted to creating an electric car truck suitable for the purpose. By the end of the year the first St. Louis Car Co. electric truck was patented and introduced to the market in limited quantities. The company's first commercially produced truck arrived in April 1892 and after some problems in service, the design was modified, and a replacement brought out in November.

> Simplicity of construction is one of the . . . features of the truck. There are but four steel castings, one of which is at each support of the car body . . . A heavy spiral spring is interposed between each oil box and its accompanying casting. These springs enable the entire truck to act as an equalizing bar . . . The old truck . . . did not possess this . . . feature . . . The wheels can be removed for minor repairs or other work by simply unscrewing the nuts which hold to the truck the plate between each oil box . . . In the old truck, there were four motor hangars, but in the present one, there are only two, of flexible hardened steel . . . The truck has been tested at the Washington University of St. Louis by the Shickle, Harrison and Howard Iron Co. of the same city. It showed a tensile strength of 80,000 lbs. . . . Tests are now being made on the Union Depot and Bellefontaine railways of St. Louis.[4]

In the early 1890s, the average size of an order had begun to increase substantially. In 1887, an order for 20 cars had been regarded as normal. By 1892, an order for 50 cars or more was commonplace, and thus the construction and opening of a new paint shop at the plant in mid-1892 was a welcome, if minor, relief from the pressures of inadequate space, for it increased the company's painting capacity by over 100 cars, at a time when streetcar painting was akin to a minor art form in its complexity.

By this time competition between the St. Louis streetcar manufacturers was intense and probably to the advantage of none. It is surprising therefore that local consolidation did not occur until the turn of the century, though there had been rumors of merger schemes before then. A typical rumor of merger was circulated in 1892 by the *Street Railway Journal* which reported that a group of promoters was seeking to make a special issue of bonds to the bondholders of the individual streetcar manufacturing concerns. The issue apparently was to be backed by the financial reputations of Henry E. Scott and W. H. Thomson. In connection with this scheme, the *Street Railway Journal* published financial statistics on the companies involved and it is striking that despite the prosperity of the previous years, the trade depression of the period was temporarily affecting the com-

(Top) Electric mail car, 1891. *(Street Railway Journal)*

(Center) Grip car #20, trailer car #122 of the Missouri Railroad Co., St. Louis, built in the early 1890s. These cars were not built by St. Louis Car Co. but their design is typical of the many cable cars that were. *(William J. Clouser collection)*

(Left) Car #4 of the St. Louis Railroad's Baden & Cemeteries line at Baden, sometime in 1894. Typical of the early electrics built by the Car Co., this vehicle is mounted on a St. Louis #8 truck.

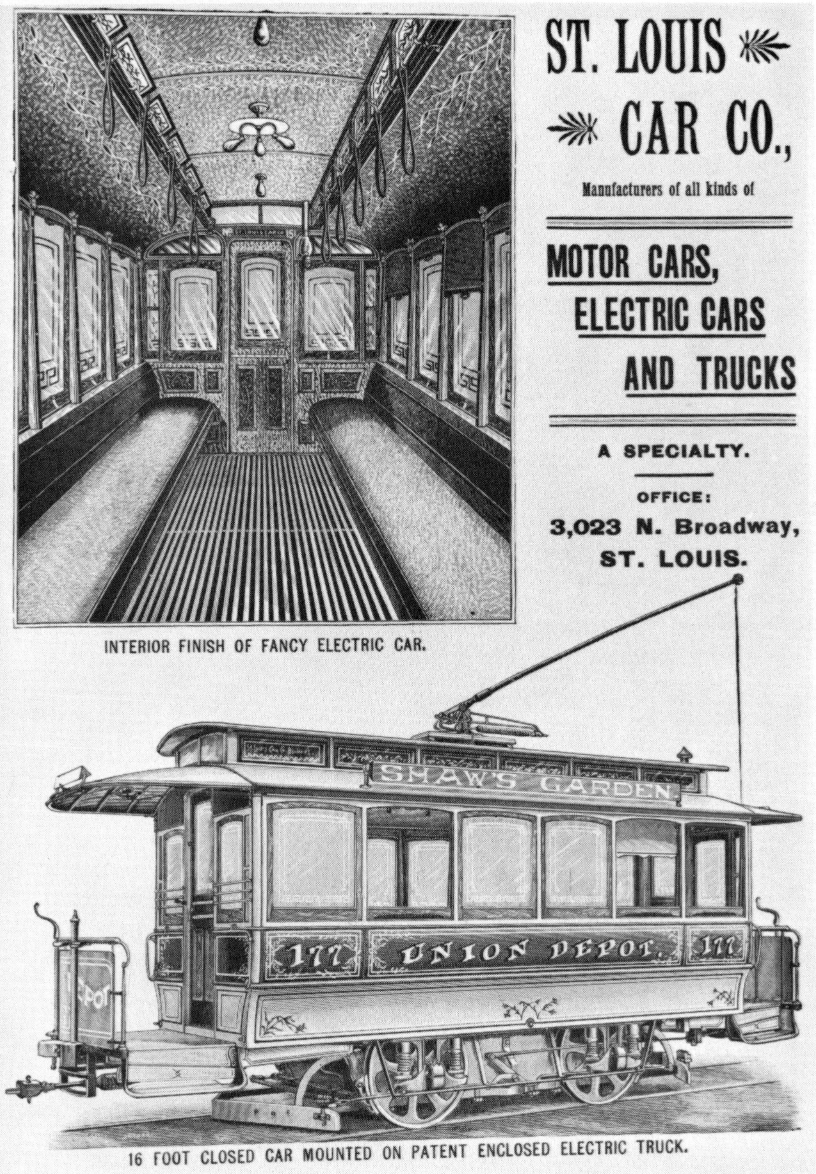

This advertisement was placed in every *Street Railway Journal* to be published between 1890 and 1896.

Union Depot Railroad #375, and a bob-tail horsecar of the Mound City Railroad Co., St. Louis, 1895. *(William J. Clouser collection)*

1895-built car for the Lindell Railway of St. Louis, seen in the colors of the St. Louis Transit Co. in 1905. *(United Railways of St. Louis, Edwin J. Klasky collection)*

Earlier cars built for the Union Depot Co. were mounted on the Robinson Radial #30A truck. This is car #220 in 1893. *(Street Railway Journal)*

United Railways of San Francisco private car "Hermosa" was built at North Broadway in 1896. Originally on a single truck, it received double trucks shortly afterwards, but was otherwise unchanged when photographed a few years later. *(Lorin Silleman, Edwin J. Klasky collection)*

These three woodcuts show typical designs built at North Broadway in the early 1890s, for St. Louis operators. *(National Museum of Transport)*

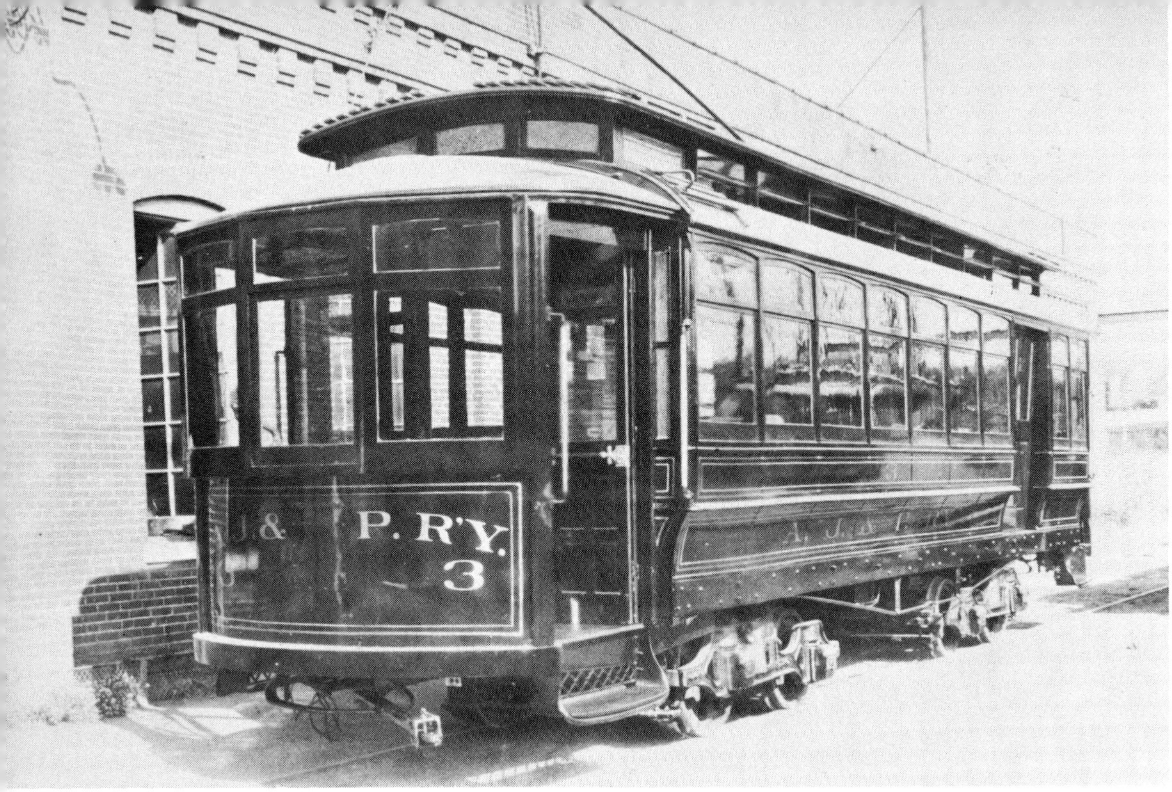

A typical wooden-bodied suburban car of the late 1890s, with small windows, small platforms and double trucks. Alton, Jacksonville and Peoria #3, ex-United Railways of St. Louis #345, shown outside that company's shops in 1908, prior to delivery to its new owner. *(United Railways of St. Louis, Edwin J. Klasky collection)*

panies. Moreover they were all severely undercapitalized, and seemed to be making little attempt to raise further money. St. Louis Car Co. with $150,000 of issued stock had but $88,000 of it paid up, despite an 1891 profit of $187,000. The new American Car Co., formed in 1891, had issued stock of $600,000, but almost all of this was tied up in the costs of its new plant. Brownell, with capital of $100,000 was said to utilize double that amount (probably as a result of developing the designs for his "Accelerator" car, the only significant design innovation of his career) while Laclede with $80,000 was in a similar position.[5] A few months later, the consolidation scheme apparently forgotten, *Street Railway Journal* again took a look at the St. Louis streetcar manufacturing industry and this time published a handful of production figures, the only ones known to survive from this period. The magazine suggested that over 350 cars a month were being produced by St. Louis Car Co., Brownell and Laclede together during 1892, and that figure represented a 30 percent increase in production over previous years.[6]

Consolidation was hardly an issue at that time however. With every manufacturing company in the city a different Brownell faction in its origin, judgment in these matters was swayed by emotion and not objectivity. Moreover despite the slight setback during the Depression of 1892/3 for the street railway industry, this was a time of unparalleled prosperity. Streetcar companies across the world were seeking to electrify their existing routes and build new lines as quickly as possible. New cars were required in abundance, and throughout the 1890s at least there was a need for every manufacturer in the car building trade, judging by the performance of those companies in that decade. Certainly that was true so far as the St. Louis Car Co. was concerned. With orders such as the 250 New Orleans cars in its hands at the end of 1891, St. Louis Car Co. could see absolutely no benefits in any kind of merger. By its own estimate, it was turning out 100 cars per month by January 1892, and in that year at any one time had orders for 400 new cars waiting for erection space. With the factory working day and night, consolidation was out of the question for the St. Louis Car Co.[7]

It was difficult enough to add the new facilities required for electric car production on the scale now needed, with the limited site then available. The plant had after all been laid out to build horse and cable cars, and at a far slower rate than was now demanded. Thus in the late spring of 1892, the company had to come to an arrangement with the city to add a testing facility for the electric cars.

> On the streets, in the immediate vicinity of the works, tracks are to be laid and overhead strung, so as to try out every new car turned out of the shops before it is shipped.[8]

At the same time, however cramped the facilities, the Car Company was prepared to work exceedingly quickly if necessary.

> On June 14, 1892, the car house of the St. Louis and Suburban Railway at De Hodiamont burned . . . (and) all cars were destroyed . . . As soon as all hope was abandoned, orders were placed for forty motor cars with double trucks.[9]

All were delivered by the end of the summer.

Further relief for the facilities was obtained during 1892 by the lease of additional working space from the St. Louis Railroad Co., but such was the rate of growth of the electric trolley car in the world that throughout 1894 the Car Company generally had between 500 and 700 cars on order as yet unbuilt.[10]

In 1894, the Car Company's single truck was modified substantially, and renamed truck #8.

> The extended spring base was not found long enough in the discarded type, and a new casting has been adopted so that . . . elliptic springs can be mounted thereon, and prevent the car from pitching.[11]
>
> In the old truck, the concussion spring over each oil box brought back the disadvantage of oscillation of the car body, to eliminate which the truck was designed . . . and lengthening the wheelbase has done away with this, although the concussion springs are retained. The four castings are riveted together with distance pieces in order to make any desired wheelbase . . . Over 500 of the old-style trucks have been sold.[12]

At the same time, Kling was experimenting with his new design of double truck which came on the market later in the year.[13]

The Car Company regarded its future prospects as highly encouraging, and present business as "brisk." It had every right to be encouraged.

> The Company . . . has recently received a contract from the People's Traction Co. of Philadelphia for 400 electric motor cars . . . One half will be closed cars with 20′ bodies, and the remainder open cars with 28′ bodies.[14]

What this report didn't say however was that the last 150 cars were optional, and as it turned out the customer did not exercise the option so that only 250 cars were built. However a year later in 1895, 300 cars were ordered by the Philadelphia Traction Co., while a great number of other cars were sold to Baltimore, Boston, Camden, various New York companies, and Paterson. The years 1894 and 1895 thus saw the Eastern market finally penetrated by the Car Company and from then until it went out of business, the company's market was national in scope.

Besides standard orders, however, many customers demanded custom work. An 1893 order from the Union Depot Railroad Co. of St. Louis was typical. These 28′ cars (sixty in number), were equipped with wide-domed roofs of cherry wood, ceilings of white maple veneer, and were mounted on Robinson radial trucks. Similar 28′ cars built for the Lindell Railway of St. Louis had an interior finish of antique oak and cherry.[15] The variations in finish were innumerable, although any change from standard inevitably meant an increase in the cost. Yet for some, cost was nothing if in return they could get the very best. Typically, customers in that category were those who bought private cars, vehicles where opulence and luxury reigned supreme. The idea of the private car came from the mainline railroads, but with the street railway industry seemingly even more of a moneymaker than the railroads, private cars became fashionable among that industry's leaders. One of the first such orders received at the Car Company came in 1893, when the Wilkes-Barre and Wyoming Valley RR. ordered a car with a mahogany interior finish, a floor covered with Wilton carpet, and willow chairs and a settee upholstered in white damask. The windows were of the "heaviest French plate glass" while the window sashes were finished in natural cherry. There was even a ceil-

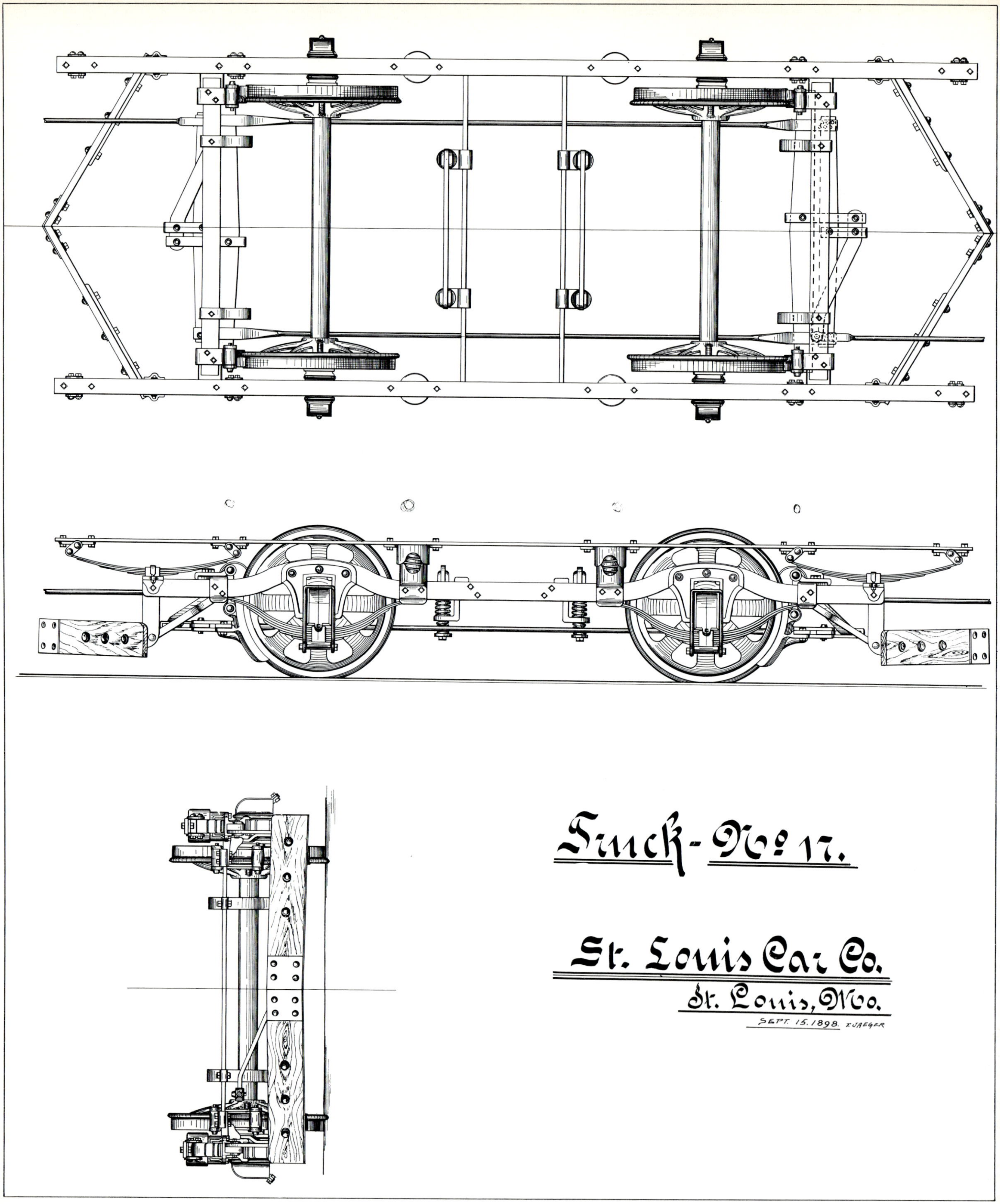
Truck - No. 17.
St. Louis Car Co.
St. Louis, Mo.
SEPT. 15. 1898. F. JAEGER

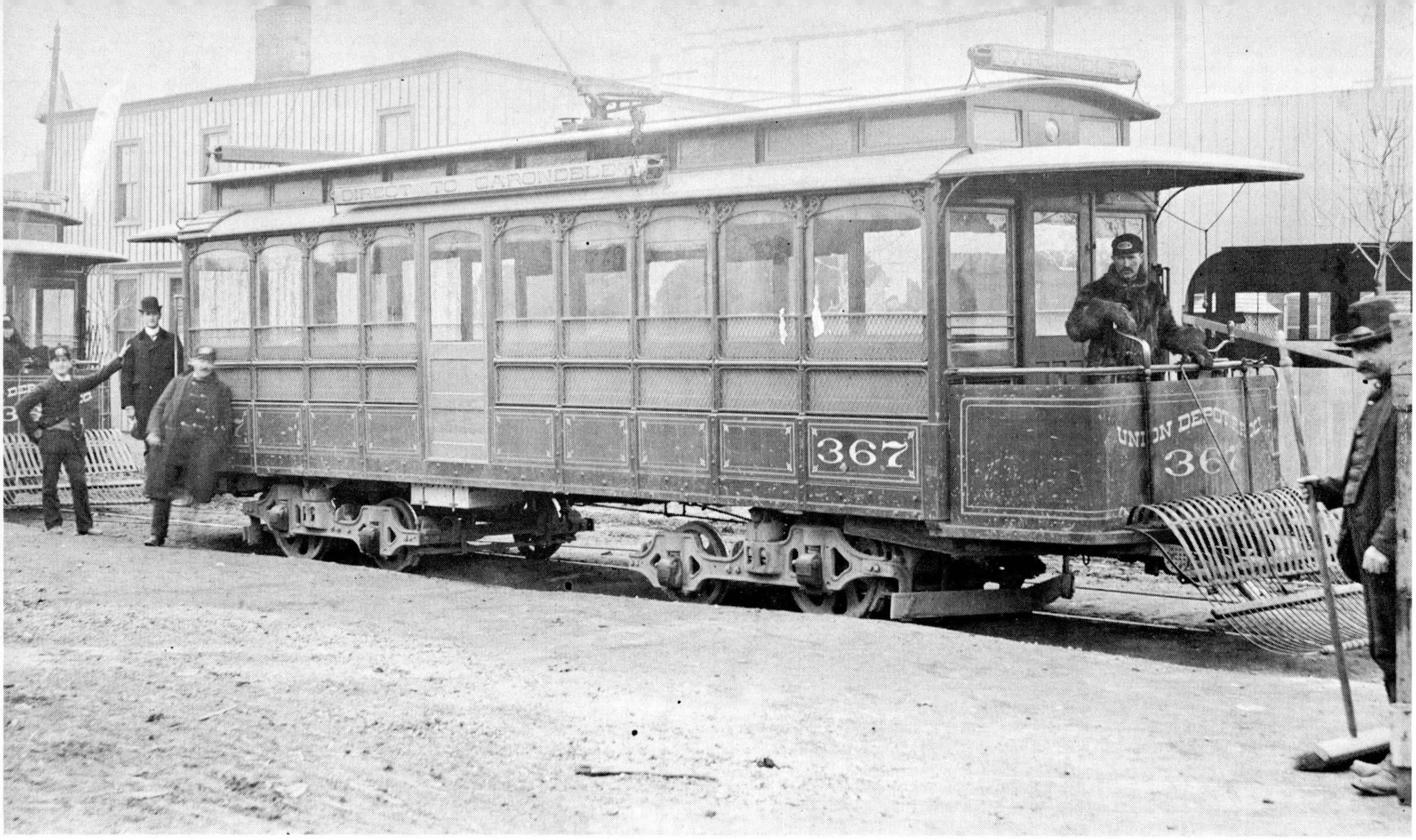

Double-truck car #367 of the Union Depot Railroad, St. Louis, 1895.

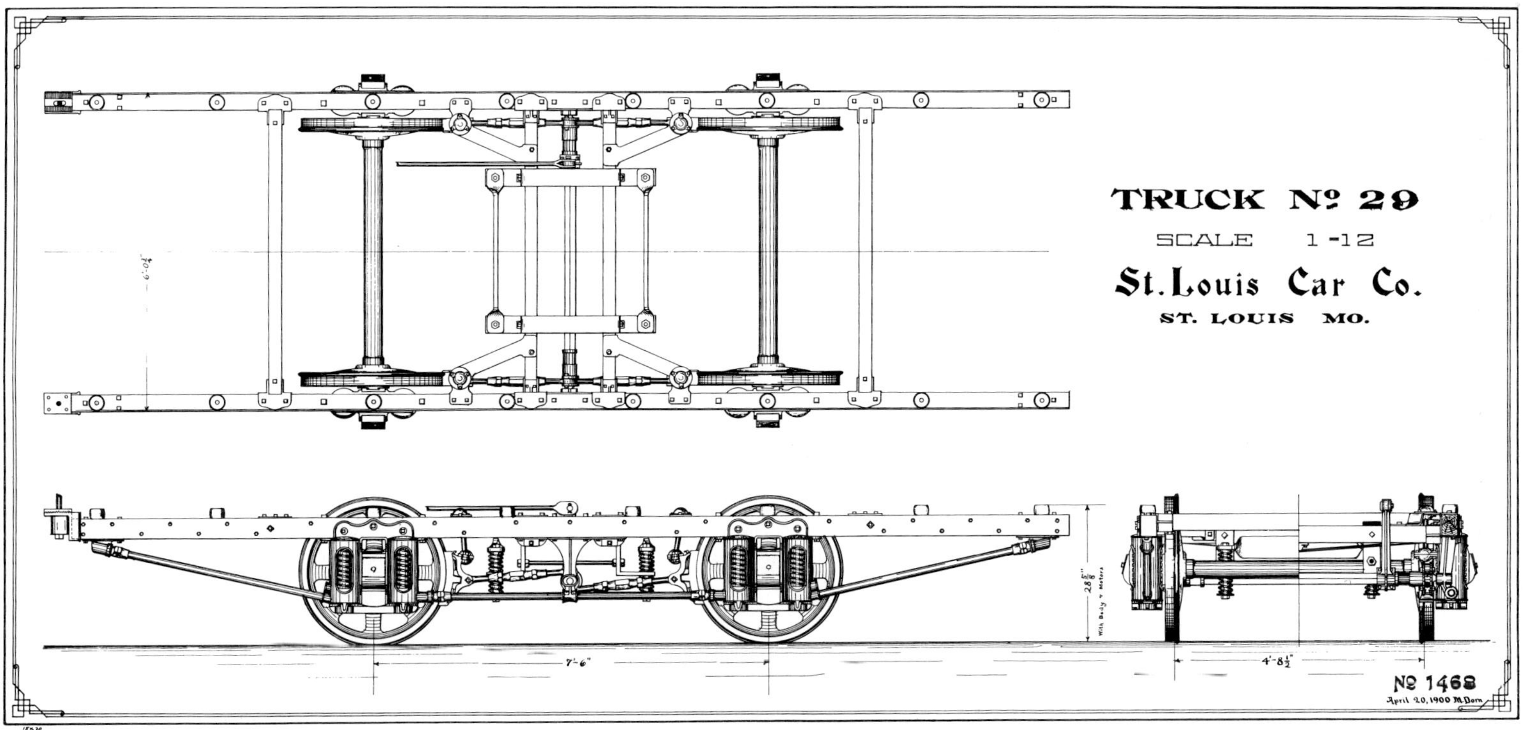

Many single-truck open cars built by the Car Co. had surprisingly long working lives. This 9-bench open, built for use in Boston in the late 1890s, is shown here at Boston's Allston car house on June 30, 1914. *(Kevin T. Farrell collection)*

Though ordered in 1898, it is not known whether this early interurban for the Birmingham Railway and Electric Co. was built at Baden or the old North Broadway plant. The car is at Fairview Station on Birmingham's Ensley line in 1905. Notice the whistle on the roof, above and to the left of the driver's windshield. *(Edwin J. Klasky collection)*

ing of bird's-eye maple, ornamented in oils and inlaid with diamond shaped mahogany panels. The exterior of the car was painted a dazzling white (highly inappropriate for so industrialized an area) and was finished with gilt lettering. A similar car was shipped to New Orleans in the same year.[16]

There was no respite from the pressure of work in 1895 and the company continued to be "pushed to the full capacity of its shops."[17] April 1895 was typical. In addition to the 300 cars already noted as being on order for Philadelphia, ninety open cars were ordered by the West End Street Railway of Boston, 75 closed cars by the Detroit Railway Co., ninety open cars for Baltimore, and sixty closed cars for the Hestonville, Mantua and Fairmount Park Passenger Ry. Co. of Philadelphia.[18]

Throughout the 1890s, references to the Car Company in the trade journals continued to speak of sustained growth and expansion, matching that of the industry it served. The street railway business seemed to have a limitless future, and it must have seemed that the opportunities for profit open to those financing and promoting street railways or their support industries, were almost as great as those open to them in the coal, steel or railroad industries.

Certainly that is what George J. Kobusch must have felt. But with his father in legal control of the St. Louis Car Co., Kobusch was somewhat restricted in his activities. John H. Kobusch showed no inclination to further expand the company, let alone expand the company's interests into other ventures, and the March 1894 capital increase, from $150,000 to $500,000, was made more to demonstrate the present worth of the company rather than its future potential. The financial statement filed at that time showed $576,742 as company assets, and only $28,996 as liabilities.[19] George Kobusch thus had to make his money without the help of the Car Company as long as his father was alive, and to a certain extent he did so. It is thought that during 1894 he became involved with the Citizen's Street Railway of Kalamazoo, Michigan,[20] and in 1895 it is known that he became a member of the syndicate promoting a line between St. Louis and Belleville, Ill. From this time onwards, he was almost as active in promoting street railway companies and other public utilities as he was at the Car Company.

#23B truck, 1900.

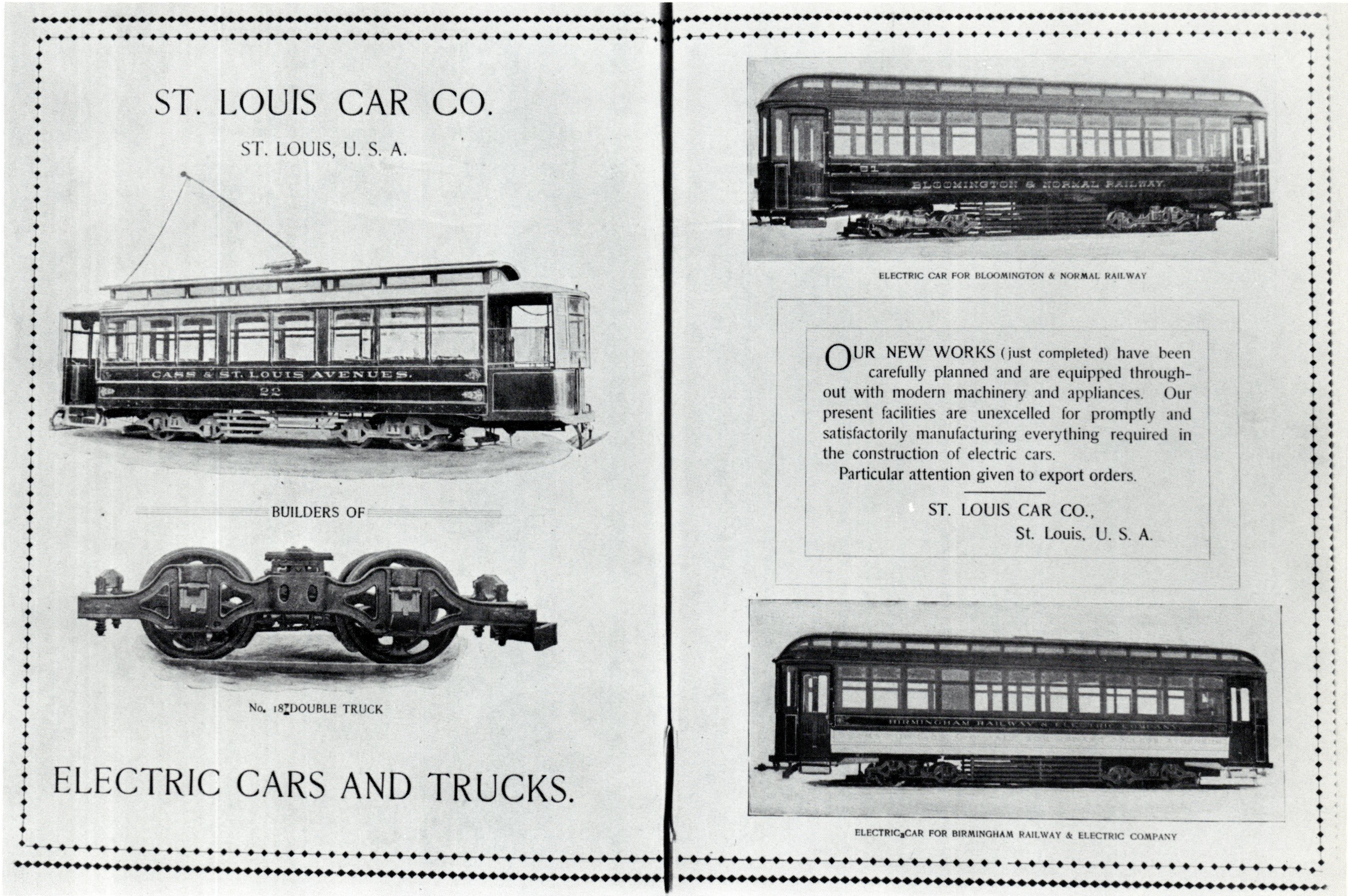

The first advertisement for Baden built cars, March 1899. *(Street Railway Journal)*

CHAPTER 3

By 1895 John Kobusch had died, and his son succeeded to the presidency of the St. Louis Car Co. With George Kobusch in control, a new and dynamic business style began to characterize the company's affairs. It was obvious for instance that the existing plant was incapable of keeping up with the demand for new cars, and that the only reasonable solution was to start again with a new plant on a new and more spacious site, laid out to produce electric trolley cars in quantity. It was not long before a suitable site was found and in 1897, the St. Louis Car Co. purchased the entire plant of the Union Car Co. of Missouri.

> This Company had been established at the end of 1895 when three men who (had) . . . been for many years identified with the manufacture of streetcars in St. Louis, left their positions . . . to form the Union Car Co., and to build a high grade of streetcar for the American market. H. P. Wehrenbrecht, the vice president, was originally with Brownell . . . then with Laclede . . . still later with Lindell Railway, and until November 1895 with the American Car Co. . . . as master car painter . . . H. Polst, the Company's master mechanic . . . held the same position with Laclede for many years . . . H. W. Rocklago . . . (was) appointed . . . company president and was a well-known contractor and capitalist in St. Louis . . . C. Knickmeyer was secretary and treasurer.[1]

The Union Car Co. had a 16-acre site located in Baden, North St. Louis. They had built a one-story brick building 100′ x 340′, divided into a mill and an erecting shop. There was a separate blacksmith and machine shop 50′ x 120′ together with an engine room and a boiler room, and a large dry kiln was also installed. Most of the lumber was purchased locally and seasoned in the yard by the side of the main building.

Union Car Co. was not ready for business until October 1896, when it placed advertisements in all the trade journals. In its entire existence only one order was recorded, placed in the spring of 1897 by the Consolidated Traction Co. of Pittsburgh for thirty 9-bench open cars on Mcguire trucks. It isn't even known if that order was successfully executed by the company, for it proved to be a major loss to them. While its advertisements continued to be placed up to the end of 1897, the company was in business less than a year.[2]

How Kobusch managed to involve himself with Union Car Co. is not clear, but the end result was the purchase of its plant and land together with much additional acreage by the St. Louis Car Co.

Kobusch's plans for the new Baden site were grandiose. He wanted nothing less than the largest and most modern streetcar manufacturing plant in the world, and throughout 1898 that plant began to take shape in the open country by the side of the Mississippi. Huge new buildings were erected and a vast new lumber yard laid out. The advantages of a Broadway site were retained—the street ran close to and almost parallel with the river, making lumber delivery very easy but rail access to the new plant was vastly superior. It took more than a year for the site to be prepared and the buildings designed and erected. Consequently the move to Baden was protracted, not being finally complete until March 1899. It is not known for certain if the Car Company remained in business between the final closing of the old plant and the opening of the Baden plant in 1899. The evidence is conflicting. On the one hand, the unbroken series of advertisements placed in the trade press from June 1887 to October 1897 abruptly ceased, not being resumed until March 1899. Nor did *Street Railway Journal's* directory of car builders list the company as a manufacturer between October 1897 and January 1899. On the other hand, the surviving list of job orders, which continued in unbroken sequence until closure in 1973, commenced in August 1898. Moreover, there still exist Car Company drawings from this interim period, showing details of work executed at that time. It must be concluded then that while the

City car built for Boston in 1899, shown at Boston's Milton car house in 1907. Although the car body is very large, the entrance is steep and narrow. *(Kevin T. Farrell collection)*

Indiana Railway Co. #206, a typical early St. Louis Car Co. interurban, delivered in 1900. *(Edwin J. Klasky collection)*

Wooden-bodied elevated car built for Boston at the turn of the century, seen at Boston's Sullivan Square car yard on August 24, 1904. *(Kevin T. Farrell collection)*

Double-deck cars for the Isle of Thanet, England, built in 1900. *(Street Railway Journal)*

Car for Berlin at the Baden plant in April 1900. *(Street Railway Journal)*

Little Rock Railway and Electric Co. #253, a 13-bench open car built in 1903.

company may have curtailed its activities during the move, it did not entirely cease to trade.[3]

With the new plant complete and operating, it is probable that for a time at least, the Car Company's unsubstantiated claim to be the biggest streetcar builder in the world was true.[4] Rail access to the plant was via the St. Louis Keokuk and Northern, and the manufacturing area was over twenty-acres. The shops were laid out so that the car bodies could be moved as little as possible, a great contrast to the monumentally inconvenient arrangement at the old plant where work had to be done on three floors, connected by elevators.

Everything necessary for car production was available on the new site. Behind the factory were the lumber yards, serviced by four electric switching locomotives. Over four miles of track were electrified on the company's property, on which materials were distributed to the shops, all of which were connected to the track system. The electrification extended to the company's rail siding, its primary link with the outside world.[5] Opening onto the yards were the blacksmith and machine shops, and the mill. The mill had three sections, one dealing with heavy materials, one producing sills, bottoms and platform materials, and one with the lighter materials used to finish car interiors. Parts from this last section of the mill went on to the cabinet shop where the detailed work was done, passing from man to man, and machine to machine until ready for final assembly in the erecting shop.[6]

G. J. Kobusch. *(St. Louis Public Libraries)*

In the blacksmith shop could be found long lines of forges, presses, lathes, steam hammers and bolt cutters, together with the truck department. A 750 hp. engine was located next to the shop, providing the plant's source of power, while a smaller engine connected to a generator produced the electricity for lighting the plant and operating the smaller machines.

Emergency motors were widely distributed throughout the plant, and the entire system could be connected to the local electricity company's line in case of failures. Refuse from the mills fueled the company's boilers, minimizing fuel costs.

Along the eastern end of the blacksmith shop was a 60′ transfer table, running the full length of the erecting shop and equipped with winding drum and block and tackle. Using this equipment, two men could load cars, trucks or other equipment and with ease move them to any part of the plant. This system's efficiency was demonstrated by the fact that completed cars could if necessary be moved from the interior of the erecting shops to a flatcar at the railhead in less than two minutes.

The erecting shop was an immense building, measuring 300′ x 624′. Covered by a single roof, the building was 20′ high, and had over 55,000 sq. ft. of glass in its windows. There were 40 separate tracks on the floor of this building and its size made possible the manufacture of 300 cars at one time. Illumination was provided by 1100 arc and incandescent lights.

The company's general offices adjoined the shops on the western side of the plant. Sumptuously furnished, they were equipped with extensive darkroom facilities to assist in photographing cars built at the plant. Finished cars were delivered on a fleet of one hundred, sixty-foot flatcars belonging to the company, which were operated all over the country.

Less than three years later, at the beginning of 1902, additions were needed to this huge plant. Another erecting shop 563′ x 100′ was built, increasing production capacity by over one hundred cars. One section of the new shop had a second story in which the newly expanded curtain and seat departments were located. In 1903, the mill area was increased by over 50%, and the original erecting shop more than doubled in size, and with such huge financial outlays so soon after the plant had been opened, more money was required. A capital increase was made on May 18, 1903, from $500,000 to $1,500,000. The company financial statement filed at that time showed assets at $3,022,940 and its liabilities as $777,091.[7] This spurt of growth gave the company an estimated manufacturing capacity of 3,000 cars per year, utilizing a labor force of 2,500 men.[8]

Estimates of the manufacturing capacity of the company have to be used with caution. No two car orders were ever alike as to weight, size or finish and the overall dimensions of cars had grown continually since 1887. In 1903, the latest transportation craze was for the electric high-speed interurban car, a vehicle far longer and heavier than the typical city car, with equipment, design and finish of an elaborateness closely akin to mainline railroad cars. Interurban cars thus took longer to build, and orders for them were much smaller in size than those for the average city car. Tooling for orders of this nature was time-consuming and expensive, producing economic problems with short production runs and time wasted in switching from one order to another. The result was that the Car Company was barely able to reach half its estimated potential production capacity, even in its most prosperous years.

Car #40 of the Greenwich Railway Co. This was a ten-bench, fifty-seat open car, 31′ long and 8′ wide. Note the full monitor roof, reinforced with steel carlines at each post. 1901.

Freight cars for electric railroads were a company specialty. This car, built in 1901, was a 44′ long vehicle for the East St. Louis and Belleville Electric Railway, mounted on the St. Louis 23B high-speed interurban double truck.

Perhaps the most striking feature of the Car Company was its style of management, which consisted of extremely close personal control exercised by an owner-manager. This was the normal method of control in industrial enterprises in 1887 but, for so large an establishment as the company had become by 1903, it was regarded as being anachronistic. Yet curiously it was a style of management adhered to throughout practically all of the company's subsequent life, an increasingly anomalous situation in a manufacturing industry more usually run on behalf of owners or stockholders by professional management. A "vanity" biographer of 1906 in reviewing George Kobusch's career remarked on this, and suggested that it was George Kobusch who had persuaded his father to establish the company in the first place. Certainly since his father's death, the biographer went on, it was due to George's

> energetic and indomitable spirit, and the honesty of (the company's) products (that) its chief success (may) be attributed. Mr. Kobusch made it known by his tact and skill, both west and east, and then around the world, overcoming apparently insurmountable obstacles.[9]

It is surprising that despite such fulsome praise, so prominent and enterprising a man as George Kobusch should have left little trace of his existence in his native city. The foundation of his wealth was his inheritance, but the earnings of the Car Company soon augmented it and he quickly became a millionaire. His greatest wish was to become known as a financier in the tradition of Morgan and Carnegie, and his great attention to the Car Company after his father's death thus was not only an end in itself, but also a means of ensuring the fulfilment of this wish; for the good name (and profits) of the company were stepping stones to the power and privilege he craved in politics, in society and in the world of business. His St. Louis friendships were carefully cultivated to include those who would be most useful to him in the street railway world, particularly those who promoted, financed and constructed. To do this successfully he needed the skill of a political statesman, and indeed he found politics a congenial occupation, very quickly becoming a local Republican party office holder. Those whom he sought to befriend most assiduously were primarily financiers or bankers, not of the rank of the "robber barons" of the time, but formidably wealthy and powerful nevertheless, men of the tight social world of St. Louis politics and finance. Young, affable and good looking, Kobusch had no difficulty becoming a part of that world. Once firmly ensconced in it, he continued to impress those with whom he came in contact, and steadily made a financial career for himself. He was soon a familiar figure on the boards of many St. Louis banks, and he conformed to all the rules and conventions of business and social behavior of the day and all went well with him.

All went well until 1898. In that year, as a result of his strenuous efforts to raise money to build the new Baden plant and fill it with work, Kobusch unwisely got himself involved in a city bribery scandal of epic proportions. The scandal concerned the purchase for $250,000 of 34 votes in the St. Louis House of Delegates. This figure was the sum necessary to buy a majority vote in any division in the House concerning the proposed Central Traction Bill of 1898, a franchise distribu-

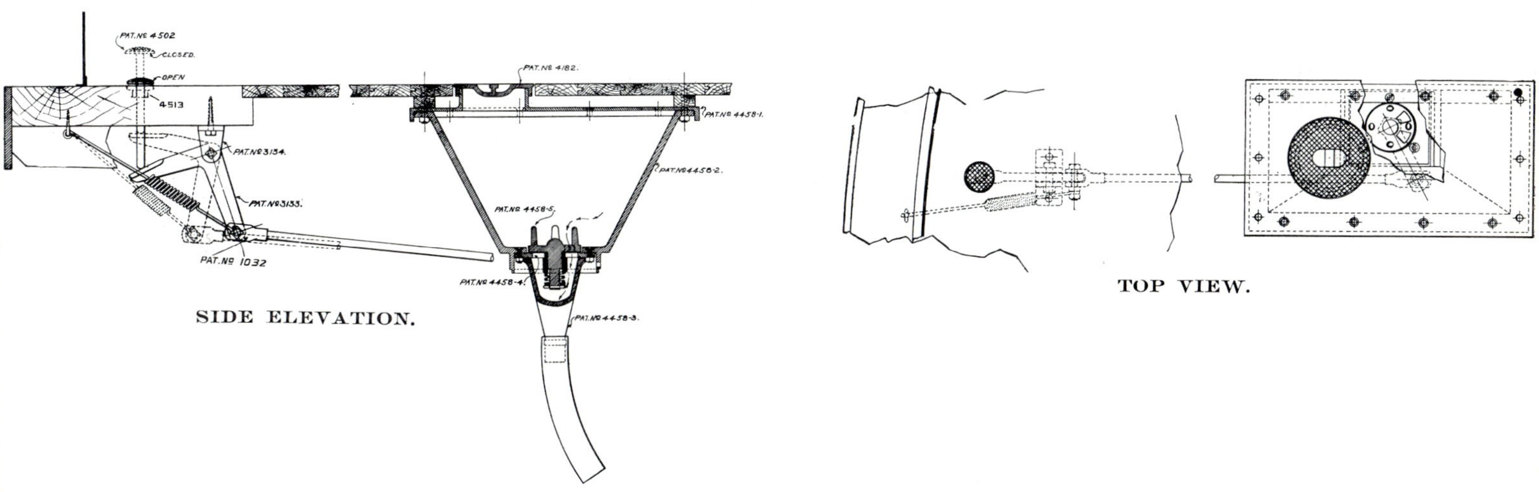

With the opening of the malleable and gray iron foundries in January 1901, the Car Co. began large-scale production of ancillary products of its own design and expanded the range of items it distributed on behalf of others. This is Sandbox #3.

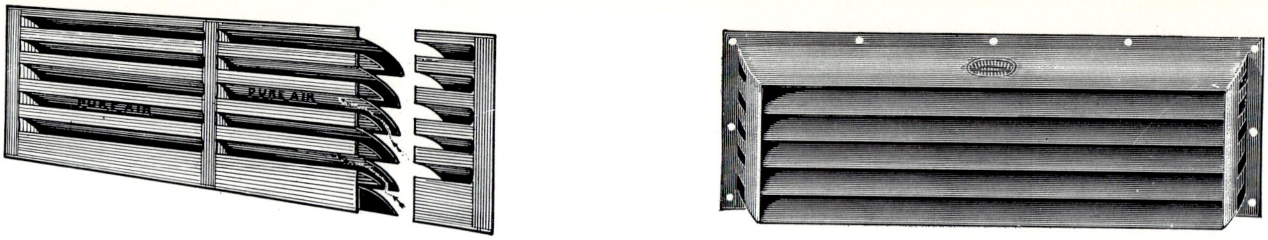

Perry ventilator.

Interior lamp #2.

tion bill intended to consolidate the many street railway firms then operating on St. Louis streets, into one city-wide company.

The promoter of this bill, and the financier behind the bribes, was Robert Snyder, a Kansas City investor with whom Kobusch had recently become involved, and a man with a dubious reputation. The St. Louis circles with whom Kobusch had hitherto been associated were unequivocally opposed to Snyder, his consolidation bill and his bribery, not for moral and ethical reasons, but because they felt the time was not ripe for a consolidation, as long as their money could not be in sole control of it. So far as they were concerned, no man who was not of their number, had any business making profits in their town, and Snyder was an outsider whom they felt to be "moving in" on them.

Prepared to stop at nothing to keep Snyder out, they turned to Ed Butler, a local political "controller" and for years their "representative" in the city government. Butler was in fact a "fixer." For a sufficient fee, paid in advance, Butler would "fix" things so as to ensure the passage of legislation favorable to the interests of his clients. He managed this generally by financing combines of at least two-thirds of the members of the bicameral House of Delegates. This was not an uncommon practise. Those controlling the St. Louis street railway interests were themselves paying seven St. Louis councilmen $5,000 per year to prevent passage of bills not in their best interests.

Now it was well known that Butler himself was committed to his St. Louis patrons, but every man has his price and Butler could not always guarantee the loyalty of his watchdogs who for an extra fee acted as whips over the others on Butler's payroll, to see they voted as instructed. Snyder knew this too, and with his promotion of the streetcar consolidation bill, a contest began between

Headlight #1.

his backers and Butler's to see who would be prepared to pay their combines more. The Butler patrons matched Snyder's offer price for price, until Snyder managed to contact one of Butler's watchdogs and gave him a sum considerably in excess of that paid by Butler, whereupon the watchdog and his men changed sides, and cast their votes for Snyder's consolidation bill, which thus passed. For a total expenditure of $250,000 in bribes, Snyder had the St. Louis Central Traction franchise in his hands.[10]

Politically, St. Louis was still a frontier town in the 1890s, wide open to anyone who wanted power or profit by whatever means. Despite the formidable clique of conservative St. Louis business interests, striving desperately to keep such people off their territory, Kobusch was as aware as anyone that bribery was the usual way of getting anything done that mattered in the city. Why he became involved with Snyder, rather than with his traditional "friends" is not at all clear. It is probable that with his new plant practically complete, his personal ambition had already outgrown St. Louis and the money it could provide. With the Central Traction franchise in his hands, Snyder should certainly have been able to offer Kobusch a more substantial amount of new business than the local businessmen (many of whom had money in rival streetcar manufacturers) could have offered had they possessed the franchise. Such was the nature of the times that this venality was accepted as perfectly normal business practise, if perhaps a trifle reprehensible morally. Though the facts of the bribery were widely known and publicised nationally, nothing was done for some years, until a crusading city attorney named Folk started an investigation into this and other municipal scandals. Eventually a Grand Jury was convened, and Kobusch was required to give evidence before it in February 1902. As he himself was not directly under investigation, his reputation would have remained largely untarnished had he not chosen to perjure himself at the hearing. The day following his testimony was a Saturday, but this did not prevent the judge in the case from issuing an arrest summons against Kobusch, a summons served the same evening in the Car Company offices, to Kobusch's acute em-

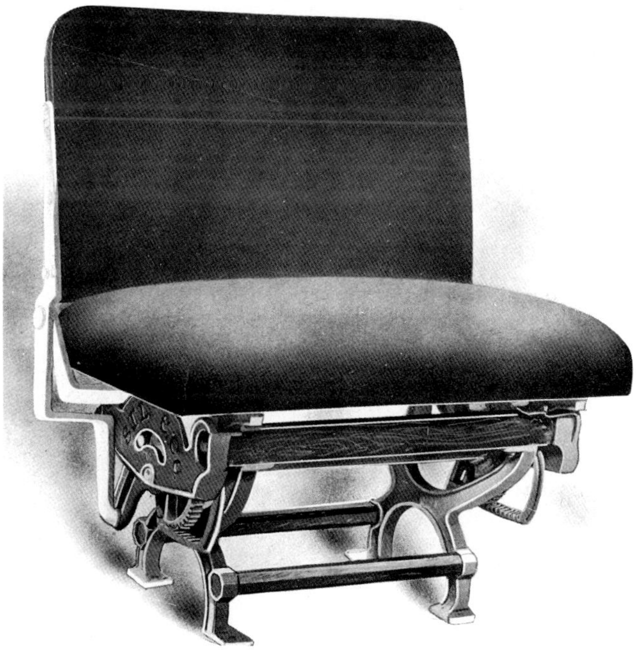

The company also specialized in seat manufacture. The best twill-weave, canvas-lined enameled spring rattan was used on the company's design of reversible back seat. Optional types of seat cover included plush, leather and pantasote.

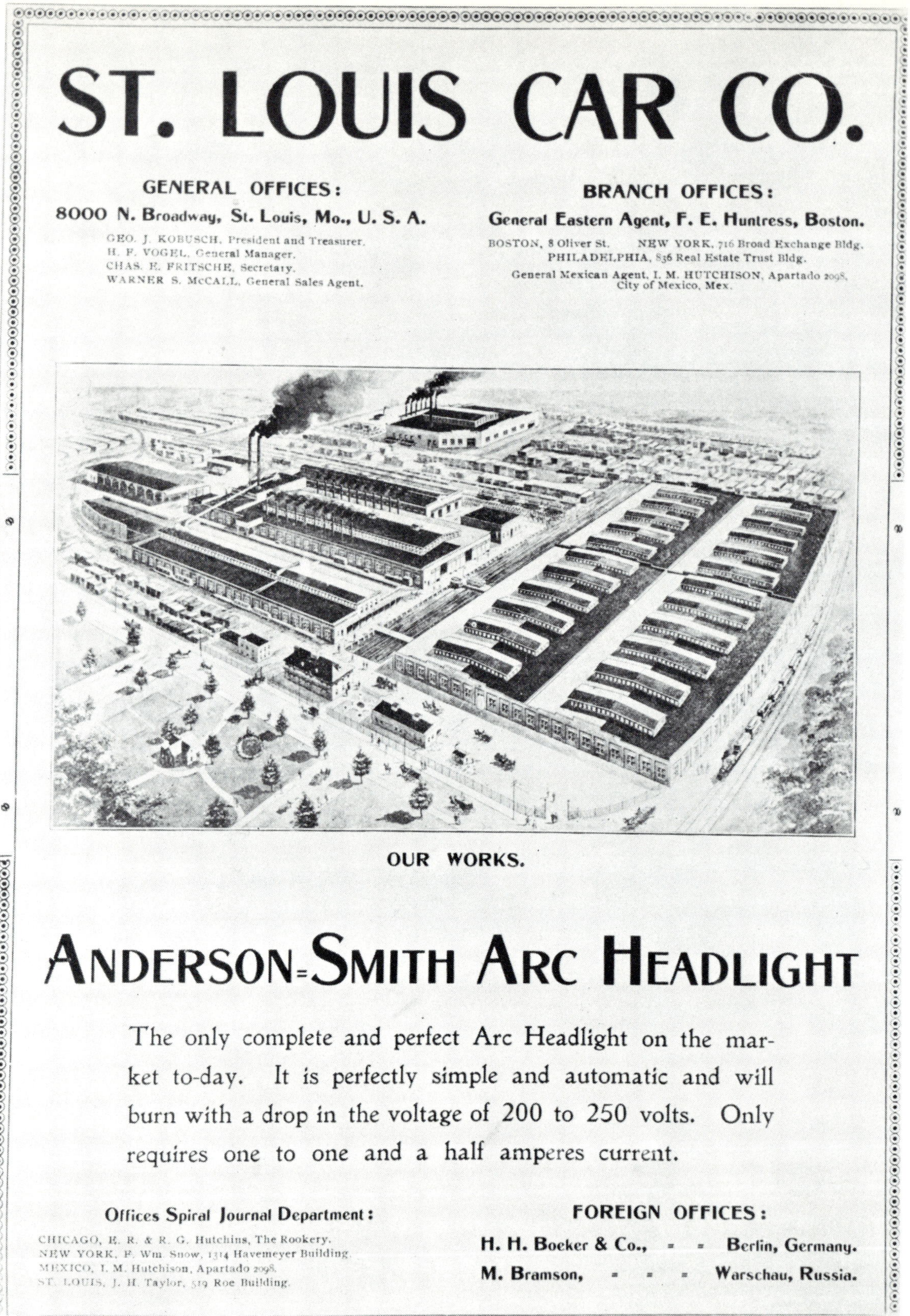

Advertisement placed in 1900. *(Street Railway Journal)*

barrassment. It then became necessary for Kobusch to find the judge and post bail, and a frantic search was begun, ending when the judge was located in a local theatre. Bail was set at $5,000 after which, badly scared, Kobusch made his way home.[11]

The local papers made considerable play with this story, but for the next few months, Kobusch stolidly refused either to explain or defend himself. As the year went on, Folk finally located sufficient evidence to implicate Snyder as the man responsible for the financing of the successful Central Traction bribe, and he was brought to trial in September, 1902.

Kobusch was the prosecution's star witness, and though he denied in court that any arrangement had been made between him and Folk to drop the perjury charge in return for testifying against Snyder, the fact is that Kobusch's evidence did convict Snyder, and he was not subsequently tried for perjury. But he was a most unwilling witness, giving his evidence under what seemed like great emotional stress, and at times was almost on the point of breaking down. The dominant impression given by the reports of the trial is of a man deeply ashamed and humiliated; not on Snyder's behalf, but on his own, for his testimony did not put his own business methods in a very favorable light. He gave evidence that he had personally bribed Councilman Gaus in the Central Traction deal on Snyder's behalf, and that he had acted as "bagholder" for Snyder in several other bribery transactions. Why? So he could get more orders for the St. Louis Car Co. In an interview given to the *St. Louis Post-Dispatch* by Gaus, it is made quite clear that Kobusch knew he was going to get that business.

> Mr. Kobusch, who is my friend (sic), wanted me to vote for the bill. If the bill went through, his company was to get the contract to build 2,000 streetcars.[12]

Between 1898 and 1902, Kobusch had indeed received substantial orders from the new consolidated street railway company, though the figure barely approached one thousand cars. Even so, it is surprising any orders came to him at all for Snyder had quickly sold his interests in the new consolidated company at a profit of $1 million! Seemingly the new owners were prepared to honor Snyder's obligations to Kobusch, at least until they themselves ran into financial difficulties, which they soon did.

It was not simply the public exposure of his curious methods of doing business that disturbed Kobusch at the Snyder trial. Almost equally as embarrassing to him was the fact he had been forced into a situation where he had been compelled to admit in public and under oath that he, himself a local politician, financier and businessman, had been involved in political bribery. Moreover, he had sought to mitigate his offense by suggesting openly what had quietly been accepted for years: that bribery was so common a business procedure that using it carried no stigma. That was indeed the case, but no one yet had had the temerity to suggest such a thing in a court of law in St. Louis. It was in any event a very weak explanation of his conduct, and certainly could not excuse it. While it was true that bribery was accepted business practise, it was not acceptable if one was caught at it, and Kobusch had been caught. In thus trying to implicate his former business and social colleagues in his own dishonesty, he had compounded his sins in their eyes.[13]

Of more immediate concern to the Car Company, was the damaging publicity arising out of the Kobusch testimony, and the exposure of the firm's business difficulties, and they were fortunate that in spite of it, orders did not fall off markedly. This was a period when a considerable amount of South American business was being done, and it must be assumed that Kobusch's problems in the USA had no great influence on that market.

Kobusch was compelled to resign his directorship in at least one St. Louis bank as a result of this scandal, and for a period was unable to muster substantial new credit locally for any business activities. Thus though the Car Company continued to do well in 1902 and 1903, Kobusch was forced to seek money from other sources.

Birmingham Railway Light and Power Co. #211 of 1901, a Robertson sill car on St. Louis 23B trucks.

Los Angeles Railway wooden-bodied combination car #262 of 1901.

Pacific Electric Railway wooden-bodied combination car #250 of 1902. These cars could run 65 mph and are said to have covered the route between Los Angeles and Long Beach in 35 minutes.

CHAPTER 4

Vice President Kling remained the Car Company's general manager and chief engineer after the move to Baden, but there were increasing signs of incompatability in both temperament and technique between himself and Kobusch, for the new plant demanded production techniques of a kind Kling was largely unfamiliar with. The plant itself was far bigger than anything previously seen in the street railway manufacturing industry, and Kling (like Brownell before him as he aged) became a man with a conservative view of his craft and found it difficult to adjust his work style. A professional acquaintance later recalled that

> to anyone methodical or systematic, Mr. Kling's way of running things was a puzzle. All preparatory work in starting an order he called red tape, and whenever he thought he saw this color of tape, he became annoyed. A common speech for him to make on starting an order was "Get out the material from (the) patterns and templates we have, build the car, and make the drawings after. Then we will know the drawings are right."
>
> But let us not judge too hastily . . . To understand this attitude of mind we must be reminded that there were no draughtsmen or engineers on the job then. Such work (which was very little) was done by the superintendents, and they, being better mechanics than draughtsmen, found . . . it easier . . . to express their ideas in wood than on paper.[1]

With a dynamic young president of a radical frame of mind, and a conservative general manager and chief engineer working in a new plant with the most modern of equipment, what else could there be but tension? Eventually Kling found it impossible to continue at the Car Company, resigning in 1900 to accept a similar post at the Stephenson Car Co. in their new (but much smaller) New Jersey plant.

The new General Manager was a very different man. H. F. Vogel had joined the Car Company in 1893 as traffic manager, being promoted in 1898 to assistant general manager. He was promoted to company vice president in 1903, and resigned in 1906 to take over the presidency of the Danville (Illinois) Car Co. As a contemporary biographer explained:

> As Vice President and General Manager of the St. Louis Car Co., the largest plant of its kind in existence . . . (Mr. Vogel) is the dean of his profession in the United States. That it is entitled to be called a profession is granted by all who know the depth and . . . breadth of technical knowledge of the presiding genius of a great car factory . . . The intelligence necessary to carry so large a burden of responsibility is centered in Henry F. Vogel more than in any one man. As a businessman, he is known for his sterling integrity, his untiring energy and his unfailing good nature . . . He has always been known as the friend of labor and all of its higher aspirations and this trait has made it possible to deal with more than a thousand (sic) employees with so little friction that the establishment of which he is the head has been held up as a model in this regard.[2]

At this distance in time, it is difficult accurately to assess the reliability of so sycophantic a statement, but evidence does suggest that Vogel was an extremely able manager, a fact demonstrated in the many organizational changes he made in the company which greatly improved the operation of the plant at the shop floor level. One of the most significant changes was the establishment of a bi-weekly series of department head meetings, by which he was constantly informed of the state of work in progress. At these meetings current problems were discussed and analyzed, and work schedule adjustments made. Normally 40 to 45 men would attend, including department chiefs, the superintendent, the foremen and other men in charge of work.

The foremen were crucial to the manufacturing process as Vogel understood it, and were as-

Richmond Street and Interurban Railway #101 of 1902.

Single truck cars were in reduced demand by 1902. Birmingham Light and Power Co. #317 and its crew shown on the South Highlands line in 1906. *(Alvin W. Hudson, Edwin J. Klasky collection)*

H. F. Vogel. *(St. Louis Public Libraries)*

A 52-seat city car for Chicago, built in 1903.

Canton-Akron Railway Co. #17 of 1902.

Car #6 of Texarkana Light and Traction Co.
on St. Louis #46 single truck, built in 1903.

A classic Robertson car, showing the large windows which dropped vertically into the straight sides, and the steel channel underframe. Originally built as part of a group of 100 cars for the Chicago City Railways, St. Louis United Railways #600 and 19 others were diverted to that city in 1903 before delivery to Chicago to replace cars lost in the St. Louis Maple Avenue carbarn fire. The car acquired the number shown here after a 1911 renumbering. *(United Railways of St. Louis, Edwin J. Klasky collection)*

signed to the erecting shop, paint shop, blacksmith, machine and cabinet shops. In addition, the foremen supervised car rigging and finishing, the brass foundry, the lumber yards, receiving, drafting and shipping. Vogel insisted on so dividing every piece of work in the plant that one individual would ultimately be responsible for the progress of each part of the job. So important was the supervision of the foremen to Vogel in his concept of efficient production that in 1903 William Sutton, formerly president of the American Car Co., was appointed to the post of general superintendent of the St. Louis Car Co. charged with overseeing all the activities of the foremen, and relieving Vogel of the day-to-day responsibility.

Social life was not neglected at the plant.

> Besides the semi-weekly meetings for business purposes, held after lunch, there is a monthly dinner and meeting of the superintendents, foremen and employees in responsible charge of work, which is familiarly known around the works as "Mr. Vogel's good time." These meetings are held the first Saturday of each month. Dinner is served in the company's lunch rooms and after dinner a general discussion follows which is taken part in by all employees. At these meetings matters of improvement in shop methods or shop equipment are discussed. Any proposition brought up is open to discussion by everyone, and debate is encouraged . . . Everyone stands on the same footing without regard to the position they may hold in the company organization.[3]

It is impossible to review more than the highlights of the Car Company's output between 1896 and 1903, for during this time thousands of streetcars were built to every conceivable design. Some of the most interesting cars were those sent to Germany in crates to the Car Company's agent H. Böker of Berlin. This German manufacturer was appointed agent in 1899, and sold many streetcars to Berlin which in fact had been manufactured in the Baden plant. Cars built by the St. Louis Car Co. were also sent to Hamburg, and to Lisbon, Portugal, while 40 double deck cars on Car Company trucks were sent in 1900 to the Isle of Thanet Co. in Kent, England. Hundreds of single truck cars were sent to Buenos Aires; at one point it was estimated that 250 cars per year went to that city alone.[4]

It was, however, the domestic market which was of greatest financial importance. The average order remained at between 30 and 50 cars, but huge orders became quite common at the close of the century. Typical were the orders from Brooklyn Heights in 1898 for 75 cars, and from the Boston Elevated in 1899 for 100 cars, an order repeated in 1900. Chicago ordered 120 cars in 1901 and the new owners of the Consolidated St. Louis Street Railway ordered 450 cars in late 1903. The Car Company had agents in many of the principal cities of the USA by 1903, and was continually seeking business wherever it could be found. Nor did it confine its activities solely to streetcars, for even before 1904 full-size railway cars were occasionally built, one customer being the Chicago, Burlington and Quincy Railroad.

There was one major flaw in this picture of untroubled prosperity. No single order was ever like another. The manufacturer had to follow the design his customer felt would do the job adequately. Indeed since 1896, when the electric streetcar had become both reliable and capacious, St. Louis Car Co. began to find it difficult to persuade its customers to accept any new streetcar designs, and design evolution stagnated for a period. Until 1896 or thereabouts, the typical electric streetcar had been the ornately finished single truck open or closed car. But after 1896 most of the cars built were long and capacious double truck vehicles. Because for the first time the street railways had in these cars vehicles which could cope with traffic without wearing out, their master mechanics were reluctant to tamper with the design. Generally most companies ordered cars with the views of their master mechanic very much in mind, and if he wanted the car to fulfill a particular task by being designed a particular way, he usually got it. Typical of the reluctance to change design was the persistence of the cramped and inconvenient platform on even the longest cars of the day. A holdover from the more leisurely horsecar era, the platforms proved to be a considerable bottleneck in busy periods, much to the annoyance of the passengers who found the overcrowded cars uncomfortable, badly ventilated and difficult to get on and off.

Once on the car, the passenger could choose between freezing or suffocating, depending on the season. Heating and ventilation were exceedingly primitive. It is incredible that wooden-bodied streetcars should have relied so largely on coal or wood-burning pot belly stoves for heat, but they did. Ventilation was entirely dependent on the effective operation of relatively small windows, which all too often were stuck in the closed position. When they were not stuck, they generally set up annoying rattles in their frames, and if the car body was weak they could be seen to move, at the same time letting in drafts. The use of the deck roof in the 1890s brought some measure of relief, but only at certain times of the year.

The extremes of climate found in the continental U.S.A. and Canada presented further design problems. Many operators at this time had to maintain two separate sets of vehicles, one of open cars for summer use only, and one of closed cars, for winter and bad weather service. This was an expensive and inadequate way of dealing with the climate, and most design ingenuity in this period was exercised in developing a car which could be completely closed during the winter but could be thrown almost completely open in the summer. Countless versions of these "convertible" and "semi-convertible" cars were thus put on the market, those of the J. G. Brill Co. gaining the widest commercial acceptance.

St. Louis Car Co.'s design, while not the most successful commercially, was for the period perhaps the most simple to operate, and the least demanding of interior space. First introduced in 1899 for a 100 car series of the New York Third Avenue Railway Co., the design was the invention of that company's Superintendent Robertson. The St. Louis Car Co. bought the rights to the design, and from then until the end of wooden car production at the plant, this style of convertible car, together with the associated steel "Robertson" sill, became the characteristic product of the Car Company.

In the Robertson convertible system, the upper window sash was raised into a roof side pocket and the main window sash lowered into a body

side pocket. If the car was also built with the Robertson steel sill (as was almost invariably the case), then the lower belt rail which this sill made possible left room for the entire main window sash to disappear into the side pocket. The gap left by the lowering of the window was closed by a wooden hinged flap upon which a passenger could comfortably rest his arm and elbow. Unlike many of the other convertible systems, the entire operation could be entrusted to the passengers and could be completed very quickly, an obvious advantage in hot showery weather. Moreover, the upper sashes did not slide into the roof proper as they did on the Brill designs, and the interior of a Robertson convertible car had a normal appearance, unlike the claustrophobic internally curved ceilings of the Brill cars.

The steel sill pointed the way to the next development in car design to be offered by the Car Company.

A type of car bottom construction which is (now) finding very extensive use . . . , is that . . . known as the steel channel car bottom of the St. Louis Car Co. The peculiar feature of this bottom sill is the opportunity it gives for a very low car body in city service, without interfering with the strength of the car by cutting down the strength of the sills.[5]

These design refinements added to the price of a car, but the period in which they were introduced was also that in which St. Louis Car Co. began to earn its long-held reputation as the "Quality Shops," and most cars turned out by the company from this time on had very long lives.

If streetcar design in general had stagnated between 1896 and 1903, the same is largely true of interurban design. Interurban cars were mostly based on scaled-down railroad designs which by 1903 could no longer even be considered scaled down. Their narrow, congested and inconveniently high entrances were a hazard to all but the most able-bodied, and their wooden construction pre-

City car #2481 of St. Louis United Railways, built in 1903. The car is passing the 12th Street and Franklin intersection in downtown St. Louis some years later.

sented fire and collision risks in view of the relatively high speeds at which such equipment was normally operated.

It was the customer who normally set the specifications for his cars, and the customer in this period regarded price, quality and passenger capacity as the most important design criteria, for these were the elements which maximized profits. Operating trolley cars was very big business, and highly profitable. Design improvements solely for passenger benefit ate into those profits. The operating companies, at a time when their monopoly of urban transit was complete, saw no reason now to spend money needlessly on unnecessary frills which produced no extra revenue. As a result, by the turn of the century, the elegant, ornately decorated multi-wood finish coach-painted electric streetcar of the early 1890s was utterly obsolete. It had been replaced by a larger, heavier and more reliable vehicle, with a far more spartan finish, and no discernible improvement in passenger convenience or comfort. For their owners however, these newer vehicles had the advantage of relative cheapness, high capacity and reliability, guaranteeing profitable operation and the payment of regular dividends to the stockholders. Moreover the sturdy and durable construction of most of these new cars ensured a long working life eliminating the need for frequent replacement. The design standards of 1896 thus largely remained the design standards of 1903, and in consequence the public perception of the street railway operator changed drastically in the early years of this century. Whereas once the trolley operators were enthusiastically welcomed as benefactors to the communities they served, they were now being seen as rapacious, greedy monopolists, who ignored the needs of those they served. It was not until public discontent became widespread that the industry's attitude began to change, but the movement toward design improvement was to remain extremely slow until the slump of 1906/7.

Horsecars for Tampico, Mexico, built in 1901 by Laclede.

CHAPTER 5

It was in the first years of the new century that consolidation in the streetcar building industry finally occurred in St. Louis. Competition, except in the most prosperous years, had been financially crippling to all, and not every company president had Kobusch's talent for finding fresh sources of money to maintain the appearance of an enterprise still flourishing greatly. The Brownell Co., after many years of financial stringency caused largely by Frederick Brownell's refusal to alter or compromise his design standards in the face of customer preference, was taken over by the American Car Co. in 1900 (yet another St. Louis company formed by ex-Brownell staff). This establishment shortly thereafter found itself in similar difficulties and negotiated with the J. G. Brill Co. for nearly 18 months before being acquired by Brill in 1902.[1] The Brill Co. was expanding greatly at that time, buying out its competition all over the U.S.A., and closing down unprofitable operations where necessary. In St. Louis neither the Brownell nor the American plants were closed immediately (indeed the American plant remained in profitable operation for over thirty years after the takeover), and their production was switched to standard Brill products, thus bringing solid competition right onto Kobusch's front doorstep. Naturally, he felt threatened and in spite of the shortage of money and his (by now) suspect reputation, felt he must retaliate in kind. He thus began negotiations with the Laclede Car Co. (which was also in financial difficulties) and on April 25, 1903, acquired Laclede. The publicly stated reason for the purchase was to give the St. Louis Car Co. an overflow plant in which to build extra cars. At the time of the takeover, 2500 men were working at the two plants and after renovating and retooling the Laclede plant Kobusch hoped to increase that number.

The Laclede Car Co. had been established in 1883 when (as previously noted) the Brownell Co. experienced its first major split. James P. Keily and Thomas F. Colfer were the prime movers in this enterprise, and through their efforts it became an important manufacturer. In August 1891, it went through a major reorganization when its then President and Secretary William Sutton and Emil Alexander resigned, selling their Laclede interests back to Keily and Colfer for $40,000, and establishing their own American Car Co. As a result of this transaction, Laclede had increased its capitalization to $80,000, broke into the Eastern markets and began to do even better.

The Laclede plant was located between North First and Second Streets in St. Louis, between May and Douglas Streets.

> The main feature of the company's shop . . . is found in the way in which cars are built from the foundations up in one place; the erecting shops where they are painted and made ready for shipment. This obviates the necessity of moving the car from shop to shop as the work progresses, and it is thus possible to reduce the labor account quite materially.[2]

In a sense, this was making a virtue out of necessity. Laclede had a relatively inefficient plant layout, largely as a result of the odd-shaped site on which it was located, and their production methods were the most efficient that could be devised under the circumstances. But the volume of business, and the quality of Laclede's products were outstanding all through the 1890s, and their reputation was high. By 1896, the Philadelphia Traction Co., one of their better customers, was operating a fleet of 1000 open front electric cars built by Laclede, finished throughout in cherry wood, with bird's-eye maple ceilings, plush covered seats, automatic twin doors and solid bronze trimmings. Hundreds more cross-bench open cars and closed cars were built by Laclede for this operator, all with the same high standard of finish. Cars sold to other eastern cities were just as well finished, and New York, Pittsburgh, Baltimore, Washington, Cincinnati, Buffalo and Jersey City all bought large numbers of Laclede-built cars. In

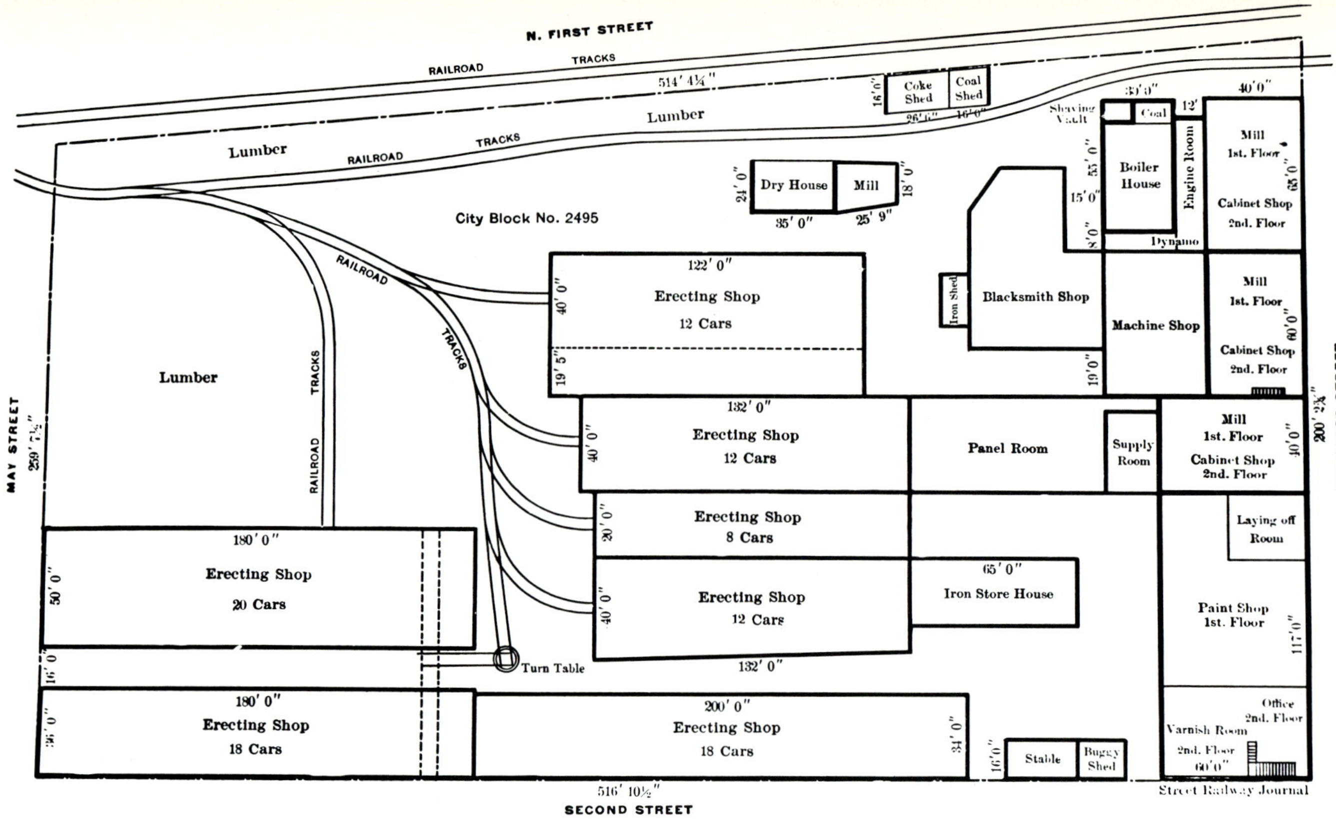

Plan of the Laclede plant, 1896. *(Street Railway Journal)*

Laclede Car Co. erecting shop, 1896. Notice the cramped working space. *(Street Railway Journal)*

St. Louis Transit Co. #1930 of 1900, seen at left in St. Louis United Railroad's colors at the Lee carbarn, St. Louis in 1908. *(William J. Clouser collection)*

Manhattan, Kansas #700, a typical Laclede-built city car, mounted on St. Louis #13 trucks. It is seen as rebuilt for sale by United Railways of St. Louis (its original owner) to Manhattan, outside United Railways 39th and Park shops in 1909. *(Edwin J. Klasky collection)*

Baggage express car for the Levis County Railway, Quebec, 1903.

Horse-drawn funeral car for a South American customer built in 1903 by Laclede.

addition, the company had built its own designs of electric car trucks in the 1890s.[3]

Kobusch had grand ambitions for his newly enlarged St. Louis Car Co. He was now the acknowledged giant of streetcar manufacture in the Midwest, and the operation of electric streetcars, his company's principle product, was among the great businesses of the age. The one hundredth anniversary of the Louisiana Purchase of 1803 (Missouri was a part of that territory) was to be marked in St. Louis by a World's Fair which would provide an international showcase for American industry. Although the fair was in fact held a year late in 1904, this indeed proved to be the case. The street railway industry in general, and St. Louis street railways in particular were "on show" to the world during the Exposition, and with the Fair being held on his own territory Kobusch was exceedingly anxious to see that his own company's products were greatly in evidence. How better could he do this than by constructing the new cars which would be needed by United Railways of St. Louis to carry passengers to and from the fair?

It may now never be known how he got the contract for the 450 World's Fair cars United Railways decided it needed, nor how he got the additional contract for the 60 cars needed for the Exposition's seven-mile-long intramural railroad. But it was obvious that the efficient running of the new cars, together with the Car Company's exhibit in the Exposition itself would probably provide sufficient favorable publicity to stimulate sales to a point beyond the Baden plant's manufacturing capacity. The acquisition of the Laclede plant therefore was, in addition to its long-term strategic value vis-a-vis the Brill Co., an attempt to quickly provide the Car Company with extra manufacturing capacity, whatever the long-term cost.[4]

The combined manufacturing capacity of the plants was said to be $5 million per year in 1903, making the enlarged St. Louis Car Co. one of the largest manufacturing companies in St. Louis.[5] Indeed at a convention of the American Street Railroad Association held later that year in Saratoga, the Car Company's booth proudly proclaimed the company as possessing

> The largest electric car plant in the world . . . owning and operating the St. Louis and Laclede factories. Manufacturers of electric cars, motor and trailer trucks, car seats, car fixtures, arc headlights, interior arc lamps, spiral journal bearings (and) car trimmings.[6]

And with that kind of publicity, Kobusch propelled his company towards the great promotional climax of the World's Fair.

CHAPTER 6

THE TIME OF the 1904 Louisiana Purchase Exposition was for many people a golden era in St. Louis' history. The Exposition, as was expected, brought visitors and exhibitors from every part of the world, focusing the attention of the whole world on the city for the first time in its history. Transportation was one of the important themes around which the Exposition was organized, for transportation was rightly seen as being intimately linked with the wonders of the new industrial age. The Exposition Chief of the Department of Transportation, Willard A. Smith put it succinctly:

> Transportation is the life of modern civilization. It is the circulatory system, without which it could not have come into existence, and the stoppage of which would cause stagnation and decay.[1]

Recognition of transportation's importance to modern life was hardly a new idea. The Chicago Columbian Exposition of 1893 had a major transportation exhibit in which the primary theme was an examination of the railroads' role in closing the American frontier. The St. Louis Car Co.'s exhibit at the St. Louis World's Fair in 1904 restated and expanded this theme, through examining the development in the quality of city life made possible since the Chicago Exhibition by the immense growth of electric streetcar facilities. In addition it took a look at the future, and the promise for the development of rural America that the electric interurban railway represented. The commemorative booklet produced by the Car Company began by suggesting that when it was considered:

> in the early sixties, the greatest traffic in St. Louis was carried on the Mississippi River, and . . . required some steamers practically sixty days to make the trip from St. Louis to Fort Benton, Montana, and from there the freight was distributed by pack trains to the lower country, one can readily appreciate what the opening of the Union Pacific Railroad has done for this country.[2]

The provision of efficient transportation facilities that was now possible in the West by the adoption of the electric interurban, would bring about just as profound a revolution in transportation as the steam railroad had done a generation earlier, and the entire West, previously considered frontier, would in a matter of years be:

> honeycombed with interurban lines, enabling one to travel from village to village, city to city, state to state.[3]

The exhibit contrasted old and new in transport and included a stage coach used to carry passengers over the Rockies in the early 1860s. A horse car of the 1870s was used as the starting point with which to demonstrate the streetcar's evolution. One vehicle displayed was the first cable car to be put into service in San Francisco in 1873, which the Car Company recognized as being the first successful application of mechanized traction to street railways.

Of greatest interest was the display of a car built by the Car Company at the end of 1887 for the Topeka Railway Co., among the first electric cars they had ever built. The vehicle had been in continuous service until just prior to the opening of the Exposition.

But the exhibit's principal theme was trolley transportation in the modern world, and most of the displays were of cars currently in production. Among the most interesting were the pre-fabri--cated electric cars intended for South America, many hundreds of which had been boxed and exported since 1900. Certainly the most advanced car exhibited, in terms of design and construction, was an all-steel subway trailer car built for the Interborough Rapid Transit Co. of New York (the IRT subway). Fifty-one feet long and nearly nine feet wide, the tapered roof design allowed maximum seating and headroom, while providing the necessary clearance for tunnel operation. Sheathed from top to bottom in copper, the car was said to be virtually fireproof. The interior was finished in African mahogany.

North Western Elevated Railway of Chicago trailer car #53.

Other cars in the exhibit included a 46-foot combination motor and trailer built for the North Western Elevated Railway Co. of Chicago, and a street railway postal car. This last vehicle was exhibited in the U.S. government building as part of the postal display. But probably the high point of the exhibit was the display of private cars.

Two magnificent examples were on view: the "Milwaukee" and the "Mabel." At the end of the 19th century, the private railroad car had represented the ultimate symbol of luxury and wealth among American businessmen. In their "private varnish" these men could live free of the doubtful accommodations of the small towns they frequently passed through, and entertain on a scale consistent with their wealth and social status. The tradition of private cars was inherited by the street railways, and like their mainline counterparts, these cars emphasized personal comfort and elegance. Since the disappearance of the original small, ornately finished electric car, these private cars provided almost the only opportunity that a manufacturer of quality such as the Car Company had to demonstrate its remarkable craftsmanship. Between 1900 and 1904, eleven private cars were built, and while they were by no means the first such vehicles built by the company, they were undoubtedly the finest. Private cars had an individuality which was emphasized down to the smallest detail of construction, and frequently they were given their own names. Two complete private cars were exhibited by the company at the World's Fair, and together they represented the skilled craft of the wooden bodied streetcar manufacturer at its zenith.

The "Milwaukee" was designed by and built for John I. Beggs, a member of the North American Co.'s Board of Directors. This was a large new holding company, specializing in the acquisition and control of public utilities. Beggs was the company's largest individual stockholder, but for undisclosed personal reasons declined to act as its president. North American's primary concentration of ownership at that time was Wisconsin, particularly that state's electrical supply business in which Beggs was a dominant force. He was president of North American's Milwaukee Electric Railway and Light Co., a company he had single-handedly put together. He was also president of Union Electric Co. and Laclede Gas Co. of St. Louis, both North American properties, and at the beginning of 1905 assumed the presidency of St. Louis United Railways, after its acquisition by North American. It is also believed he held a con-

After the World's Fair, the private car *Mabel* was rarely seen, until in later years it was bought by the St. Louis United Railways for use in charter service by trolley parties. The car was renamed *St. Louis Sans Souci. (National Museum of Transport)*

siderable amount of stock in the St. Louis Car Co. at this time. He was an immensely wealthy and powerful man, and his private car had been designed to demonstrate that fact to the world. The car was divided into compartments, each furnished and decorated in a different style. Each end of the car had an observation room with a motorman's cab and an upper and lower berth, finished in East Indian vermilion wood with marquetry inlay. One compartment was finished in Hungarian ash, and included a sofa, a lower berth, a dressing case and a washstand among its many personal comforts. Another compartment was fitted with a folding bed stored in a cabinet under a bookcase. There was a kitchen with a 26″ x 30″ range, and a toilet compartment which sported zebra wood walls. A typewriter and desk were installed at one end of the car, while in the center was a dining room finished in Philippine rosewood with tables, a sideboard, silver lockers, chairs and a fireplace. There was even a double refrigerator which extended into the kitchen.

The car ceilings were of Empire design and decorated to harmonize with each of the rooms. Passageways were vermilion and white silks and tapestries were used throughout as both decoration and furniture upholstery. Heat and hot water were provided by an independent electrical system, which also lit a series of electric lights, covered by holophane globes. The full impact of this somewhat garish opulence was to some degree diminished by Beggs' insistence on the separate compartments, but in any event it hardly mattered for the car was destroyed in a carbarn fire in December 1907, and he must have had very little use from it.

The private car "Mabel" was built for Edward Gardner Lewis, the founder of University City, Missouri, and the publisher of *Women's Magazine* and the *Women's Farm Journal.* Unlike Beggs, Lewis did not make the mistake of dividing his car into compartments. The car in fact had only two sections: a buffet or smoker, and a parlor. A pea-green Empire ceiling, with carved and inlaid woods, stretched the length of the car. The carpets in both sections matched the ceiling, and in the center of the parlor compartment was a handsomely carved and upholstered settee. The upholstery was of a light yellow fabric, complementing the ceiling and curtains. The ventilator lights were of a colonial pattern, and the upper sashes were of bevel plate, with centerpiece designed in art glass. The lower sashes were of plate glass and dropped into pockets covered by flaps. In both compart-

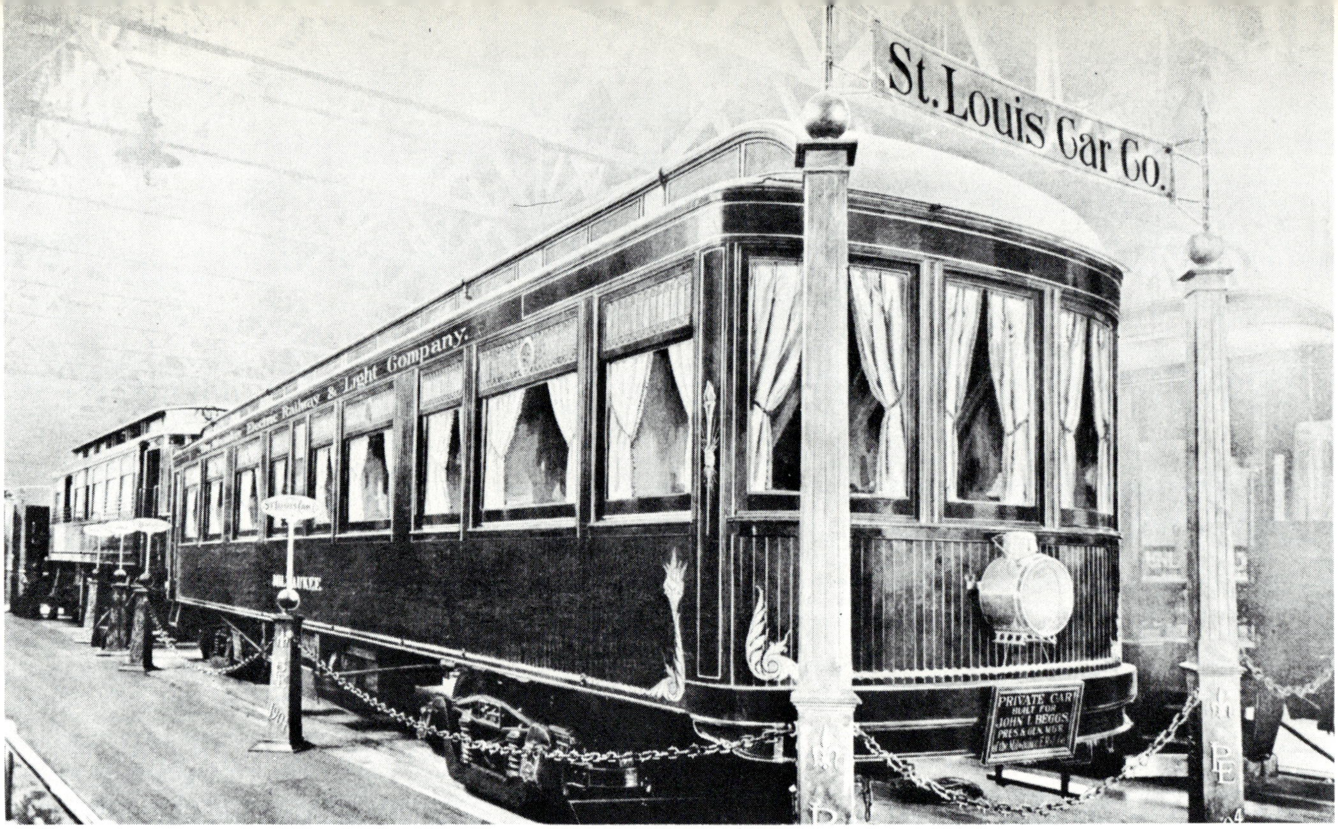

Private car *Milwaukee* at the St. Louis World's Fair in 1904. *(William J. Clouser collection)*

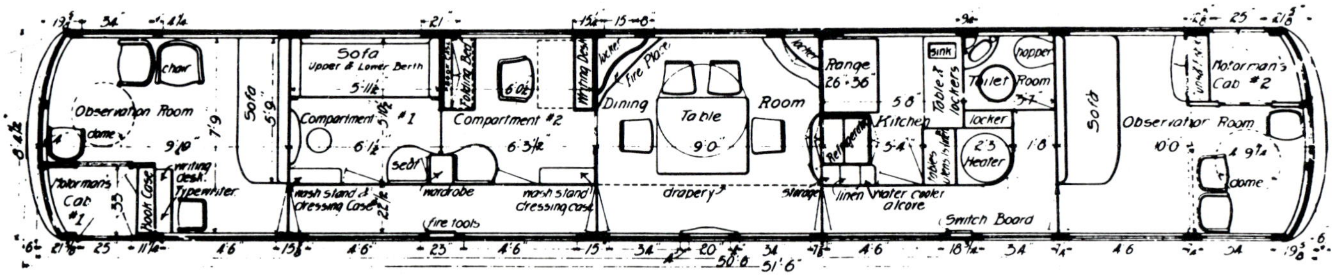

Floor plan of the *Milwaukee*. Notice the many separate compartments. *(Street Railway Journal)*

The private car *Alabama* was not completed until April, 1905, and is seen here in California.

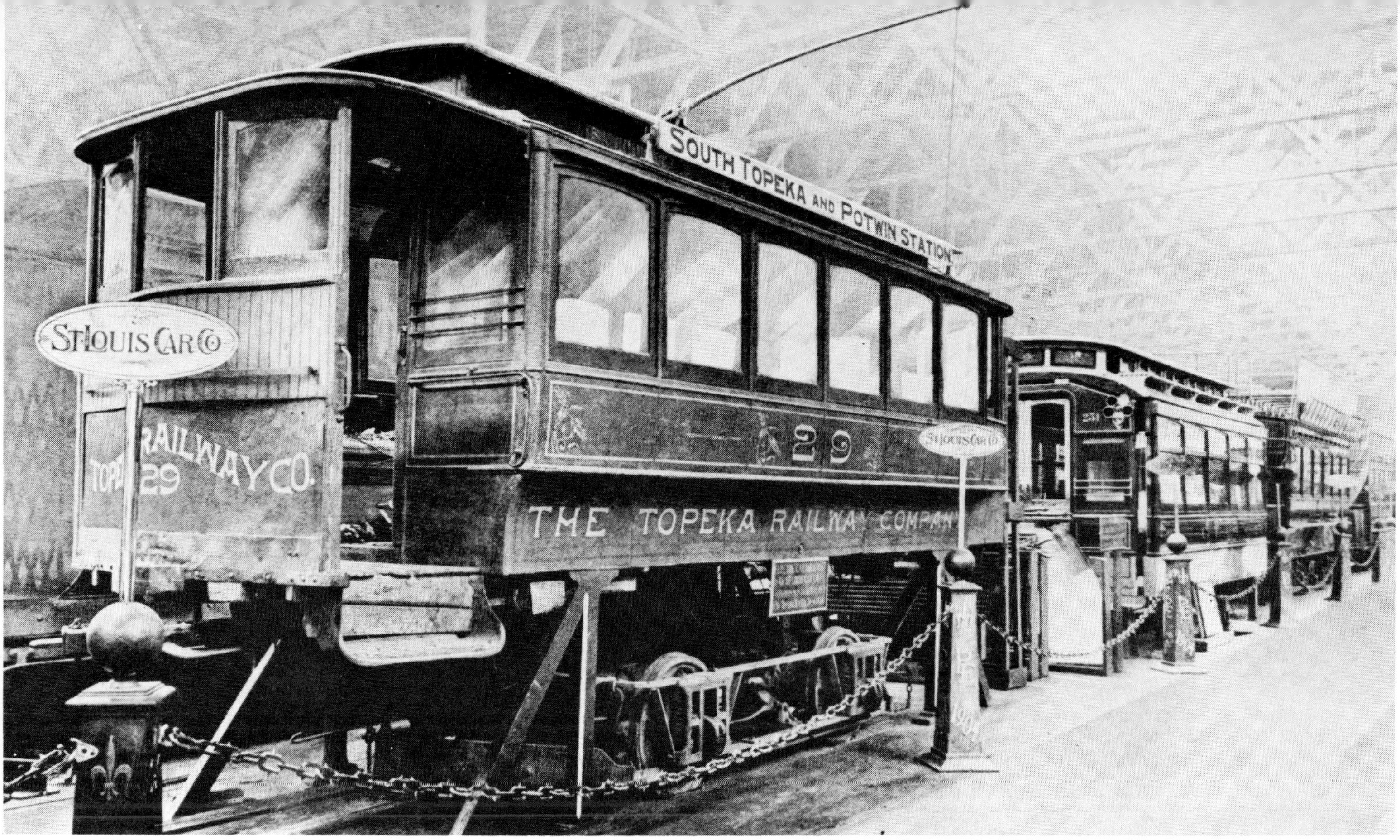

This group of cars represents streetcar evolution as understood by the Car Co. It formed part of the World's Fair exhibit. The Topeka car, built in 1887, had just been withdrawn from service. The car behind was a typical export model for Buenos Aires. Behind that was a sample double-deck car for Dublin, built in 1900 but never sold. At the end of the World's Fair, the car was sold to British Electric Car Co. in Manchester, England, and then was resold to Huddersfield Corp. as car #67.

The ornate World's Fair office of the Car Company. The large variety of electric arc lights is striking. *(William J. Clouser collection)*

The Indiana Railway Co.'s #53 was one of the last wooden-bodied city cars built to this elegant design. It was delivered in 1904. *(Edwin J. Klasky collection)*

Interurban cars continued to be more ornately finished than city streetcars. Alton, Granite City and St. Louis #51 is a good example, with its etched glass and lined-out paintwork. *(William J. Clouser collection)*

ments, and along each side of the deck sill was a row of frosted electric lamps.

As well as complete cars, the exhibit included displays of the specialized products manufactured at the plant. Seats, arc lamps, curtains, trucks, vertical wheel brakes and spiral journals were all included as other products from the company's brass and malleable grey iron foundries. Evidence of the success of the company's products at the fair was the award to them of the Grand Prize for excellence in the manufacture of streetcars and equipment by the Committee of the Exposition.[4]

The World's Fair exhibit was a great triumph for the company, and with the plant in the St. Louis area, it was easy to arrange visits, using private cars for the purpose, including the "Mabel."[5] In addition, Kobusch's publicity sense led him to arrange various "stunts" one of the most striking taking place on July 30th, the Exposition's "Transportation Day." About 3,000 employees took part in a parade, and for many days production had been shut down while this huge body of men was rehearsed and drilled. The employees of the various departments were all in different uniforms, carrying tools or other implements illustrating the different branches of car construction. This was a big point for Kobusch to make, since at the time there were over 30 separate departments in the company. Some of the more important departments constructed floats, the most flamboyant being crowned by a huge globe, sitting on top of which was a small open trolley car, while the entire display was emblazoned with the slogan "The sun never sets on the products of the St. Louis Car Company." Other placards carried in the parade were equally as buoyant. Typical was the one which stated, "We lead the world in car building."

Still it was not the local visitors Kobusch wanted to impress; he was far more concerned with the foreign visitors, especially those in the market for new electric streetcars. Though 1903 had been a good year, preparing special displays for the fair, and the general holiday spirit prevailing in the city through much of 1904 had made that year less profitable. Kobusch was particularly anxious to solicit new customers, especially foreign customers whose business might not be as profitable, but carried more prestige than domestic business. In 1904 therefore, the Car Company began an active campaign to seek wider export markets, and a branch office run by Aaron S. Everest was set up in Queen Anne's Chambers, London. The office was regarded as their European headquarters, and as a branch office for their agent H. Böker of Berlin, who since his appointment in 1899 had helped the Car Company secure orders in South America, Russia, Germany and Italy.[6]

To further expand export markets, an extensive business trip was made shortly after the Fair closed by E. I. Robinson, a Car Company vice president and head of the Laclede plant. In the *Margaret* a chartered yacht from Baltimore, Robinson, together with W. T. Van Brunt, head of the St. Joseph Railway Light and Power Co., Dr. Eugenio Dahne, Brazilian Commissioner to the Exposition, and several others, first visited the West Indies, sailing then to Brazil, and on to Europe.[7] A series of letters survive, written by Robinson to his son (then in temporary charge of the Laclede plant), which describe something of the trip, and provide an insight into the characteristic way in which the St. Louis Car Co. did its foreign business. On January 25, 1905, "from off the coast of St. John's in the West Indies" Robinson wrote to his son, urging him

> to be very diligent concerning the business at the factory. As I wrote you before, have the office in first class condition . . . you know the annoyance to both yourself and me about keeping the entire plant in first class condition and clean . . . Have a place for everything, and everything in its place, especially in the lumber yard and the iron department and as Mr. Kobusch told you, and very explicitly, see that every foreman in his department is competent and carrying out his orders through you so that there may not be any complaint of the Laclede branch during the entire year.[8]

Proceeding from St. John's to Barbados, the party visited Bridgeton, the capital, where they examined the mule car system, hoping the city might be a customer should electrification be decided upon.

St. Louis Car Co.'s parade at the World's Fair *Transportation Day*, July 30, 1904. The float was symbolic of the fact that "the sun never sets on the products of the St. Louis Car Co."

They run their cars every half hour. At the terminus down in the city they have four or five cars . . . The superintendent told me that they owned twenty 6-bench open cars of the very cheapest type. They operate ten or twelve morning and evening, and during the day five cars, and they are drawn by two little mules, not much bigger than our ordinary goats. The gauge of their track is 3′ 2″ and very light rail. The young man employed in their office whom I met at the car barn before I saw the superintendent told me that they carry 2,000 passengers a day. They have two rates of fares; 2d a mile (i.e. four cents) on the mile sections and a through ticket for 3d (six cents) on the two mile sections.[9]

Throughout all this series of letters, there is the sense that Robinson and his party considered themselves as much emissaries of the U.S.A. on a diplomatic mission, as they were businessmen looking for new customers. In Brazil for example:

> We . . . called on two State Presidents, also on the National President, and found them all dark men. The President is a little fellow, but lives in a large and beautiful mansion.[10]

There is no mention at all in this letter of any particular business they were sent to conduct.

Despite this, the correspondence continually returned to a single theme: keeping up the business in St. Louis. Addressing his son at the conclusion of the Brazilian visit, Robinson exhorted him to be

> very diligent in your business, watching every point about the place, not forgetting the Blacksmith shop.[11]

From Brazil, the party made its way to England, and from there to France before returning home in May 1905.

Though this was by no means the last foreign trip made by Car Company executives (Vogel was already in England on his way to Germany at the end of 1904),[12] such junkets to the pleasant places of the earth, done at the leisurely pace and style of the *Margaret*, were far too expensive for a company with chronic liquidity problems. Such jaunts were in a tradition started after the Civil War by railway magnates such as Gould, Morgan and Huntington, and it is reasonable to suppose that Kobusch and his executives thought that the importance of their industry to the U.S. economy merited this same appearance of leisured ease in transacting international business. But by 1905, the street railway boom was ending and the industry never again recovered that kind of buoyancy and optimism about its future.

The Baden plant in 1904. The inset shows the Laclede plant.

The first announcement of the American Mors was patriotically printed in red, white and blue, appearing in the *Automobile* on November 29, 1906.

CHAPTER 7

In both prosperity and influence, 1904 was St. Louis Car Co.'s peak year under Kobusch's guidance. He had succeeded in re-establishing the Company's credit in St. Louis after the Snyder affair, he was successfully cultivating new friends outside St. Louis who had access to money, and the World's Fair had brought him some badly-needed acclaim from the public.

A partial indication of the company's financial recovery was shown by the capital increase of March 1904. Taken together with that made in 1903, the net result was to raise the Company's capitalization by $1½ million in less than a year, company capital by 1904 being $2 million.[1] Kobusch was in a particularly euphoric state of mind at this time, and full of new projects. The Fair had provided him with his international showcase, and it seemed to have resulted in the new orders he wanted. With the Car Company's immediate future taken care of, he turned his attention away from streetcar manufacture, and began to look at other manufacturing possibilities.

The automobile had been well represented at the Fair, and the Societé Anonymée d'Electricité et d'Automobiles de Paris, with its Mors vehicle was awarded the Grand Prix for design and workmanship in automobiles. The Mors was a large, powerful luxury touring car, and Kobusch was highly impressed by it. Though the automobile was a rich man's toy at that time, he felt that there would be an excellent market for it in the U.S.A., especially as in the first few years of this century the French were regarded as the world's best automobile designers and manufacturers. Negotiations with the Mors Co. were started early in 1905, and a final agreement signed a year later, which gave Kobusch the exclusive marketing and manufacturing rights in the U.S.A.[2] A new "Kobusch Automobile Co." was set up as a wholly-owned subsidiary of the St. Louis Car Co. to deal with the Mors.

Readying the automobile plant took some time, and it was not until mid-1906 that the first vehicle was produced in St. Louis, going out on sales demonstrations at the end of August.[3]

It had been planned to use a leased factory in which to build the cars, but with the decrease in streetcar orders commencing with the beginning of the 1906 slump, the Laclede plant was no longer fulfilling its function as an overflow for Baden, and it was decided to convert that plant to an automobile factory.

The new automobile corresponded very closely to the 1907 French Mors, the only substantial difference being the dimensions of the wheel tread and the height of the body. The 1907 American Mors was available in 3 models, 14-18 hp., 24-32 hp. and 40-52 hp. All the vehicles were fitted with pressed steel frames with gusset plates at each corner. Four-cylinder motors were used, cast by the Car Company in their own foundries at Baden. All the latest design improvements were incorporated, including an automatic carburetor and "make and break" spark ignition.[4]

A feature of the car which was made much of in advertising was its "all-American" manufacture. Everything on the car was made in the U.S.A. and practically everything of importance at the Car Company plants. The list price of the vehicles was between $3500 and $5000, depending on the model, not much less than the average streetcar of the time. With so high a selling price, it is difficult to understand how Kobusch possibly could have hoped to make money on the venture, though in fairness it must be said that this was an exceptionally high-grade vehicle.

The automobile was first exhibited at the New York Grand Central Palace Auto Show in December 1906, but as an expensive 4-cylinder vehicle it was at a distinct disadvantage when compared to cars of similar quality fitted with the 6-cylinder motors first exhibited that season. Undoubtedly 6-cylinder automobiles were the "hit" of the show, and Walter Scott Miller and George C. Johns (the plant and sales managers respectively) did well to book orders for 125 American Mors cars, about half the anticipated 1907 output. Thereafter sales

A Mors limousine, exhibited at the World's Fair. *(William J. Clouser collection)*

A Mors touring car. *(William J. Clouser collection)*

A 1908 American Mors touring car. *(St. Louis Public Libraries)*

were very slow throughout the model year, and management problems in the St. Louis Mors plant exacerbated the situation.[5] Moreover the use of an old fashioned chain drive in the car, rather than the more modern and reliable drive shaft, further added to the vehicle's lack of sales appeal. There is no exact record of the number of American Mors cars sold, but there is no doubt that the project quickly got the St. Louis Car Co. into grave financial difficulties.[6] Owing to the last minute change of plant, the first car had been delayed almost a year, and the very high price and obsolescent design guaranteed slow sales. It is certain that the large capital investment was a total loss, and yet more money was lost when at an unknown date, the automobile plant was moved to another new location, this time a plant at 5200 North Broadway.

At the time the Mors franchise agreement had been signed, it is probable that money was no object to Kobusch, for much of 1905 had been taken up with the ultimate in consolidation schemes.

> In the *Railway Age* of June 9, 1904, a report was published upon good authority concerning plans for effecting a combination among practically all . . . (builders of) street cars in this country. At that time we were not at liberty to state who constituted the outside interests which have been securing options upon the various plants . . . Announcement is now made that the syndicate, consisting of 19 companies will be managed by Kean Van Cortlandt & Co., bankers, New York . . . and that the promoters are E. H. Power and W. T. Van Brunt. The capital will be $43 million, consisting of $15½ million 6% cumulative preferred stock, and $27½ million common stock. The average annual net earnings of the individual companies is stated to have been $1,263,390, which the promoters propose to double by the combination . . .[7]

The companies involved were as follows: Brill, Stephenson, Laclede (which still had a separate corporate existence) Saint Louis Malleable Casting Co., St. Louis Car Co., American, Kuhlman, Cincinnati, Wason, Osgood Bradley, Cummings, Jewett, J. M. Jones' Sons, agents, Laconia, McGuire-Cummings, Peckham Mfg., Niles, Journal Bearing Co., and Easy Access Door Co. While both Stephenson and Peckham were in financial difficulties at the time, it was hoped that such a combination would do for the street railway business what the combination which led in 1899 to the formation of ACF had done for the railroad freight and passenger car business. Even though the scheme eventually fell through, by April 1906 Kobusch was still sufficiently confident to start the procedures for raising the company's capital, a process completed on April 16, 1906, when the total worth of issued Car Company stock at face value was increased to a total of $2½ million. At the time of the increase, the Car Company listed the net worth of its assets at $4,696,657, while its liabilities were $1,942,817.[8]

Kobusch's continued lack of concern over money in the circumstances seems strange, for the slump was now getting worse and (for the first time in its history) the street railway industry was being adversely affected by such a slump. The most likely explanation of his attitude probably lies in his developing involvement in the financial empire of George Gould.

The history of the Gould-Kobusch relationship is obscure. Gould's empire had its origins in 1896 in a dispute over freight rates between Andrew Carnegie, the Baltimore & Ohio and the Pennsylvania railroads, which threatened to overprice Carnegie's Pittsburgh manufactured steel in the eastern markets. Gould and Carnegie sought to break the monopoly of these two railroads by working out an agreement to stitch together an alternative rail route from Pittsburgh to the East, utilizing the Wabash, Missouri Pacific and Wheeling and Lake Erie lines. Carnegie sold out to J. P. Morgan in 1901, but Gould continued to build his empire, using the Carnegie arrangement as the nucleus for a more grandiose scheme, nothing less than the first coast-to-coast transcontinental railroad, a direct east-west line that did not pass through Chicago. To that end he spent the next few years in filling the gaps in his eastern network, and formed a new company to build west from Salt Lake City. One large gap in the East was filled by extending the Wabash into Pittsburgh, there connecting with the Western Maryland Railroad, bringing Gould's roads within striking distance of the East Coast. There remained only a forty-mile gap between the end of the Western Maryland at York, Pa., and another Gould company, the Philadelphia and Western Railroad.

Formed in 1902, this line had been authorized to build from 63rd Street, Philadelphia to Parkersburg, Pa. If extended west to York, and east to the Philadelphia city wharf, this line when completed would also complete Gould's line to the East. At this point then, the success of the Gould enterprise lay with the Philadelphia and Western. It isn't clear in what way Kobusch was involved, for while rumors abounded, the Philadelphia and Western scheme was never made public, and Gould's connection with it was roundly denied. It became clear some activity was contemplated when in May 1905, immediately after Robinson and Van Brunt returned from their cruise in the *Margaret*, Van Brunt was appointed president of the Philadelphia and Western. Van Brunt, in addition to his other posts, was an officer of the New York banking house R. B. Newcombe, with whom he had been connected since 1885, and had many connections in St. Louis banking circles, which of course would have brought him into contact with Gould (via the Missouri Pacific, headquartered in St. Louis) and Kobusch, who still retained some bank directorships in St. Louis.

But what the exact connections were remains quite a mystery, for there was an almost pathological desire to maintain secrecy concerning the true purpose of the Philadelphia and Western. In July, 1905, the Gould organization issued a statement to quell rumors that it controlled that line, stating quite flatly that the only persons involved were George J. Kobusch, Van Brunt "and their financial friends." But within a month the secret was out when Van Brunt was replaced by Kobusch as president of the Philadelphia and Western.

There is little doubt Kobusch was acting in good faith. Though the line was never in fact completed west of Strafford, Pa., some ten miles west of the proposed 63rd street terminal, this was due entirely to lack of funds, and not lack of intent. The financial drain of building west from Salt Lake City to the Pacific affected all Gould's empire, but at the time it was thought those problems were temporary. Thus during 1906, Kobusch and Gould were extremely active in Philadelphia and Western affairs. Surveying and grading of the line west of Strafford was begun, the extension to downtown Philadelphia was in the planning stages, while many complex financial and political deals were entered into in an attempt to get the location of the route to the wharf fixed.

By May 1906, the line's management began to admit openly their intention to build an electric road to York, Pa., paralleling the Pennsylvania Railroad, and joining up with the rest of the Gould network lying to the west. Indeed in the summer of 1906 it seemed for a time that the entire coast-to-coast project was going to succeed if the temporary financial difficulties occasioned by the Utah-California extension could be overcome. But the nationwide slump grew ever more serious and money was difficult to raise. By July 1906, the continued Philadelphia and Western activity was little more than a sham, a way of raising new capital for the little line which was by now so short of cash that the completed section was as yet unable to open for revenue-producing traffic. It was obviously felt that this continued activity would help keep the entire Gould transcontinental scheme alive through the slump. The small size of the Philadelphia and Western would keep operating expenses down, while it served areas which could quickly become revenue-producing. This it was thought made the line a more attractive investment during a slump than the West Coast extension being built through wilderness, over immense distances.

Cash was scarce for the line, largely through Gould's own fault. The secrecy surrounding the line's true function was not the most tactful way to attract investment capital, particularly as it was obvious that the scale of engineering was totally out of proportion to the line's stated purpose. It had been expensive to construct because it was designed almost entirely as a high-speed line, with relatively easy curves and grades by the standards of the day. This was exactly right for a long distance mainline, but quite extravagant on a short commuter route, which it had rather foolishly been insisting was the line's true purpose. Originally scheduled to open in October 1905, lack of money to complete it kept it closed for a long

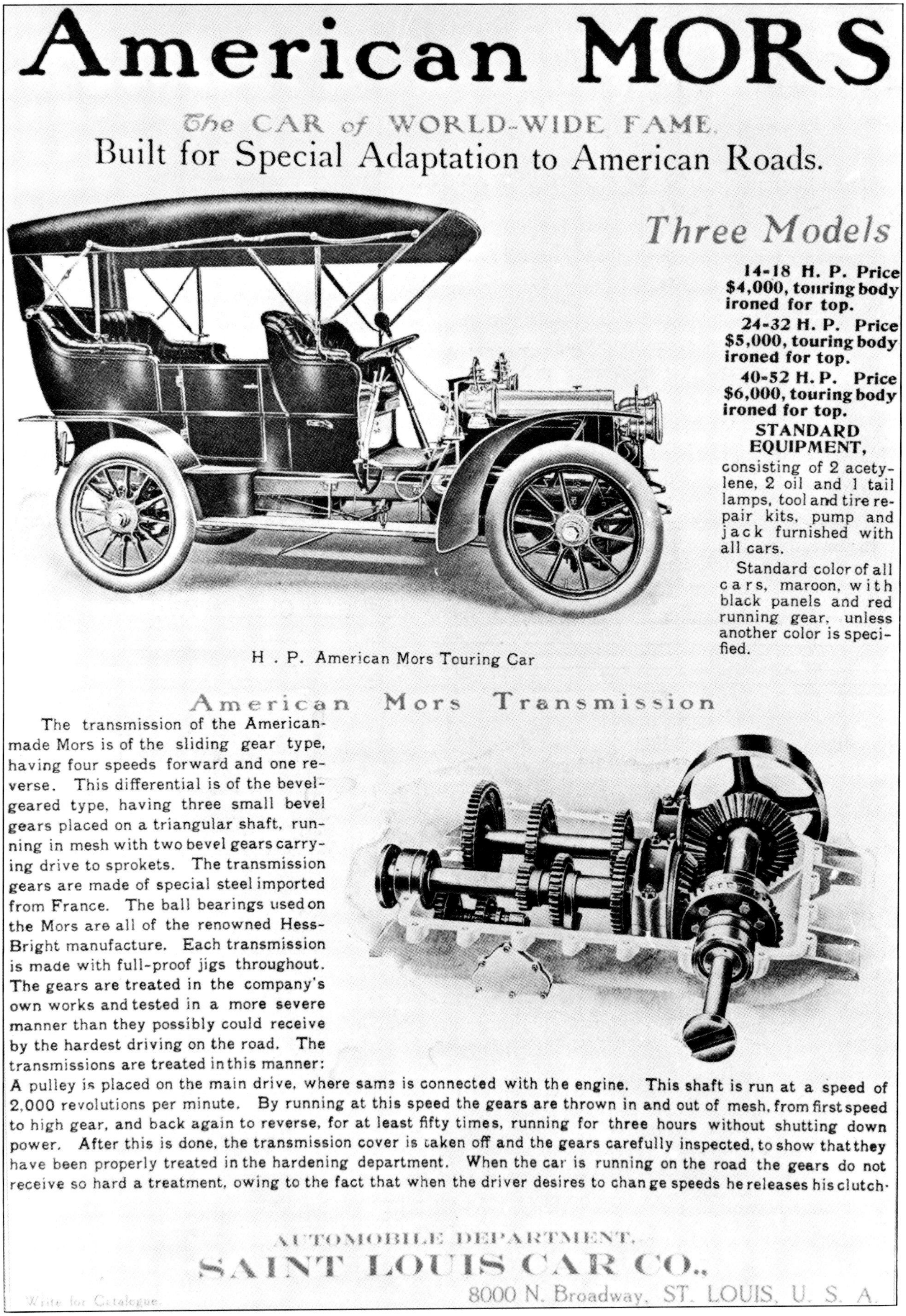

A 1907 advertisement explaining the special adaptation to American driving conditions. *(St. Louis Public Libraries)*

period, and Kobusch was much chagrined to have 22 high-speed electric cars built especially for the line left unsold. They remained at Baden for over a year before being disposed of to other customers.

By the end of 1906 it was clear Gould had overreached himself, and Kobusch, having set his financial course in Gould's direction, was in deep trouble. Moreover because of the slump, he could not wholly rely on the hitherto unfailing profitability of the St. Louis Car Co. to bail him out.[9] In an attempt to retrieve the situation, Kobusch immediately tried to raise money by increasing the Car Company capital from $2½ million to $3 million. From the Company's point of view, this increase, completed by November 28, 1906 was not an imprudent move. In that month, the company had $6½ million of equipment contracts unbuilt, sufficient to guarantee full-time operation throughout 1907. Orders for 1908 delivery were already being taken, and a further $1,600,000 was tied up in vehicles completed but not yet shipped. A further large, but undetermined sum was frozen in various parts and materials on hand for cars about to be assembled.[10] Clearly the shortage of liquid capital at the Car Company at the end of 1906 had nothing to do with its own business which seemed to be weathering the slump quite well.

Kobusch's activities as a financier were drawing money from the company at a time when it needed all it could get to keep itself financially stable. During the early part of 1907, a number of orders were cancelled, and it became more difficult to replace the working capital needed to finance work in hand, much of which had been put to other uses by Kobusch. The new steel car plant, which had been opened in 1906 was the hardest hit by the slump, for practically no customers wanted steel cars, and the department lost money from the day it opened for business.

Kobusch, now without adequate financial backing, was forced to retrench as best he could, phasing out the costly railroad car building program started in the wake of the World's Fair, finding other uses for the steel car department, and trying to disassociate himself from Gould. He resigned the presidency of the Philadelphia and Western in April 1907[11] and sold his interest in it for ready cash to George R. Sheldon a New Yorker, who was a director of St. Louis United Railways. Even more money was urgently required to keep the Car Company, his financial bedrock, in sound condition throughout the slump. A certain proportion of the money could still be raised locally, but Kobusch's reputation was now such that commercial loans of this nature were only available to him at outrageous interest rates. Moreover, in the changed economic climate, the streetcar was becoming a much less attractive investment, while the automobile was beginning to seem as promising a mode of transport as the electric streetcar had twenty years before. Kobusch already owned an automobile plant, and while it was presently losing money, there were good grounds for thinking that if properly undertaken, automobile manufacture would be the U.S.A.'s new growth industry.

This was a sufficiently tempting vision to prompt Kobusch at this point to turn to the Mors Co. in Paris for help. He planned on selling $3 million of new Car Company stock to Mors, and presumably he hoped to pay his debts, provide working capital for the Car Company, and expand the automobile plant. Unfortunately, while his judgement was sound, his timing let him down. The automobile industry was not yet developed to the point where such major investments could safely be undertaken, neither in France nor the U.S.A. Automobile manufacture was still not much more than a craft industry, and profitability was still questionable. Investment on the scale proposed by Kobusch was thus extremely unwise, and the deal fell through when the French company failed to pay even the first installment. Kobusch was thus deprived of his money, but no one else knew that, for he carefully saw to it that the $3 million of new paper which should have been taken up by Mors, was deposited in the company safe as if it had, in fact, been taken up. Shortly thereafter, he used this paper as backing for another capital increase, needed to solve the cash shortage.

This increase of capital, the third in 18 months, was an unwise, indeed flamboyant gesture to make in a slump, and yet one characteristic of an age which had produced the brash business promoters of Kobusch's stamp. For with a flourish, Kobusch simply decreed to the world that the company was now to be capitalized at $6 million, a sum double that of only eight months before which had already proven so difficult to raise. To attract investors, and to gain plausibility, this new stock was designated a preferred stock, bearing interest at a rate of 7%.

> It is reported that a French syndicate which was expected to take up $3 million of the preferred stock . . . has failed to do so . . . Kobusch has succeeded in reorganizing the (Car) Company . . . with financial support from St. Louis residents. It is reported that the automobile department will be divorced from the streetcar end entirely, and the reorganization will be followed by additions to the company's equipment and by an enlargement of the plant. The repository of the Company is the St. Louis National Bank of Commerce, and Benjamin F. Edwards, Vice President of the bank said that it was his understanding that while the streetcar company was in excellent condition and paying all its obligations promptly, a reorganization would nevertheless take place. The $3 million stock is to bear interest at . . . 7% . . . Upon delivery of this stock to the bank, $1 million cash would be deposited there to the credit of the company immediately, and that a similar amount would be forthcoming on October 1st. The Company has filed notice of an increase in its capital stock from $3 million to $6 million. Its outstanding bonds amount to $695,000.[12]

Despite this optimistic press report, it is doubtful if this increase were anything but water, and that fact was quite apparent at the time.[13] The state of the industry was anything but healthy, and there was a prevalent feeling that only marginal expansion of the street railway network therefor was now possible, for the country was saturated. The manufacturers' market would in the future, therefore be largely confined to replacing existing equipment and the new capital increase made no sense from a business point of view. Kobusch's career as a minor street railway tycoon had closely paralleled the fortunes of the industry. By the end of 1907 he must also have been able to see that the financial glamour of this hitherto most exciting of industries had now largely evaporated, and that most investors and financiers were looking at oil, automobiles and real estate. Moreover, there had been a change in the political climate over the previous few years. There was now an anxiety to curb the power of big business — and anything to do with streetcars was thought of as big business. Breaking the monopolies of the big industrial corporations and the public utilities was seen as a national priority. The street railway industry, despite its recent poor financial showing, was a prime target for this point of view. It was forced into a defensive posture and Kobusch with it.[14]

An American Mors at a bodyshop for repairs in 1907.

A Standard Six automobile on a demonstration run in St. Louis during 1909.

Hundreds of wood cars were shipped from St. Louis to California between 1895 and 1915, and with judicious rebuilding, some enjoyed remarkably long lives. Car #423 of Los Angeles Railways was built in 1905 as a California type car with open ends and an enclosed center compartment. It was later rebuilt and is shown here in service during 1944. *(Los Angeles Transit Lines, Edwin J. Klasky collection)*

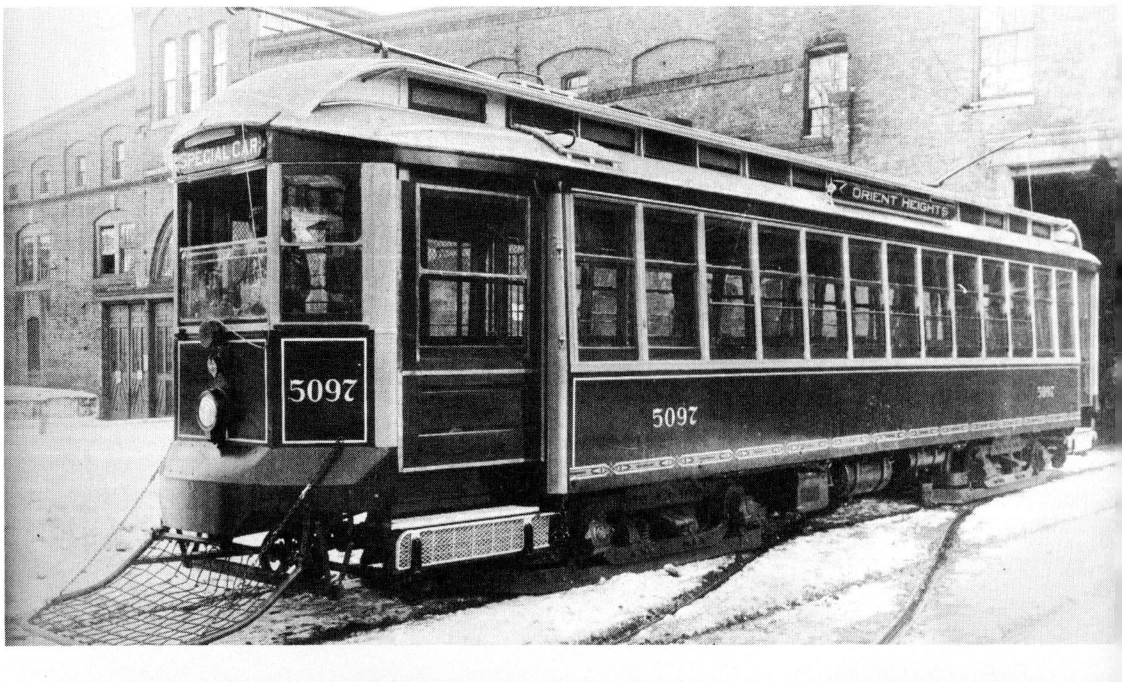

A handful of these Boston type 3 cars are in use today as snowplows. They were built in 1907. Car #5097 is seen when brand new at Boston's Bartlett Street shops. *(Kevin T. Farrell collection)*

CHAPTER 8

THROUGHOUT ALL HIS other activities, Kobusch persisted in his attempts to make automobile manufacture profitable, and in 1907 added a completely new American Mors automobile to the existing range. Designated model "E", the new car featured shaft drive and a six-cylinder motor, being exhibited first in October 1907 for the 1908 model year. It is not known whether the design was entirely original, or whether it was a copy of the French 6-cylinder Mors, first exhibited at the 1906 Paris motor show.[1] However, it is known that the Car Company had contemplated entering a six-cylinder American Mors in the elimination trials for the Vanderbilt Cup as early as March 1907[2] and it is probable that the new Model "E" was a copy of the French machine. Nothing came of the Vanderbilt cup entry, and with the departure of George C. Johns from the American Mors sales team in June 1907, trouble with the sales staff became acute.[3]

The model "E" was a very large seven-passenger tourer, with a 127″ wheelbase and a price of $4,250.[4] It is not known if it was a commercial success[5] but it was listed as available until production of the American Mors ceased in mid-1909. But whether available from stock or on special order only, the car could not have sold well at so high a price, and could not have helped the Car Company's finances.

By 1908, the French no longer had the lead in automobile design that they had possessed four years earlier when Kobusch first considered the Mors, and it was decided to substitute for the Mors a wholly American vehicle (and it is believed a purely Car Company-designed vehicle) for the 1910 model year. The last American Mors was delivered in April or May 1909, and the first "Standard Six" (subtitled "the car complete") was on demonstration runs by June. The car's all-American design and manufacture was a major theme in the promotional campaign, as was its ability to go from 4 mph to 65 mph in top gear. With a 124″ wheelbase, vanadium steel front and rear axles, an inverted cone clutch and an aluminum body, the car certainly lived up to its billing as a "good car at a fair price" for it listed at $3,000. One chassis only was available, in the interests of "standardization," but touring, roadster and miniature bodies could be had, and for an extra $1000, a limousine body would be supplied. The car was the first in the U.S.A. to be fitted as standard with a Carter Carburetor, but in spite of all these features, and a competitive price, the car was perhaps even more unsuccessful than the American Mors. There is no record of the number of cars manufactured or sold, and so far as is known, by May 1910 production of the car had ceased, though the Car Company continued to advertise the vehicle until December 1910. It is possible however that the grave financial difficulties in which Kobusch found himself towards the end of 1909 may have affected the car's sales.

Whatever his difficulties, and whatever his losses, Kobusch was unwilling to dispose of the automobile plant. He felt that automobile manufacture gave him prestige, and it is known that his unwillingness to sacrifice that prestige led him to turn down a number of merger offers which made much sense at the time, and in the long run would unquestionably have made his fortune.

> A positive statement has been made by President Kobusch of the St. Louis Car Co. to the effect that he had been approached by the Morgan interests which were reported to be engineering (a) merger, but that his company would not enter into the combine. The three firms whose names are being most persistently linked with the (merger) . . . are the Olds, Buick and Maxwell concerns.[6]

It is also believed that Henry Ford approached Kobusch at the end of 1907 with equally as advantageous an offer. For a 50% share in the Ford Company Kobusch was to sell his entire auto plant and interests to Ford. For his part, Ford was prepared to make St. Louis his manufacturing headquarters rather than Detroit, and made some other

Another new type 3 #5116 displays its characteristic angular "Boston front" at the Cypress Street car house. *(Kevin T. Farrell collection)*

Six cars of the Denver and Interurban Railroad ready for shipment in 1908. Cars include Nos. M153, M154 and M155.

Interurban car for the St. Louis and Monte Sano Railroad. Though the order was placed in 1908, it is not known why the car illustrated was incomplete on April 24, 1913, the day this photograph was taken.

New York Central rail post office car #4394, typical of the heavy full-size railroad cars made at Baden between 1904 and 1907.

Allegheny Valley #43 of 1908. Notice the bird's-eye maple ceiling, and the stove in the interior.

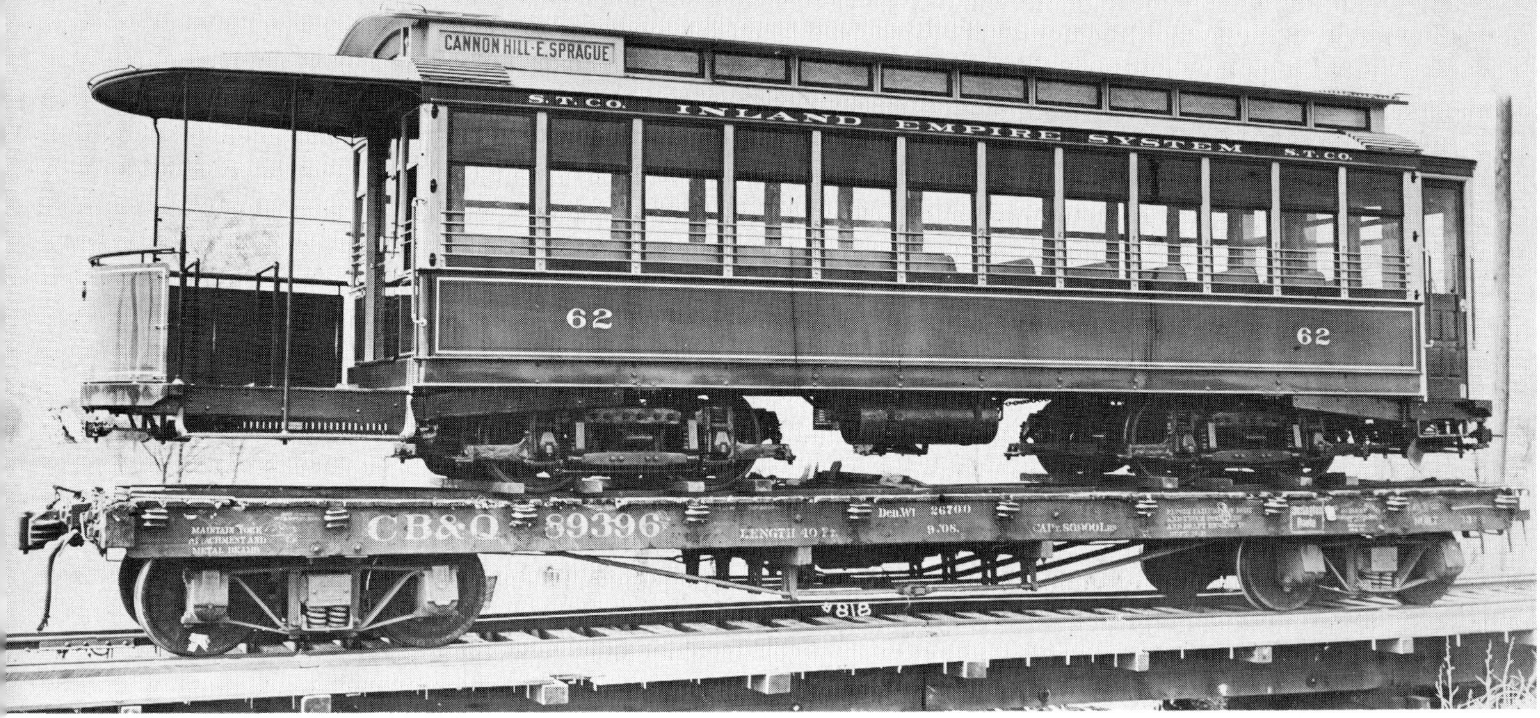

Spokane #62 of the Inland Empire system, built in 1909.

offers whose terms have since been lost. Kobusch turned him down.[7]

Automobile manufacture was not the only unsuccessful diversification he entered into. One of his least successful ventures was a partnership with W. G. Wagenhals in the production of a self-propelled steam railroad passenger car. A company known as the Kobusch-Wagenhals Steam Motor Car Co. had been formed in 1906, and ordered from the St. Louis Car Co. a large steam passenger motor car for the Missouri Pacific Railway. The design was modified, and a smaller vehicle was then produced for the Crystal City and Ulvada line. No further cars were built and Kobusch lost more money.

His earlier diversification into regular production of full-size railroad passenger cars was also a questionable move. The first orders had come in largely as a result of his Gould connections when 137 cars were ordered, mainly for the Harriman lines in the West, but also for the St. Joseph and Grand Island, and for the Pennsylvania. Without further expansion of the plant, there was not enough space for the efficient and profitable production of such units, and in any event railroad cars were highly demanding of manufacturing space and time, at the expense of the more profitable, and more quickly executed streetcar orders. Railroad production was quickly eliminated when the losses grew too great and subsequently main-line railroad equipment was built only when no other work was available, even after the plant had been enlarged.

By the fall of 1908, Kobusch's financial worries began to overwhelm him as he began to be hounded through the courts by his creditors, in a seemingly endless maze of lawsuits. In September 1908 for instance a suit was filed against him by the Oriental Bank of New York to recover $50,000.

> The note ran for four months, and as security . . . Kobusch deposited 400 shares of stock in the Union Trust Co. of New Jersey. Kobusch said that he didn't care to discuss it.[8]

No wonder, for it was evident that this was the tip of an iceberg. While the Car Company's credit had not yet been questioned, it was extremely worrying. Kobusch was raising money for the Car Company by mortgaging his personal assets on short-term notes, and those assets were of questionable worth. Typical was his use of watered stock in dummy companies which he and Van Brunt had set up some years earlier.

Kobusch-Wagenhals steam motor car for the Crystal City and Ulvada line, Missouri. Built in 1909, the second photo shows the steam motor unit being fitted.

Sample car built for the Puget Sound Electric Railway in 1908. Note the spartan finish of both interior and (below) exterior.

Coal Belt Railway #1 of 1909, mounted on St. Louis #47 trucks.

Seattle center-entrance car #661 of 1908, with interior. Note the unglazed compartment for smokers, with its wooden seats and observation platform.

Wichita Falls Traction Co. #23 of 1909. This open trailer car would not have looked out of place in an 1889 equipment order, so obsolete was the design. Notice the horse-car style pedestal mounts doing duty as trucks.

Though this questionable activity was undertaken with the best of motives (keeping the Car Company's credit in good condition) it was unfortunate that Kobusch's credit and that of the Car Company were synonymous. When questions were raised concerning the worth of some of Kobusch's securities pledged as collateral, the company's credit-worthiness and reputation was gravely compromised.

In December 1908 a number of creditors decided to test the company's solvency by filing a bankruptcy petition against it in the sum of $101.44. Why the matter came to a hearing at all, rather than the bill being paid was on the face of it peculiar, and the results were, in fact, ambiguous.

> St. Louis Car Co. will pay the claims of the Glidden Varnish Co., the San Francisco Pioneer Varnish Co., and the California Glue Works, aggregating $101.44, and will cause to be dismissed the petition of bankruptcy filed against them. The petition alleged the company committed an act of bankruptcy in giving a deed of trust for $2½ million to the Commonwealth Trust Co., to support a new bond issue for that amount. Mr. Kobusch says he has made arrangements to pay the bills . . . and then ask for the bankruptcy to be dismissed. (He) says the company's assets are $2½ million greater than its bonded and floating indebtedness and that it is perfectly solvent. He says that arrangements have been made to treat all claims as they fall due, and thinks that the creditors who filed the petition took snap judgment.[9]

Obviously Kobusch was once again attempting his time-honored technique of raising money to pay his debts by increasing the capital of the Car Company and these three firms had called his bluff. Under the circumstances no investor could have had confidence in any new paper issued by Kobusch for the Car Company, and he wisely went no further in that direction. How he managed to stave off liquidation of the company through 1909 will never be known. There was no improvement in his prospects in 1910 and Kobusch found himself faced with another court case. This concerned a deficiency judgment of $2,236,566 against the Randolph Macon Coal Co., was heard in the U.S. Court of Appeals, and involved both Kobusch and Van Brunt, the principal stockholders. The coal company had been organized by Kobusch, Van Brunt, James T. Gardiner and William N. Read in January 1906, capitalized for $5 million, and had issued bonds of $3 million. Obviously the bulk of the money in that stock had been diverted to other purposes,[10] and with so large a debt to be paid, the Car Company could no longer remain unaffected. By July 1910, the entire plant was on half time, orders ceased to be solicited, and shortly thereafter, layoffs began.

Throughout all of Kobusch's troubles, there had been no compromise in quality or workmanship at the plant, but the company's staple product, the wooden-bodied electric streetcar and its interurban counterpart, were in greatly reduced demand, and product diversification had been singularly unsuccessful. Kobusch's personal finances had badly affected the company's already poor financial performance, and fresh capital had to be found to avoid total closure. It was in the course of this search that John I. Beggs and his personal assistant Edwin B. Meissner became connected with the St. Louis Car Co.

Trailer cars for New York's IRT subway. Car #1694 ready for delivery on June 9, 1911, and the interior of car #1698.

CHAPTER 9

JOHN I. BEGGS, for many years president of The Milwaukee Electric Railway and Light Co. (TMERL), was by 1910 recognized as one of the electric railway industry's most influential figures. Born in 1847 at Media, Pennsylvania, of Irish parents, he was an excellent example of Horatio Alger's self-made man, rising from poverty to immense wealth in the course of his life.

He began his career as an apprentice in a Philadelphia brickyard, saving enough money to take courses at a local business college, where he was so good a student that he was shortly afterwards hired by the college to teach accounting at a salary of $1500 per year. Being young and ambitious, he saw little chance of further promotion in the college and in 1868 left to go to Harrisburg, where he went into real estate and insurance. He built up a profitable business, but while attending church one day, became interested in the commercial possibilities of electric lighting.

> When incandescent lights were first made, I saw some of them in a store. The proprietor said "They (sic) things is a kind of fake" and I thought so too at first. Then I got to thinking how nice a cluster of these lamps would look on the big chandelier in Grace Church. I went to New York to look into the matter and found we would have to produce electricity on a big scale to light up the church and that while we were about it, we might as well furnish light to others also. I got some other businessmen interested, and we talked at first of forming a $10,000 company, but then decided to do the right thing and form a $100,000 company (and) I consulted with Thomas Alva Edison on the plans for the Harrisburg plant.[1]

From then on Beggs' career was in the electrical promotion business. In 1886, he was appointed vice president and general manager of the Edison Co., and in 1890 was sent to Chicago as western manager of the Edison General Electric Co. which was deeply involved in the installation of electric street railway equipment. He soon tired of this and went to New York in 1893

> to retire from business and spend my life tramping, like my favorite fiction character, Bulwer Lytton's Kenelm Chillingley. (But) William Nelson Cromwell, the New York lawyer, came on me as I was studying steamship folders, and told me that the North American Co. wanted me to go out to Milwaukee to look over the . . . lighting and traction properties and see what could be done with them. I went out . . . and returned and told them what ought to be done. I told them the properties would pay if they did certain things, some of which meant spending money. They said they wouldn't put up the money unless I took the management. I didn't want the job, but they insisted, and got my Scotch-Irish up, and I went.[2]

Thus began a phase of his career which Beggs later described as the "rehabilitation of broken-down plants." He stayed with North American for the rest of his life, and of all their companies, TMERL remained his personal favorite and the one to which he devoted most of his time.

The North American Co. was the first of the big holding companies to appear in the U.S.A. Founded by Henry Villard, it had a checquered career until the 1890s, but then began to acquire and rehabilitate a considerable number of valuable traction and lighting properties. As a member of North American's Board, Beggs became intimately involved with the running of many of these companies, and through them was able to build his immense fortune. By 1905, with North American owning the gas, electricity and streetcar system of St. Louis, Beggs had responsibilities in St. Louis, Milwaukee and New York, spending much of his time commuting between the three cities.

A partial explanation of Beggs' success in an industry characterized by spectacular failures was

Pre-payment car #4 of the Elgin and Belvedere Railway was ordered in November 1911, and was ready for delivery on February 13, 1912. This was testimony to Meissner's achievement in turning a bankrupt company into an efficient and viable concern in less than a year.

John I. Beggs.

Kankakee Electric Railway #25 on St. Louis-Warner #71 truck. This car was ordered in December 1910, and was ready for delivery on June 29, 1911, an obvious indication of the return to more normal times at the Car Company with Meissner now in charge.

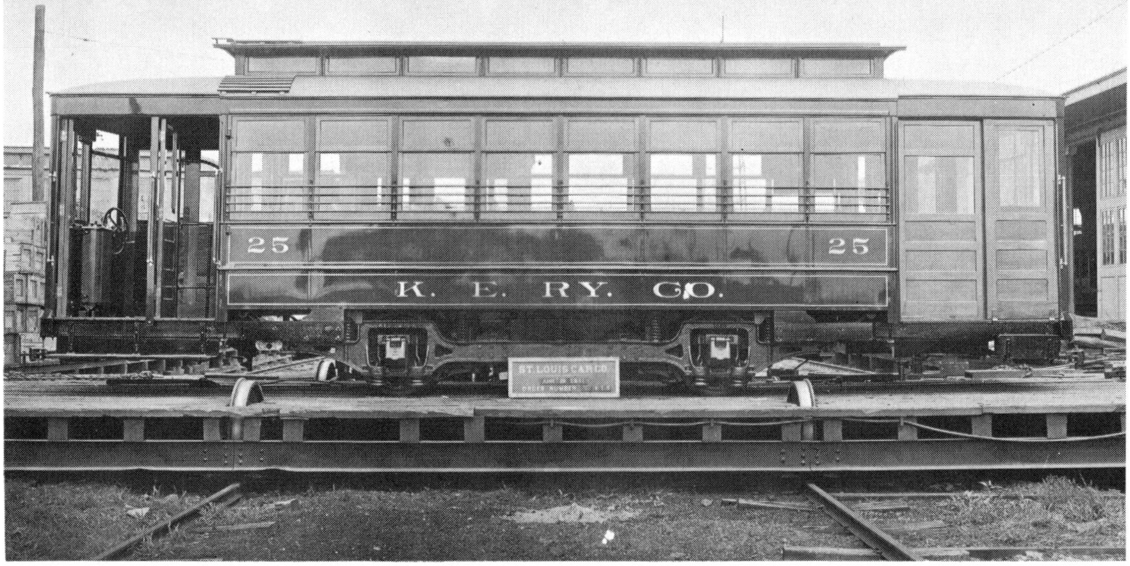

his association with a company which was soundly and (probably as a result of his influence) conservatively run. At a time when liquidity problems, and questionable business ethics appeared to be the usual order of things in industry, Beggs and North American seemed to prosper without effort. To a large extent, it was Beggs' thorough grounding in the principles of accounting, and his application of those principles to the books of every company with which he was associated that explained North American's success. It was Beggs' talent that he could cheaply acquire a company in dire financial straits, raise credit for it on the strength of his name and that of North American, set up a proper accounting system, recapitalize, and then watch the company grow. Moreover in a time of commercial dishonesty, he undoubtedly enjoyed cultivating his image as a hard, but fair and honest businessman.

By the turn of the century, Beggs' success with TMERL had given him the reputation as one of the country's most able street railway managers, and soon he was regarded as one of the country's greatest experts in the field. He was very active in the various industry associations, and was elected president of the American Street and Interurban Railways Association for 1906-7. Naturally he used this post to great advantage in preaching the gospel of honest accounting. In a speech he gave to the Association on October 14, 1907, Beggs described how he had urged with every business that he had

> ever been connected, that every accounting room be run in such a manner that if the Angel of Death appeared between sundown and sunrise and transplanted every one of them to a sphere where they do not run on trolley wheels . . . that a new set of accountants coming in the next morning could . . . take up those books, ask no questions, but go ahead with them. That, gentlemen, is accounting. It is not the running of simple columns of figures. It is understanding the principles of debit and credit . . . of honest, straightforward accounting.[3]

It was hardly surprising a man such as Beggs should have enemies, and during 1909 they appeared at North American. In that year, a major "war" had broken out between Beggs and his supporters, and James Campbell, North American's acting president. This clash became the subject of much comment and speculation in St. Louis when it became apparent that Beggs, for so long the colossus of St. Louis' public utilities, was on the losing side. By the end of the year, he had been forced by Campbell to resign his posts in all the St. Louis companies, but the war continued into 1910.

During that year, the St. Louis *Post-Dispatch* reviewed the history of the war.

> Campbell's reported enmity towards Beggs is the explanation generally accepted for Beggs' removal from control of Laclede Gas . . . Union Electric and United Railways . . . Campbell was by then virtually executive head of North American, owing to the disability of President Wetmore, although he was not formally elected until the summer (of 1910).

> After Beggs' withdrawal from St. Louis, he devoted his entire time to . . . (TMERL). Beggs "got back" at Campbell, it is generally believed, when he prevented the sale of Laclede Gas to Campbell's friend Emerson McMillin more than one year ago. Following the U.S. Supreme Court decision in the Standard Oil case, Attorney Isaac Lionberger advised North American to dispose of one of its two St. Louis lighting properties to avoid prosecution under the Sherman Act. Laclede was the one decided upon and negotiations for a sale, headed by McMillin with Campbell a prominent figure, was almost concluded at $94.50 a share. As the vote on the sale was about to be taken, Beggs appeared with an offer of $97.50 a share from the Busch-Walker syndicate, and McMillin had to withdraw. After this . . . the breach between Beggs and Campbell became seemingly irreparable. In his duties at Milwaukee, Beggs had little occasion to conflict with Campbell, but it is said that the latter has not relented in his purpose of removing Beggs as a factor in . . . North American. In accordance with this belief is the report circulated lately in Milwaukee that Beggs was letting go of his North American stock. He at one time held the largest block of the company's stock, and was fond of saying that he held all the North American stock he had ever had, and that his stock was not held for speculative purposes.[4]

Much of the enmity between the two had arisen out of a conflict of philosophy. Beggs and his faction continued to believe in the efficacy of the high-speed electric interurban, and the modernization of city streetcar systems as a legitimate way for North American to invest its money profitably. Campbell's faction believed that the day of the electric trolley was over so far as high yield investment was concerned, and that North American should be investing in the electrification of America by setting up and running electric lighting and distribution companies.

In August 1910, the war between Beggs and Campbell once again flared, and Kobusch's attempts to settle with the St. Louis Car Co.'s creditors were the cause of this fresh outbreak. In June Kobusch had been on the point of piecing together a complex refinancing arrangement with a local investment syndicate headed by Saunders Norvell of St. Louis. Many members of this syndicate were Car Company creditors, and there was little doubt therefore that this deal would have gone through, until Beggs unexpectedly made Kobusch a better offer. There had been no written agreement with the Norvell syndicate, and Kobusch was quite within his rights to accept Beggs' better offer. What was not made clear was why Beggs chose to make the offer, but in due time the reason became apparent when Campbell, in a related move, cut Beggs' salary as TMERL president from $50,000 to $30,000 a year.

> Beggs refused to make a statement (but) dispatches from Milwaukee state that Beggs is fighting mad at Campbell, whom he believes is trying to force him out of North American. Beggs' sudden entrance into St. Louis Car Co. affairs is now regarded as a move to establish himself in this city for a fight on Campbell and his St. Louis interests. Their latest open clash came when Beggs opposed Campbell's proposal to increase . . . North American's dividends from 5% to 6%. Campbell, as head of North American, is said to have believed Beggs' salary should be cut to correspond with the reduction made during the past year and a half in his (Beggs') duties and authority.[5]

Publicly, Beggs said nothing of the affair, and the statement made by him concerning his offer for the Car Company made no reference to it.

> Finally yielding to long and increasing pressure of many of the largest and most influential bankers, merchants and manufacturers of St. Louis, who are vitally interested in its growth and prosperity, and the strengthening and enlargement of its manufacturing interests, which as you know, I have repeatedly and strongly urged for many years, I have tentatively agreed under certain circumstances and if certain financial arrangements are perfected and consumated, to take in association with Mr. Kobusch, a large financial and administrative interest in the reorganization, strengthening and enlargement of the St.

Louis Car Co. . . . I am merely aiding in putting the St. Louis Car Co., which has been in difficulties for the past year, back on its feet.[6]

The move was not popular in St. Louis, and the St. Louis *Post-Dispatch* next day published a savage cartoon of Beggs, whose tone reflected local opinion on yet another local company falling into the hands of an outsider.[7] Beggs indeed for a time became local public opinion's scapegoat, at a time when a major campaign was under way in St. Louis to exhort the citizens to buy only locally-made products. The fact that negotiations with Kobusch were exceptionally protracted was good neither for Beggs' image, nor that of the Car Company.

The negotiations were lengthy owing to the failure of the various parties involved to make good on their promises of cash. Beggs' first offer, made in August 1910, was based on his owning one third of the stock, with Kobusch retaining the other two thirds and the company presidency. Beggs had his money ready, but Kobusch did not, and once again he became involved in a frantic effort to raise it.

So poor was his credit by this time that he had to go to New York to find an investor. By August 16 he had started a lengthy round of negotiations in that city

> with a London syndicate, for the sale of the company's preferred stock, and for the financing of several Kobusch mining properties, two deals which are expected to supply him with the required ready money to finance the Car Company deal . . .(A) representative of the London syndicate recently made an extensive investigation of the Car Company property, and of the mining properties.[8]

The success of the deal would provide a surplus for the Car Company to meet all claims, and give a sum sufficient to cover running expenses during the reconstruction. To prod the London syndicate into making a decision, Beggs stated that so far as he was concerned his interest in the deal was due solely to a promise he had made

> to see the Car Company through its financial difficulties until the delivery of one hundred cars for the Milwaukee lines was made.[9]

thus implying that with the cars safely delivered, his interest in the Car Company would cease. But his obvious need of the Car Company as a tactical weapon in his war with Campbell was apparent by then, and that bluff failed. The Englishmen were not only reluctant to involve themselves with a set of companies which retained Kobusch, they were equally unwilling to share control with an "investment tycoon" such as Beggs, whose concern for the company's profitability would probably be secondary to his own interest. The deal therefore fell through.

Later, Beggs made a new offer, based on the merger of his interests with the Saunders Norvell group whom he had previously outbid. Beggs now insisted that his offer was dependent on his being company president, rather than Kobusch. The Norvell syndicate, while very willing to drop Kobusch, was adamant that as it was to provide two thirds of the money, it should have control of the company, and with the two sides unable to agree, that proposition foundered.

> The proposition as the . . . syndicate understands it, said one member, is that Beggs and Kobusch have been unable to raise the money necessary to finance the deal. Not less than \$1½ million is needed. Beggs we understand has fulfilled his agreement with Kobusch which called for him to put up \$350,000. Kobusch was to raise the remainder. He went to New York for that purpose and on his return, we were invited to take stock, which makes it very plain to us that Kobusch is finding difficulty in raising the money. Beggs is willing for the members of the syndicate to get in as individuals holding a minority of stock; in other words Beggs wants us to put up the money, and he wants to run the company.[10]

With the collapse of this offer, matters lay dormant for nearly a month, and with no new orders being placed, work at the company began to run out. This clearly was a situation which seriously could damage the long-term financial prospects of the company, and if prolonged would have made successful reconstruction impossible. Clearly this was a turn for the worse, and Beggs, still needing his St. Louis base, realized that Kobusch was a liability. He thus dropped the notion of retaining Kobusch as president, and began to work independently to save the St. Louis Car Co.

On September 20, 1910, Beggs held a conference in St. Louis to review the situation. It was not encouraging. As expected, Kobusch had been completely unable to raise the money needed, and the company's credit was now entirely gone. The plant was on half time, with less than 500 men still at work and complete closure seemed imminent.[11] Yet in spite of this discouraging situation, Beggs was still reluctant to alter his offer; $350,000 was all he was prepared to put up, and he pleaded with other St. Louis investors to do their duty and save a local company by buying its preferred stock. In this way, he hoped the plant could be reopened on a basis which would eventually enable it to employ 5000 men.[12] But again Beggs was bluffing, and his bluff was called. St. Louis finance had no further use for Kobusch and his company, and it was a matter of indifference to them whether he went bankrupt or not. As for Beggs, they had no wish to aid an immensely wealthy outsider fight a war from whose outcome they could not profit.

Their misgivings concerning Beggs were quite justified. On hearing Beggs was holding a conference concerning the Car Company's future, Campbell had laconically remarked that

> if Beggs went into the St. Louis Car Co., he could hardly expect to be retained as executive head of North American's Milwaukee properties.[13]

For Beggs, such a remark represented a serious threat. He had little sentiment left for the world after the death of his wife in 1902, and what remained was largely for TMERL, which above all other things had been his own creation. In thus threatening to fire him from TMERL, Campbell had unmistakably signaled that it was to be a fight to the finish between them.

Beggs' immediate response to Campbell was ambiguous . . .

> Mr. Campbell said that if I accepted the Car Company's proposition, I would probably want to resign . . . Whether I shall . . . or not is another question.[14]

But his actions were not ambiguous. He needed the company badly now, and saw he would have to raise the money himself if there was to be any hope of success. By late October he had persuaded Moses Schoenberg and David May to head a new syndicate which would find the $400,000 the Car Company now required, and give Beggs outright control. This transaction was negotiated in great secrecy, although Beggs' regular appearance in St. Louis could not be hidden. When asked on one occasion why he was there, Beggs blandly replied

> To see what progress (is being) made on 100 TMERL cars for which TMERL is providing money to keep the shops (open) . . . until the order (is) completed.[15]

The deal was finally announced on October 31, 1910, and a letter explaining the arrangement was sent to the Car Company creditors the same day. Signed by Beggs, May and Schoenberg, it stated that:

> An arrangement has been made . . . for reestablishing the St. Louis Car Co. . . . Under this arrangement, $850,000 of new money is to be put in by Messrs. John I. Beggs, D. May and M. Schoenberg and associates. For this, they are to receive 7% cumulative preference stock at par.
>
> The co-operation of the creditors is essential to carrying out this plan, it being necessary that they take 7% cumulative preferred stock for their claims . . . The preferred stock issued to the creditors will stand on the same footing as the preferred stock issued for the new money at par. The result of this arrangement will be to discharge all the indebtedness of the company, except $1 million of bonds, and a mortgage on the automobile plant of $40,000, and leave a cash balance of $400,000 for working capital.
>
> Messrs. Beggs, May and Schoenberg will be in control of the company and Mr. Beggs will be president and General Manager . . . (They) show their faith in the future of the company by their willingness to put in money for preferred stock on the same footing with like stock for the claims of the creditors.[16]

In due course, a stockholders' meeting was held on January 31, 1911, at which all stockholders were represented, and a new board elected. Board members were as follows: John I. Beggs, George J. Kobusch, W. S. McCall (of Mississippi Valley Bank and Trust Co., and formerly a Car Company general sales agent), Edwin B. Meissner (Beggs' personal assistant, manager and chief clerk), Robert McCullough (general manager of United Railways, St. Louis) and Richard McCullough (his son, and Beggs' son-in-law).

The arrangements made in 1910 for the reorganization had been modified by the time of the stockholders' meeting, for Beggs during that time decided to make a personal investment, buying 7,500 shares of the company preferred stock at par for cash (amounting to $750,000), while the others associated with him bought a further $300,000 of preferred stock. In addition Beggs acquired a great deal of company common stock.

More than $600,000 was spent to liquidate the company's debts not provided for by the issue of preferred stock. This left about $450,000 as working capital; the $1 million in bonds, and the $40,000 mortgage mentioned in the October letter remained outstanding.

Immediately after the stockholders' meeting, the Board met to elect officers. Beggs was made president and general manager, Kobusch chairman of the board and sales department supervisor, a J. M. Taylor was elected secretary and treasurer, and Edwin B. Meissner was appointed assistant to the president, specifically charged with the plant's day-to-day management when Beggs was in Milwaukee.[17]

Beggs' Milwaukee responsibilities did not last much longer. In the last week of February 1911, he admitted defeat in his battle with Campbell, and announced his resignation of TMERL's presidency. What precisely motivated this action is not known, but Beggs was not a man to embark upon any enterprise without having a clear idea of how he might best turn it to his own account. It has to be assumed that he felt it more advantageous personally to choose the time of his resignation from TMERL, rather than wait for Campbell (by now North American's president) to fire him, with all the attendant loss of prestige that that would bring. As he was by then securely in the saddle at the St. Louis Car Co. he must have felt this to be the most appropriate time to resign from TMERL.

While relieved to see Beggs go, Campbell was being less than honest when he suggested that Beggs had resigned against the wishes of everyone connected with TMERL. That might perhaps have been true of Beggs' subordinates in that company (and the City of Milwaukee went on record in regretting his departure) but it was not true of Campbell, nor his faction now in control at North American. They were jubilant in having disposed of Beggs so easily and their published utterances reflected that mood. Campbell's remarks on Beggs' resignation have all the hallmarks of a long-prepared obituary notice (save for his use of the present tense) and his eulogy of Beggs was not at all sincere.

> Mr. Beggs is an ideal executive of a great company. He is a wonderful executive; he has vision . . . I have never known a man who combined so many qualities of leadership. He is an engineer, an administrator, an accountant and a financier. (TMERL) is a monument to his ability as a manager, and his devotion to duty as a man.[18]

It is not known for certain how long Kobusch stayed with the reorganized Car Company once Beggs severed his connection with North American, but he had ceased his active involvement by the summer of 1911, and withdrew completely by 1913. He had paid many of his debts by the end of 1910 through the proceeds of the sale of his Car Company stock. But he had been left chronically short of ready cash, by paying excessive commissions on loans, and in May 1911, he brought an action against the Mississippi Valley Trust Co. to recover $409,735 he claimed he had been compelled to pay in excess loan commissions, on loans aggregating $2 million, borrowed between 1905 and 1909.

> (Kobusch) paid 3% commission for loans in addition to 6% interest, but when he repaid all the loans recently, (his) lawyers allege he was informed that there had been an additional commission of $409,725 for making the loans which he had had to pay before he could get the collateral security he had put

During Meissner's first years with the Car Company, wooden cars were built very quickly. These 24 pay-as-you-enter cars for San Diego were contracted for on December 8, 1911. By February 8, 1912, the framework of the first few cars was well advanced. In the middle of February, the first cars were being panelled, and the carlines fitted. The final erecting shop process was the fitting of the shellacked canvas roof. The cars were then fitted with their electrical gear and sent to the paint shop, where #125, the first complete vehicle emerged on March 28, 1912. The complexity of the work is shown in the pictures on the following four pages.

A batch of closed cars was built for the Bay State Railway at the same time as those for San Diego. Car 4103, ready for shipment on July 16, 1912.

ST. LOUIS CAR CO.

#900

> up with the Trust Co. The attorneys allege Kobusch had borrowed $1,048,831.30 on March 3, 1905, $150,000 on December 1, 1905, $294,000 on 6 March 1906, $536,374.06 on 27 December 1906, and various smaller sums between 1905 and 1910.[19]

Breckenridge Jones, the president of the Mississippi Valley Trust Co. said they did not owe Kobusch one cent.

> We loaned him large sums of money during the past four or five years. We aided in financing some of his deals, out of which he made a profit of $750,000. The commissions we charged him were authorized by written agreement. Now he has paid off his debts to us, he wants to recover the money he paid in commissions by written agreement.[20]

The hearing dragged on for over a month, with little prospect of settlement. Breckenridge Jones on June 13 finally admitted that they had made a large charge for their services, but tried to mitigate the enormity of the charge by having Kobusch agree in writing to pay that sum.[21] Still later in the month it was revealed that as a part of the loan from the Trust Co., Kobusch had paid $40,000 to finance a trip to Belgium by Jones, to help sell a portion of a $1,750,000 bond and stock issue in Kobusch's San Antonio Waterworks Co., which Kobusch had contracted with the Trust Co. to dispose of.[22]

L. M. Lyon, Kobusch's French and Belgian agent was summoned from Paris to testify that he had transferred stock of the San Antonio Water Power Co. to the banking firm of Maas and Movis of Antwerp in January 1910. Kobusch had accepted the terms of that transfer, and a copy of the terms was also sent to the Mississippi Valley Bank and Trust, with a list of the men the Antwerp bank wanted to serve as directors of the San Antonio concern, among whom was Breckenridge Jones. Lyons then said that it was his original understanding that Jones was going to Europe in connection with the transfer of that stock to the Antwerp firm, but Kobusch had later told him that the Mississippi Valley Trust Co. had no further connection with the proposed transaction. When Jones reached Antwerp, the Belgian firm again insisted he (Jones) be put on the Board of the San Antonio company, and when Lyon later asked why, an official of the Antwerp firm replied

> "How do you expect us to trust Mr. Kobusch, when Mr. Jones spoke of him as he did?"[23]

The matter was eventually settled without the court coming to a verdict, but there was no doubt that Kobusch had been thoroughly at the mercy of the bank, and such a revelation hardly enhanced his prestige as a businessman, nor that of any company he belonged to. Beggs thus decided Kobusch was an embarrassment and began to ease him out of the Car Company. The pretext he used was a genuine one—another unpaid Kobusch loan.

Beggs had been unwise enough to loan money to Kobusch in 1911, and Kobusch had almost immediately defaulted. It wasn't until 15 July 1913 that Beggs filed suit against Kobusch to recover the sum of $19,606.75. The suit alleged that Kobusch had given a promissory note for $50,000 to the First National Bank of Milwaukee, pledging as collateral his 400 shares of common stock in the Union Trust Co. of New Jersey, and 500 shares of St. Louis Car Co. common stock. The bank had presented this note for payment on September 8, 1911, and Kobusch didn't pay. Beggs therefore foreclosed on the collateral, and the bank sold the stock for $30,393.25, requiring Beggs to make up the difference, which he had done, and which he now sought to recover from Kobusch.[24] At the same time as the loan had been made, Beggs had fired Kobusch from active participation in the company, and Kobusch left by July 1911.

The hearing was delayed until 1914, when Kobusch filed an answer to the suit, making a counterclaim against Beggs. Naturally he had been unable to pay Beggs' 1913 claim, and with the court costs, he now owed Beggs $20,000. Beggs in the meanwhile was asking for $200,000 of collateral belonging to Kobusch and currently held at the St. Louis National Bank of Commerce as security for another Kobusch loan, to be held subject to the judgment Beggs had against Kobusch for $20,000.

Kobusch's answer did not deny the loan made by the Milwaukee bank, but suggested that the foreclosure on his collateral, made on May 20, 1912 by the bank was fraudulent. He claimed there had not been a public sale of the shares, but that the sale was conducted secretly after banking hours, with the Trust Co. shares fetching $80 per share, and the Car Company common stock a mere $1.00 per share. Moreover he further claimed that the bank officers had been acting as Beggs' agents in purchasing both the Trust Company and Car Company stock, for Beggs now had outright control of it, he having been the purchaser from the bank! Kobusch claimed that had all the shares been sold at reasonable market price, they would have brought nearly $70,000, not the $30,000 Beggs had paid for them. Thus he sought judgment in the sum of $68,605, less the amount owed to the bank.

He also had a counterclaim. He claimed that in October 1910, he contracted with Beggs, May, Schoenberg and the Car Company that he was to be paid $30,000 a year for five years to act as chairman of the board at the Car Company, and as the sales department's manager. After he had served for nine months, Beggs had requested him to leave, in fact "made it impossible for him to remain."[25] He had received no part of his salary, and he was now suing for it.

No more was heard of these cases, and it must be assumed they were settled out of court, but while they lasted, they could not have helped the Car Company re-establish its credibility. Kobusch's affairs had been messy in the extreme, and once he ceased to be actively involved with the Car Company, orders visibly improved. However, he was still allowed to borrow large sums of money from the company against his stock holdings until they ran out in 1922. Indeed during 1911 he even made unauthorized pledges of his Car Company stock as collateral for yet more loans he had made during the year, something entirely unknown to Car Company officials until 1925. His final departure signaled the Car Company's recovery.

CHAPTER 10

Although Beggs had planned to give up his Wisconsin residence to settle in St. Louis, his ouster from North American Co. made it more important for him to remain in Milwaukee, awaiting his opportunity to get back into TMERL and North American. The St. Louis Car Co. was no longer necessary to his strategy and the seemingly unimportant role of his personal assistant Edwin B. Meissner became crucial for the successful day-to-day operation of the Car Company as Beggs' absences from St. Louis became regular, and occasionally protracted. Beggs had come to trust and rely on Meissner in many ways, and this new assignment was for Meissner the biggest trust of all, for in 1911, at age 26, he had been given the entire St. Louis Car Co. to manage on Beggs' behalf.

Meissner had come to work for Beggs as the result of a long chain of events. With the failure of his family's business, and the subsequent death of his father, he had been compelled to leave school at the age of 13 to find work. He had found part-time employment in many places, but at the same time landed a full-time job with TMERL as messenger boy. He started with TMERL in 1899 and for him the company was a stepping stone. He was intelligent, ambitious and desperate to make up the education he had been unable to complete. His new job enabled him to find the money with which to go back to school, and the next seven years were spent taking night classes at McDonald Business College, Milwaukee. Being employed in one of the most solid operations, in the country's most dynamic industry, his choice of courses was made with an eye to further advancement within the industry and TMERL, and his studies included bookkeeping, commercial law, electrical engineering, shorthand and typing. As a result his promotion in TMERL was rapid and frequent, and by 1905, he had been appointed Beggs' chief clerk and personal assistant, assuming heavy responsibilities in TMERL's sumptuous new head office.

At the time of the Beggs' purchase, morale at the St. Louis Car Co. was understandably very low, and the presence of a young and highly energetic man went a long way towards improving matters. His greatest asset was his ability to manage. Kobusch had been many things, but he was not a manager, and Vogel's departure in May 1906, just after the opening of the new steel car plant, had left Kobusch without an experienced manager to take over. Kobusch's affairs subsequently had been so complex that he could give little time to the day-to-day affairs of the Car Company, yet despite his total dependence on the Car Company's continuing profits to keep him solvent and credit-worthy, he amazingly never hired any one individual to directly replace Vogel, and the efficiency of the company was gravely impaired as a result. W. S. McCall (one of Beggs' directors in 1911) had been promoted to Vogel's vacated vice presidency, and A. H. Sisson was promoted from assistant general manager to general manager. Walter S. Miller was at the same time promoted from superintendent of tools and machinery to works manager, a post he held concurrently with his post at the automobile plant. In effect Vogel had thus been replaced by three men, not all of whom remained with the company for very long.[1]

Lack of direction had been most keenly felt in the sales office. Without definite policy guidelines, and the constant supervision and encouragement Vogel had given, the department had become sluggish, failing in its prime task of finding sufficient business. The shortage of working capital did not make matters any easier, and this combination of problems led to a vicious circle. There was no money, and therefore there was no work. Equally, because there was no work, there was no money. Until Meissner came to the company in 1911, this circle remained unbroken.

These were the greatest of the problems that Meissner faced when he started work early in February 1911. It is not known precisely what techniques he used to turn the company around, but simple psychology must have played a very

In 1912, the open car was still popular. Cars for the Bay State Railway are here shown under construction during April and May of that year. Car #6119 was ready for delivery on June 29, 1912.

Bay State also ordered freight motors for baggage service in 1912, and these were complete in less than 3 months. Note the semi-steel construction on car #18.

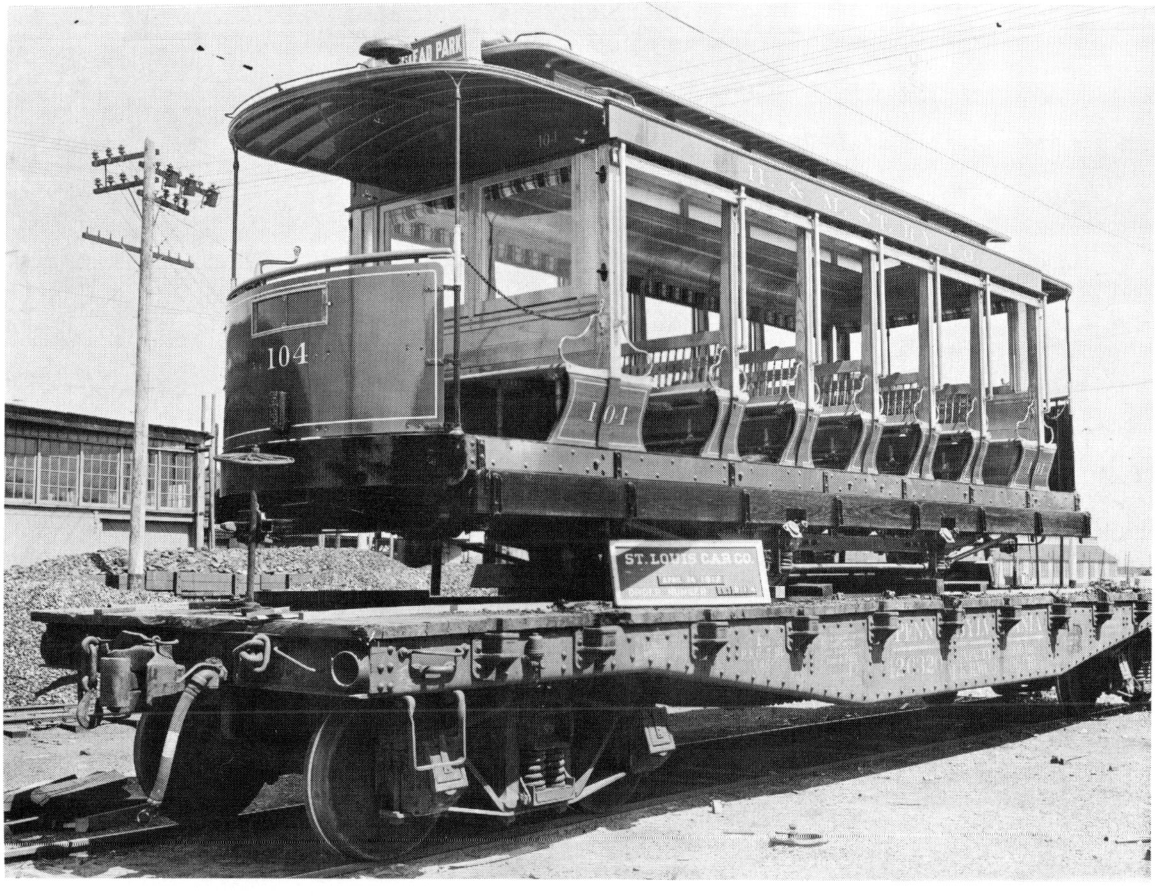

Single-truck car for the Homestead & Mifflin Street Railway, Pa.

Heavy interurban cars for the Illinois Traction system and its subsidiaries. Notice the characteristic front-end design with its three windows, and the ornate stained glass in the car interior.

Completed body shell of an Illinois Traction system interurban.

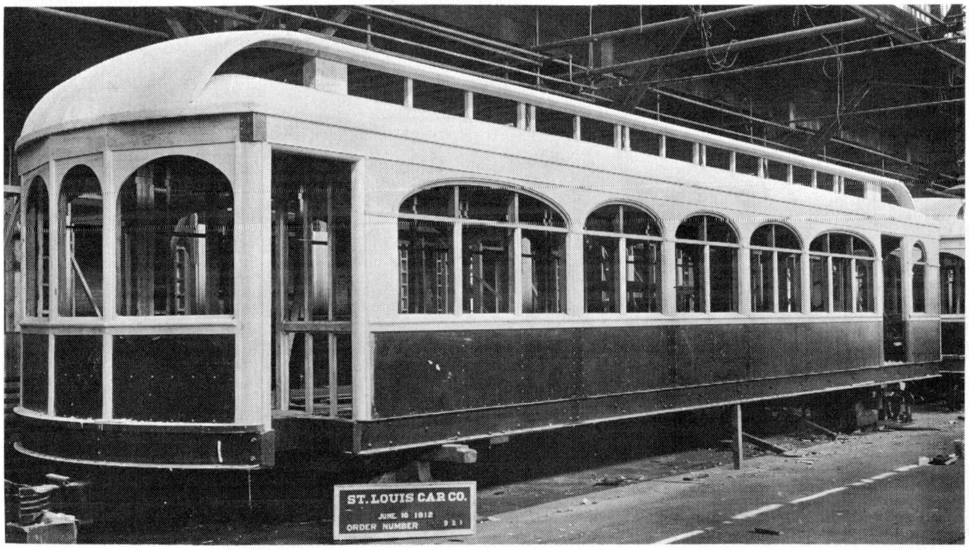

Semi-steel interurban cars built in 1912 for Arkansas Valley. Note the fare register in the upper right-hand corner of the car's interior.

Line car for Arkansas Valley.

large part. He was young, newly married, extremely hard working, and always very visible: factors which improved morale immeasurably during the spring and summer of 1911, and with it the efficiency of the plant.[2] The company's last good year had been 1907, when nearly 1000 cars had been ordered. Less than 400 were ordered in 1909, and less than 300 in 1910, of which 100 were not ordered until December 1910, when it became certain that Beggs was to take over.

Once it was seen that customers were being actively solicited in an orderly and businesslike manner by a capable and dynamic young manager, the prospects for the company's recovery seemed more certain, and in 1912, the first tangible results were to be seen. Orders for that year totalled nearly 670 cars, two of Meissner's biggest coups being orders for 175 central entrance stepless cars for New York, and a number of one-man safety cars for the local Illinois Traction System, both new and subsequently very valuable customers. Moreover, a higher proportion of contracts than in the recent past included orders for trucks, a welcome source of extra work and income to the company, and it was decided to hire a full-time chief engineer to better cope with the design problems that this new work brought. H. Wallerstadt, for many years superintendent of New York's IRT subway was the successful candidate for the post.[3]

Meissner's appetite for work was prodigious. His wife recalled the early days of their marriage as being a time when he would work 16 hours a day, nine of them at the plant and the rest at home in an armchair with huge piles of papers or contracts, which he would happily read out loud to her as he worked on them so as to keep her company![4] Nor was he any more unwilling than Kobusch to try new schemes with possible commercial application. One such project had been Illinois Traction's one-man lightweight safety cars. Another was the building of motor bus bodies on commercially supplied chassis. Railroad passenger car building was resumed for a period, and the promising engineering features of the Warner non-parallel axle radial streetcar truck, the U.S. distribution rights to which had been bought by Kobusch late in 1909, seemed to be bringing sales results in 1911 and 1912. But one of most exotic projects would have made even Kobusch pause, for Meissner took the company into the production of flying boats.[5]

In the Fall of 1915, Thomas W. Benoist, a local St. Louis aviator and airplane designer, entered into an agreement with the company to negotiate

Some of the lightest electric cars built at Baden were these all-wood Gould storage battery cars for export to Cienfuegos, Cuba. Notice the drilled plywood benches.

A special car built in 1912 to demonstrate steel car body construction. It is mounted on a Warner non-parallel axle truck.

the sale of his Benoist Type XV flying boats. The company was to build the prototype, and complete the orders which would subsequently be placed, and a complex financial agreement was worked out. Benoist was certain his plane could be sold to the British for use as an observation plane and light bomber.

Benoist deserved to be taken seriously. He was a highly competent designer and in 1914 had established and operated the world's first commercial air service from Tampa to St. Petersburg, Florida. His credentials therefore were very impressive, and Meissner took a calculated risk in backing him. Had the negotiations been successful, the company would have built nearly 5000 planes at a cost of $6,100 each.[6] But the negotiations were not successful. The British and their pilots were unwilling to accept an aircraft of largely untried design in the middle of an on-going war, particularly as their flyers were already trained on Curtiss-Wright planes. Just before Benoist's trip to England, they had (unknown to Benoist) signed a contract with Curtiss-Wright for a large supply of their machines. The Car Company thus built only two Benoist planes, and their involvement with airplane construction then ceased temporarily.[7]

Such setbacks were of no great importance to the well-being of the company. Meissner was a more conservative businessman than Kobusch had ever been, and both he and Beggs took care not to overreach company finances in schemes of this nature. Streetcar manufacture continued to provide the bulk of their business until the placing of the first defense contracts in 1916, and it was once more proving profitable. All the same, the Car Company was still short of ready money, and needed further loans on which to run its contracts. By a fortunate chance one of the banks to whom the Car Company applied for money made a full investigation of the plant in March 1917, and that report has survived,[8] giving a full and detailed financial evaluation of the company and its prospects on the eve of the U.S.A.'s entry into World War I.

Conducted on February 29, 1917, with Meissner's full cooperation, the investigation used as its base the company's financial statement dated February 28, 1917. After a brief statement of assets and liabilities as the company saw them, the report made detailed comments on the figures presented.

In the assets category, the Car Company valued the real estate at $529,250, divided be-

Tri-City Railways city car, photographed on September 16, 1913. Despite the lengthy platforms, this was a decidedly old-fashioned style of city car.

tween the Baden plant, the Laclede plant, and the automobile plant. By this time the Baden plant covered 47 acres, with five miles of railroad spurs and sidings connecting the plant with the Terminal Railroad Association of St. Louis (TRRA), the Burlington route, and the Missouri, Kansas and Texas railroad. The Laclede plant in city blocks 2490 and 2495 was vacant (though included in the assessment) and in a poor state of repair. The automobile plant by this time consisted of two lots 150′ x 300′, and two lots 150′ square, with tracks connecting it to the Wabash and the TRRA. A small section of the building was leased to the Maxwell Automobile Sales Co., and the remainder was used for "high class" machining work, primarily for the Western Cartridge Co.

The buildings at the Baden plant were regarded as being in a fair state of repair, the work and machinery were fully protected from the weather. 102 cars were under construction at the time of the investigation. Machinery and tools were also in a good state of preservation, and according to Meissner were well adapted to the company needs, but the investigator noted that it was difficult for a layman to decide whether the machinery was obsolete or up-to-date; a fact which would materially affect the Car Company's valuation of $820,043.11. There was little argument over the Car Company's figure of $968,015.39 for the buildings, nor with that for the terminal and railroad equipment ("fairly old . . . but adequate") at $114,752.40. However the patents, drawings and patterns were considered to be "seriously overvalued" at $507,915.28.

Bills receivable amounted to $95,862.21 of which $37,254.28 had been uncollected for over three years, and some items had been uncollected for seven. Most were secured by car trust agreements, and it was not considered the company would lose more than $15,000 ultimately. Accounts receivable at $308,157.86 were a more serious matter. Over $100,000 was composed of accounts charged prior to December 31, 1915, and of that sum, $88,230.88 was due from Kobusch, and had been outstanding more than five years.

> The only security (for this sum) which the company is holding is $73,000 par value of its common stock, which from the standpoint of a creditor represents no value at this time . . . $3,000 of this account is due from John Maggie and Molly Murphy, former employees, and has been carried on open account for more than two years. $9,000 is due from

This Pittsburgh design evolved from one first introduced in 1905 and subsequently built in the hundreds. The addition of the center entrance did nothing to modify the antique appearance of these cars in the #4200 series, shown here in January 1914, under construction. However, these were the first cars of the low-floor type and in passenger convenience at least, were an improvement over previous designs.

Side view of a Pittsburgh low-floor, center-entrance car when new. Notice the additional front exit. *(Pittsburgh Railways, Edwin J. Klasky collection)*

Pittsburgh #4000, built by Brill some years earlier, was fitted during this period with specially modified St. Louis #47 trucks. The most striking alteration was the provision of coupling rods to provide increased traction on Pittsburgh's many hills.

These center-entrance cars for Brooklyn were far more modern and up-to-date in design and appearance.

St. Louis Waterworks Railway #11, photographed on August 26, 1914. These specially designed cars had both entrance and exit on one side of the vehicle only. Even at this late date, the entrances were inconveniently steep and narrow.

Steel-bodied cars were no less prone to wrecks than those with wooden bodies, but as this photograph graphically shows, the claim that steel cars would retain their structural integrity after a wreck had an element of truth to it. In this example, the passenger section is largely undamaged, and the heavy steel underframe is totally unaffected. Dallas 188, built by St. Louis Car Company in 1914, photographed at an unknown date. *(Edwin J. Klasky collection)*

Battery electric car #3 for Tranvia Electrico de Cardenas, 1915.

Some railroads succumbed to the interurban fever and electrified a handful of branch lines. Observation car #312 of the Jamestown, Westfield and North-Western Railroad, New York, in 1916.

Pittsburgh low-floor, center-entrance trailer #A-300. The standard of comfort in big city cars was still low. Notice the glass-sided fare box in the center of the car.

St. Cloud Public Service, Minnesota pay-as-you-enter cars #100 and #101 on June 10, 1916.

Steel baggage car #288 of the Michigan Railway Co. in 1916.

City car for the Chicago, South Bend and Northern Indiana Railway in 1917.

A body for the Gas-Electric Motorbus Co. of Chicago, 1916.

(Below) Motorbus #1 of the St. Louis Division of Parks and Recreation, bought by them in 1916, and used normally in St. Louis' Forest Park.

A Benoist flying boat taxiing on the Mississippi in 1915.

the Companie de Tramway Electric Company (sic). This charge I am advised, resulted from some of Kobusch's operations under a grant from the Chilean government. It has proved uncollectible for more than eight years.[9]

Materials, supplies and work in progress was valued at $729,579.62, based on the inventory taken December 31, 1916. Of that figure 60% was based on raw materials in stock, the other 40% on work in hand, and the whole sum represented 70% of the company's liquid assets.

> However, included in the inventory, the company is carrying automobile material and supplies amounting to $53,289.74. In my judgment $5000 would be the very limit of the amount which could be realized out of this old material, as it is all of extremely heavy design and obsolete. The company appeared to have a very large amount of steel, lumber and supplies on hand, and Mr. Meissner informed me that practically all of the material had been purchased at prices very substantially below the replacement cost at today's market.[10]

Bonds, stocks and securities, valued at $315,304.31 would be better carried "at a nominal figure only" in the books, as they included $89,100 of Philadelphia and Western Underwriting syndicate bonds, an organization formed to purchase first mortgage bonds and common stock of the Philadelphia and Western.

> This venture was never carried to a conclusion, assessments made have not been paid by the Car Company and . . . represent no value whatsoever.[11]

$200,000 was the company valuation given to the stock of the Spiral Journal Bearing Mfg. Co.

> This is practically a good will entry, which represents the right to make spiral journal bearings. While the company manufactures a very limited amount of these bearings, the right to manufacture them is of no tangible value.[12]

$21,704.39 was still held in the name of the Kobusch-Wagenhals Steam Motor Car Company.

> This represents money expended in experimental work and in developing a type of steam motor car. As far as I can learn, it has proved a failure and the assets are of no value.[13]

Cash in hand totalled $17,627, but the valuation of $1,696,692.10 on the good will of the company, in the investigator's opinion, represented no value whatever and was indeed being used to offset a portion of the company's common stock!

The company's liabilities were next dealt with. Bills payable amounted to $464,642.80, of which $350,000 was due to the bank making the investi-

Tom Benoist, Meissner and Roger Jannis, seated in the front of a Benoist flying boat. The identities of the men in the rear are not known.

gation. This sum was endorsed by Beggs, and was also partially secured by $142,000 par value company first mortgage 6% bonds. The $40,000 mortgage on the automobile plant, taken over by Beggs in 1911, was still outstanding, but secured by a deed of trust. What was significant, and an unfortunate indication of the company's chronic shortage of liquidity, was the sum of $74,642.80 due on merchandise accounts.

> I am advised they do not represent original transactions, whereby the notes were given for merchandise agreed to at the time of sale, but that it is the result of closing accounts payable with the company's notes. The majority of these notes are given for 90 days . . . The officer advised me that they have met every note which has matured . . .[14]

Similar was the $214,991.45 in accounts payable, the company's current commitments.

> It is the practise to voucher all accounts payable once each month from the 15th to the 25th, and at the time of vouchering, they include the accounts payable which are covered by invoices actually received, and also the merchandise which has reached the plant. However, the company's payment of these vouchered claims is not always as prompt as it should be—the vouchers going through the different departments, and then being held until such time as the cash finances would permit of their payment.[15]

Mortgage bonds amounted to $858,000, and although total issue was $1 million, $142,000 was pledged to the investigating bank as collateral security. Insurance on plants, machinery and stock was carried at a value of slightly over $1,400,000. Net sales of the car department during 1916 were $937,000, and of the auto plant $76,000, and while there had been a minor slump at the beginning of 1916, which kept figures somewhat depressed, the company expected business to double in 1917.

> In conclusion, it is my judgment that the plant is in fair condition, and the prospects seem good for an increased volume of business upon which a profit should be realized. The company, however, in my opinion lacks capital of at least $250,000, and just to that proportion . . . I consider the risk hazardous. My opinion is offered on the risk represented by the Car Company's notes, and does not take into consideration the endorsement of Director Beggs . . . (signed) W. W. Smith.[16]

Such was the condition of the Car Company on the eve of the First World War; a good reflection of Meissner's business skill, but equally it was a reflection of the dismal state of the street railway market, now confined largely (as predicted ten years before) to the replacing of existing fleets.

A Benoist flying boat in flight.

Semi-steel city cars under construction on June 25, 1912, and a completed car for the Toledo Railroad Co. ready for delivery on August 23, 1912.

CHAPTER 11

MEISSNER'S FIRST YEARS with the Car Company were also the years of the first significant changes to be made in streetcar design since the 1890s. With the change in public attitude towards monopolistic public utilities, the streetcar operators had been compelled to redesign their vehicles and eliminate some of the causes of complaint. As a result, cars had become longer and heavier, and entrances became wider, frequently being moved from their traditional locations to the center of the car. New methods of fare collection were tried in an attempt to make loading easier and speedier, and wholly new types of cars were introduced in the years between 1910 and 1917. The most radical, and at the same time the most widely adopted design was that of the one man lightweight safety car, which in various forms was offered by most major manufacturers after 1914 (though its peak of popularity was delayed by World War 1). But the biggest change of all was in the actual fabrication of the cars: the change from wood to steel construction.

Traditional materials for streetcar construction had been well-seasoned oak, hickory, ash and pine, and car builders had flourished in cities which were major lumber distribution points. But in the age of iron and steel it was natural that thought be given to metal car construction. One of the exhibits at the 1904 St. Louis World's Fair had been a partially completed private car, built by the St. Louis Car Co. for Henry E. Huntington of the Pacific Electric Railway, nephew of Collis P. Huntington. What was not on view in this exhibit was the major innovation in its fabrication about which the *Street Railway Journal* commented

> bid(s) fair to mark a new era in the construction of electric cars for high-speed interurban service.[1]

This innovation was the incorporation of steel framing in the body. This break with traditional building materials was not just a question of substituting steel for wood in the load-bearing areas of the sills and sashes, but of constructing the entire car framing of steel from the floor to the carlines. As a construction method, it was a logical progression from those previously used at the Car Company where the steel sill and all-steel bottom framing had long been a speciality.

The Huntington private car was built at the same time as the fifty all-steel trailer cars for the IRT, and the success of these two designs undoubtedly had prompted Kobusch in his efforts to lead the industry in the production of all-steel cars for electric and steam service. By early 1906, the company was ready to introduce a line of commercially manufactured steel-bodied cars, built in its new steel car plant.

This plant consisted of two buildings, and their equipment gave testimony to the radical departure in building techniques needed to produce steel cars. One building was exclusively supplied with punches, lathes, shears and other machinery, while the other was used as an erecting shop, from which the completed cars rejoined the regular production flow in the paint shop.

At first, steel was substituted for wood on a member by member basis, and no attempt was made to utilize steel's greater strength to reduce car weight. Indeed at the time it was felt that heavier weight tended to make a smoother riding car and many cars in this period were made even heavier by the provision of a solid concrete floor, to provide durability in service and steady riding qualities. Consequently the argument over the use of wood or steel in car construction became very vexatious.

It was largely a question of the service to be given, first, and maintenance costs and the life expectancy of the car. The question was unresolved for years, although by 1906 there was little argument over the merits of a "fireproof" car for subway and high-speed service, where the risk of collision and fire was much greater. But maximum speed on a city streetcar system was low, and cars normally operated in single units rather than in trains, so that little need was felt for steel bodies.

Meissner's first major new order was for 175 cars of radical design. Known as "stepless" cars (and nicknamed "hobble-skirt" cars), these low-floor, center-entrance vehicles for the New York Railroad Co. were of fearsome appearance. Their all-steel construction made them very heavy, and this series of construction views helps illustrate the way in which steel members were used to replace wood members on a part-for-part basis. January 1913 saw the start of the job with the laying down of the underframe.

Structural members being riveted to the main frame.

Center-entrance door frames being attached.

New York stepless car #5000 in service.

The interior of a completed car.

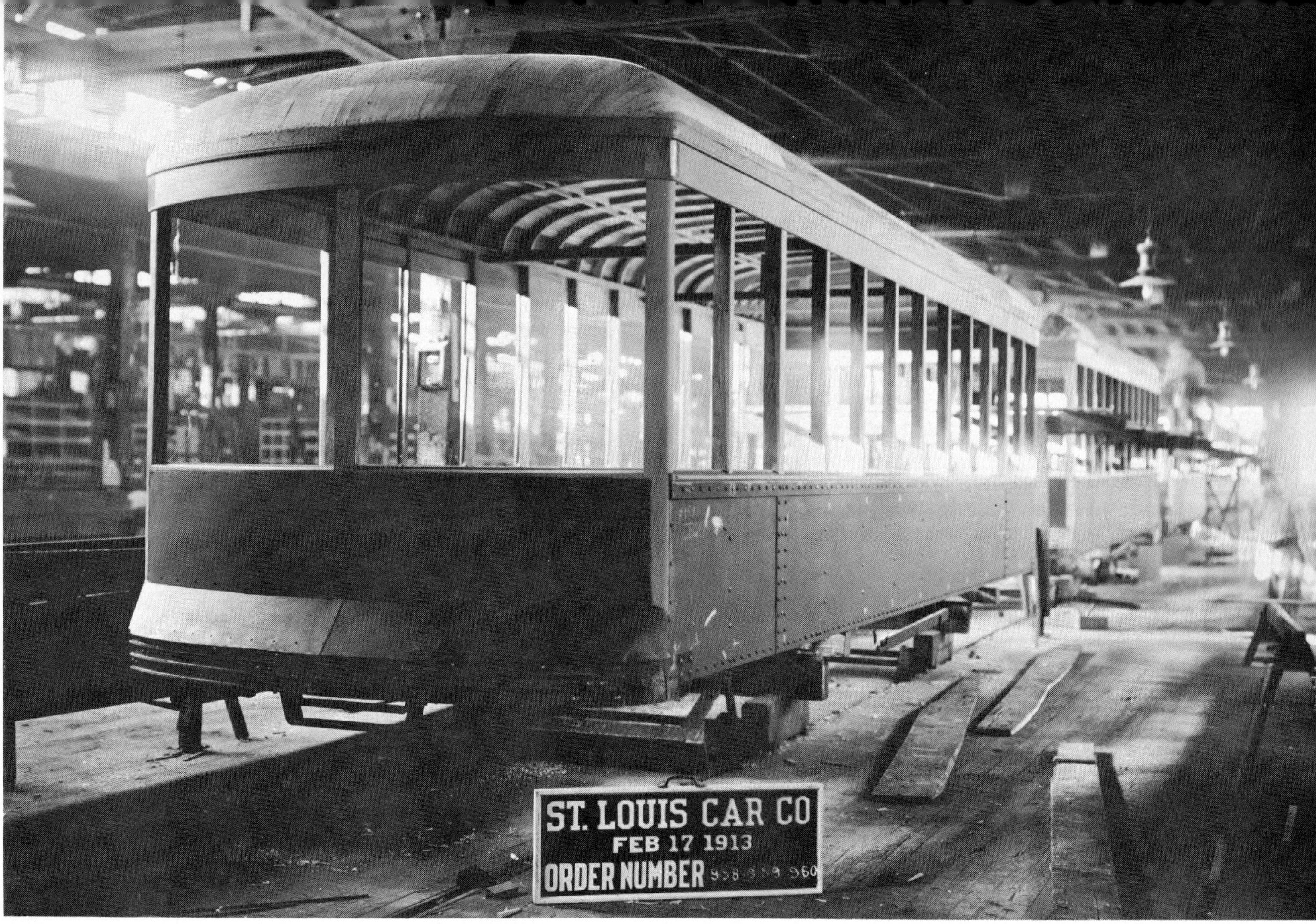

The first one-man lightweight safety cars under construction for the Illinois Traction Co. in 1913.

Conventional wisdom was that steel showed to best advantage when the strain of swaying, vibration and pulling was encountered. This most commonly occurred in multiple-unit operation in subway or elevated service. The steel car on such services gave the advantages of strength and smooth riding, but on the city streets such cars were noisier, heavier on current, and wore out the tracks. Consequently, the demand for the Car Company's steel-bodied cars was limited.

More annoying than the lack of customers was the presence of another manufacturer making steel cars, practically in the Car Company's local area. The Danville Car Co. of Danville, Illinois, introduced a line of steel cars in 1906, shortly after the Car Company had opened its steel car plant. Most serious for the company was the fact that the Danville plant was at this period owned and operated by Henry Vogel, their own vice president and general manager. His departure in May 1906 to better attend to his Danville duties had been a severe blow to Kobusch, made worse because of his intimate knowledge of steel car manufacturing techniques, and his subsequent use of that knowledge to compete with the Car Company.

The slump of 1906-8 was another factor in the limited demand for steel-bodied cars. It became quite clear the street railway industry had reached its saturation point, and further substantial investment in new cars for new systems or expansion of services on old systems was not justified. Many operators in this period of diminished liquidity also decided to retain their existing equipment which was proving more durable in service over a longer period than had been expected when first it had been bought. Thus new equipment orders were

Albuquerque City Electric #15, built in 1917, was a repeat order of a St. Louis Car Co. lightweight design first delivered to that city in 1915.

considerably reduced at the precise time the Car Company began to market its steel cars.

The failure to sell the new cars was one more problem to be faced in the financially troubled years between 1906 and 1911, and it was not until 1912 that the large scale adoption of steel-bodied cars commenced in earnest, partly as a result of the movement to improve car design. The corresponding (and unexpected) increase in the price of wood made the change exceptionally speedy and by 1914, the trend to steel construction had encompassed the city streetcar, still the backbone of the Car Company's work. Indeed there soon began to be heard complaints from those car builders still using wood that seasoned ash, used to fabricate posts and rails, was scarce, and if this were to continue, wood construction might have to be completely abandoned.

Initially, steel car construction had been characterized by high first cost and lack of standardization. There were few standard rolled shapes, and most parts had to be especially made for the job in hand, using new dies on each occasion. But the operating company that did switch to steel cars could find immediate benefit in reduction of maintenance costs, for by purchasing cheap, simple equipment, the average maintenance shop could then make its own dies and thus press its own replacement parts. Formerly, this work was sent to an outside firm for forging, or else expensive reconstruction in the company's own shops was necessary.

Steel cars were less susceptible than wood cars to exterior damage. With the later development of the portable electric spot-welder, minor damage to steel cars could be repaired *in situ* without having to take the car out of service. Steel cars were stiffer than wood, with great resistance not only to frontal collisions (a feature shared by the compromise semi-steel car which was steel to the belt rail and wood from there to the roof) but also to shearing blows and side swipes. A wooden car under similar adverse conditions could expect major structural damage or even collapse, and with the reckless driving and excessive speeds practiced by some companies (frequently with the connivance of the passengers) this was an important consideration.

The tiniest lightweight car built at Baden was this vehicle for the Illinois Traction Co., delivered in 1916. The design was by Illinois Traction's master mechanic Bosenbury.

Interior of Illinois Traction lightweight #400.

The ultra-lightweight was too small and light for practical operation, but some were sold. Car #103 of Illinois Traction's Oskaloosa, Iowa line. Similar cars went to Atchison, Kansas, and Three Rivers Traction, Quebec.

Jitney body, shipped to the Schurmer Wagon Co., St. Paul, on September 3, 1915.

This is thought to be the first batch of Birney designed safety cars to be built at the Baden plant. They are seen here under construction early in 1917.

Double-end St. Louis safety car #287 of the San Antonio Traction Co. on January 27, 1917. This was one of the last pre-Birney lightweights to leave the Baden plant.

With the First World War over, the Birney idea became immensely popular and in 1920, the plant was reorganized to produce five or more complete cars a day. This is thought to be the first St. Louis-built Birney car to be fitted with the new St. Louis #7 safety car truck. It is being driven out of the new shops. Meissner is fourth from the right.

A major improvement in steel car construction helped materially in the shedding of excess car weight. On these cars, the entire car side from the top of the letterboard was constructed as a one-piece truss.[2] The weight problem was seen as impossible to solve until the development of this technique. It had been felt that a steel car light enough to compare in weight to a wood car would have metal parts so thin in places that there would be a danger of rust shortening the car's life. This did not happen in the few cars so built, and with operating expenses rapidly climbing, the big heavy cars were coming to be viewed with disfavor on all but the most intensively patronized city services. With the development of truss construction in 1913 weight ceased to be a material consideration, and for the next decade or so, customers could choose between the older and heavier type of steel car, still more suitable for high speed interurban or intensive city service, and the lighter truss car for other types of use.

By 1915, the *Electric Railway Journal* was able to observe that the experimental period in steel car building was over, with the introduction during 1914 of the steel car to so many lines.

> The qualities that place steel in the van are uniformity and an ability to be worked into irregular shapes, in which the strength can be placed where needed. Thus the steel car is superior to the wood car only because it provides an opportunity for improved design, and if this fact is neglected the advantages of steel construction largely disappear. The mere substitution of steel members for wooden ones accomplished nothing, and it is quite likely that a steel car . . . built in accordance with the old "underframe" principle inherent in wooden car design will cost more, weigh more and involve more repairs than a similar car, built throughout of wood . . .[3]

It was precisely this need to reduce weight and cost, while retaining steel's strength that led to the interest of the Illinois Traction and Stone and Webster Corporations in small lightweight steel cars for city service. Both companies had extensive interurban and small urban services to operate, and J. M. Bosenbury, Illinois Traction's superintendent of motive power and equipment and Charles O. Birney, Master Mechanic for Stone and Webster had independently of each other begun to work on the problem of designing a suitable lightweight steel car for use on small town urban services. Bosenbury's prime concern was with lightness of weight and safe one-man operation. Birney was more concerned with safe operating procedures, standardization of parts and economy. Both men contacted the street railway manufacturers for help, and used their facilities extensively for the construction of experimental vehicles.

Bosenbury was the first to complete a design; the one-man safety cars produced by the St. Louis Car Co. for the Illinois Traction system in 1913 were the true ancestors of the thousands that followed over the next 12 years. At the same time, the Car Company itself was experimenting with ultra-lightweight one-man cars, and in the years to 1916 a fair number were sold. These cars were less of a commercial success than those fitted with safety equipment.

This equipment (designed by Bosenbury in conjunction with Westinghouse) consisted of a combination brake, sand and door mechanism, and a controller with a "dead man's handle." In normal operation, the driver would keep a button or lever on his controller depressed to keep it functioning normally. In case of his sudden illness, or death at the controls, the release of pressure on the button or lever would operate the brakes and bring the car to a swift halt. In addition, the controls were interlocked with the doors, and until the doors were closed, the car could not be moved. Equally, except in an emergency when they could be opened by hand, the doors could not be opened again until the car came to a complete halt. Cars with these features were built by the Car Company and others in some quantity before 1917, and for many years afterwards, St. Louis Car Co. described itself as being "the home of the safety car."

In a technical sense, this is quite true. The credit for bringing these design features together in a single-truck, lightweight car intended to tackle the very real operating problems of expense, durability, safety and weight was essentially Bosenbury's. But the idea of producing large quantities of such cars to a wholly standardized design, for universal use without modification on small and medium sized city systems, as a way of reducing costs while at the same time increasing service, was that of the Stone and Webster Corporation through their man, Charles Birney.[4]

Stone and Webster owned over 25 streetcar properties in the U.S.A., and already appreciated the virtues of standardization in cost cutting. Their urban properties were mainly small, and very vulnerable to automobile competition, especially that of the jitney, which had appeared almost overnight during 1914.[5] Birney's new car was intended to rejuvenate these ailing properties by providing increased service with lightweight one-man safety cars. The theory behind the design was that the provision of increased service by these small and fast cars, would bring automobile drivers and their passengers back to the streetcar by virtue of the frequency, reliability and speed of service. The car itself would be cheap to construct and operate, being standard throughout the country. Thus the operating companies would through the real savings in cost, operation and accident claims, be able to afford the extra new cars necessary to provide the increased service.

In final form, Birney's car was in external appearance almost identical to Bosenbury's and neither style was much different from that used on the majority of one-man lightweight cars built since 1912. However, it was Birney's car design rather than Bosenbury's which was followed in the years to come, even though his first car was not produced until 1916. The war delayed large-scale acceptance of the idea, and it was not until 1919 that the Stone and Webster operating idea for the lightweight steel safety car became a dominant trend in the street car industry.

The car met with a mixed response. Its enthusiasts praised its virtues to the skies, extolling it in terms that the religious fanatic might use in greeting the Messiah. Indeed the very word Salvation was heard frequently in the industry, as if the new car could be expected to work miracles. And of course it couldn't.

It could not even prove to be profitable in many cases. Though many thousands were made

Birney cars were basic in their external and internal appearance. City of Monroe, La., #24 (exterior) and #21 (interior). Jim Crow laws applied even to these diminutive vehicles.

Lightweight steel framing for safety cars.

Contrast the light framing of the safety car with the more usual heavy steel framing of full-size cars. Below is car #217 of the Guthrie Electric Co., Oklahoma.

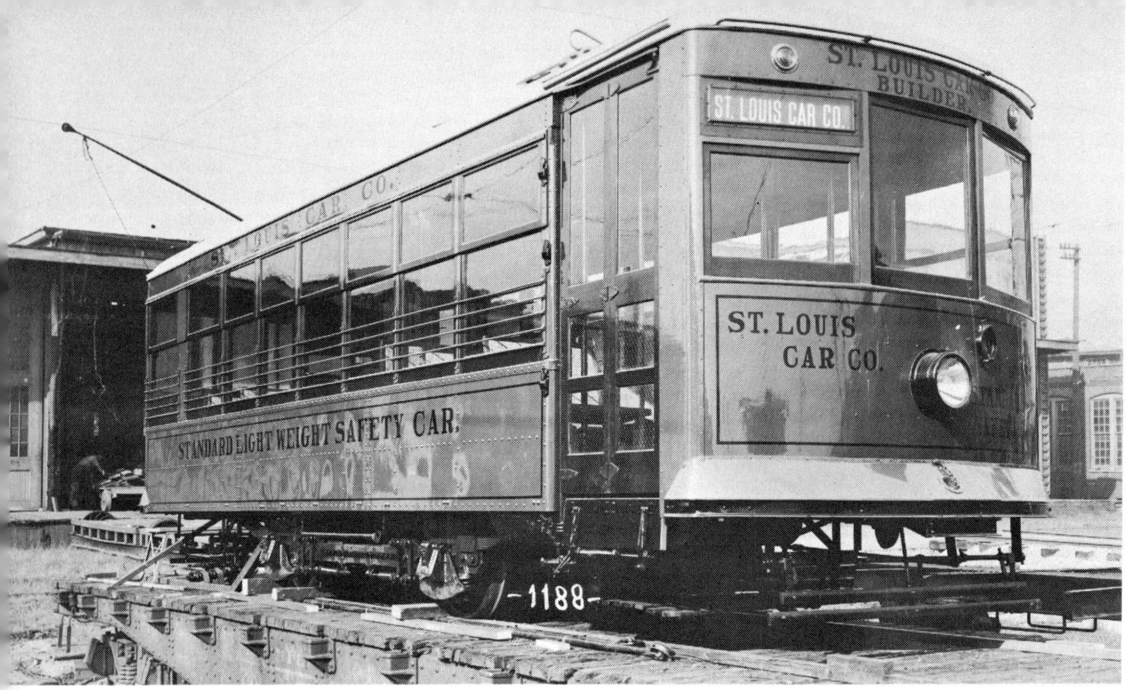

A fully finished car, the first of 50 built for distribution by Tontrup's National Safety Car and Equipment Co., St. Louis.

and sold, and although the operation of even a few safety cars was a symbol of the operating company's willingness to move with the times, there were certain areas of operation that were utterly unsuited to the little car, as the newly-formed Detroit Department of Street Railways had found out to its cost in 1923. This kind of operator was best served by the big steel city car, and the 1915 "Peter Witt" design of front entrance, center exit, pay-as-you-pass two man car, fitted with longitudinal seats in front (to give a large standing area) and normal seats in the rear, proved to be the most effective car type to deal with the conditions of big city service. Seemingly the antithesis of the safety car theory as to speed and operating cost, these cars in fact proved to be the savior of big city operation, for they could lift big crowds very quickly, crowds that were little concerned at the lack of comfort the big Witt cars offered (though curiously, the Birney cars were just as uncomfortable as the Witts).

Ironically it was the big city operators alone who could afford to purchase substantial numbers of new cars. The smaller companies could not, even if those cars were the cheap safety cars, specifically designed to meet their particular problems. Consequently, the type of installation necessary for the operating success of the safety car (suggested by the theory) could not always be met in practice. Too frequently, the car's purchasers replaced their old, steady-riding high-capacity vehicles with the poor-riding, low capacity safety car, on a one-for-one basis. This created an extremely grave public relations problem, for no matter what was said to the contrary, such a substitution was tantamount to a reduction in service, and more importantly in the quality of service. Without the increased service, speed and frequency its designers had insisted upon, the safety car was all too obviously a poor substitute for the vehicles it replaced. Yet, where the car was installed as design theory dictated, in a small or medium-sized town, or on lightly-loaded big city lines, the installation often meant the difference between closing down an unprofitable line or system, and its revival once again as a profitable investment.

By 1917, the sale of safety cars was becoming an increasingly important part of St. Louis Car Co.'s business, and with the full-size steel city car now the company's dominant product, the change-over from wood to steel car manufacture was complete. It had moreover been accomplished without affecting the company's profitability, an achievement Meissner could be proud of, for he alone had been responsible for it. Beggs, his war with North American long since over, had taken little active interest in the company's daily affairs since 1912, and the company's recovery since then had been due solely to Meissner.

CHAPTER 12

THE YEARS IMMEDIATELY preceding World War I had been the most difficult since electricity had been first used to power streetcars. The competitive threat of the automobile was altering the financial position of many transit companies for the worse, and the market for new equipment was depressed. Many of the weaker manufacturers had gone out of business in the boom years, and there certainly was no good economic reason why the Car Company itself should not have been allowed to go under in 1911. There were still far too many manufacturers for the available market in that year, and by 1917, the market had further contracted. But Beggs wanted the company to survive for his own reasons, and the company creditors chose to trust Beggs' superb reputation for restoring profitability and therefore protect their claims, rather than settle for what they could get in a liquidation. Meissner in his turn had shown what could be done to rejuvenate the Car Company, and was rewarded in January 1916 by being appointed vice president, a promotion which Beggs specifically stated was to recognize Meissner's services to himself and the Car Company since 1911. In a declining market, and in the face of slump, Meissner had on his own turned a bankrupt company into a fairly profitable enterprise.

Beggs had expressed little interest or concern in the Car Company after 1912, aside from its possible value as a profitable asset, and Meissner had felt sufficiently confident in 1916 to make Beggs an offer for the Car Company. In principle Beggs was quite ready to sell, but not at Meissner's price of $800,000. Beggs insisted that he had paid $750,000 for 7,500 shares of stock when he had bought the Company in 1911, had paid its debts, and had taken out loans from the Third National Bank, National Bank of Commerce and the Mississippi Valley Trust Co. Yet he had received no dividend whatever since he had bought it, and he explained to Meissner that the controlling block of stock, plus the interest on the loans together had cost him nearly $1½ million. In a letter concerning the matter Beggs went on to say that

> If the purchase of my interest at $850,000 had been consumated two or three years ago when the matter was under consideration, and held in abeyance for several months, it would have been much more advantageous to me than $1 million at this time. Therefore I must reluctantly refuse to concede to your earnest solicitations to modify the price of $1 million for all of my St. Louis Car Co. stock, which I am enclosing forthwith, duly assigned in blank.[1]

Meissner could not raise the money, the sale fell through, and the matter was not seriously raised for another eight years. Undoubtedly both men must have examined the company finances and its issued paper closely during the course of these negotiations, and despite the bank report which suggested the company was wanting capital of $250,000, it was quickly discovered that the 1907 capitalization of the Company at $6 million was at least half water, and it was immediately necessary to reduce the capital.

Generally such a procedure is routine, and the papers which are filed in the Missouri Secretary of State's office are legal documents, no other explanatory material being necessary. In this case however, a protest was lodged by Director W. S. McCall, who was now also representing one of the banks financing the company. Briefly, McCall claimed it was a matter of question whether the preferred stock as originally issued in 1907 was accumulative as to dividends. His position was that it was accumulative, and therefore dividends were due upon it before the common stockholders could share in any distribution.

The Corporation Attorney at the Missouri Secretary of State's office ruled the capital reduction proper, and dismissed the protest, and there the matter should have rested. But Sears Lehmann, a member of the law firm Lehmann and Lehmann who acted as the Car Company's representatives, took it upon himself to write the Missouri Secretary of State explaining why the Car

Company felt it necessary to reduce its capital. This letter, written in December 1917, remains on file at the Secretary of State's office to this day, and contains an excellent summary of the Company's financial tribulations in the decade 1907-1917, a summary not otherwise available in the other surviving Car Company papers[2]

> In . . . 1907 . . . the company . . . (got into) financial difficulties . . . Kobusch believed he could sell and issue $3 million of preferred stock to some French parties. Thereupon papers were obtained by which the $3 million preferred stock was issued to George J. Kobusch *as subscribed and fully paid by him* (Author's italics). This was done in anticipation of a sale of the stock to the French parties . . . and it was done before any affidavit of any kind was required in connection with an increase of capital stock.
>
> The sale to the French parties fell through. Thereupon, without any legal authority that we know of, Kobusch, *who had paid nothing for this $3 million of preferred stock* turned it into the treasury of the Car Co. We consider the issue was void and fictitious, but we do not think that question is now involved.[3]

The letter then turned to the situation in 1911, when the company had been faced with an involuntary petition for bankruptcy.

> Over twenty judgments on notes and admitted accounts had been obtained against it in the local courts, and it was utterly unable to continue in business in its financial condition. It was believed that if the company were allowed to go through bankruptcy, not only would the stockholders get nothing but . . . the creditors themselves would take a large loss. The company still had in its treasury the $3 million of preferred stock issued as heretofore stated. An arrangement was made by which Mr. John I. Beggs and Mr. Kobusch put $950,000 (sic) in cash into the treasury of the company for an equal amount of this preferred stock. Creditors of the company took approximately $600,000 at 100% on the dollar for their claims. These creditors in bankruptcy would certainly have gotten well over 50¢ on the dollar on their claims, but they believed preferred stock to be worth more than this. This preferred stock is preferred as to assets on distribution, and it is so stated on the certificate. . .
>
> The preferred stock has paid no dividends since issued over five years ago . . . The last sale of preferred stock, as we understand it, was around $30 per share, and was within the last couple of months. It is therefore plainly apparent that at the present time, there is absolutely no value behind the common stock of the company. It is also apparent that the people who took this preferred stock some five years ago, and saved the company from bankruptcy, would have been better off *if they had let the company go into bankruptcy, and taken what they had realized on that.*[4]

This was a harsh verdict, but one with solid foundation. It had been Beggs' insistence on having a St. Louis financial base to fight his war with Campbell which alone had saved the company. The Norvell group knew it, the London syndicate must have had more than a suspicion of it, and Campbell certainly knew it. Obviously, in making these arrangements with Kobusch, Beggs had connived at the fraudulent issue of preferred stock, and had not let anyone else know of it. At the same time, with Kobusch now in his debt, he had almost a blackmailer's power over the man, and could get rid of him whenever he proved an embarrassment, which of course he had done at the first opportunity. In saving the company, Beggs' interests had been served at the expense of the creditors.

And what of Meissner? It is extremely unlikely he was privy to these "arrangements," and his subsequent discovery of the truth years later must have been hard for him to accept. His enthusiasm for the company had been genuine, and his hard work had been devoted not just primarily to serve Beggs' interests, but to making the company viable once more. Now, here was Lehmann suggesting that the work of over six years had been for all practical purposes futile. As a result Meissner went through an unhappy period in which he began to doubt his future with the company. Twice he had

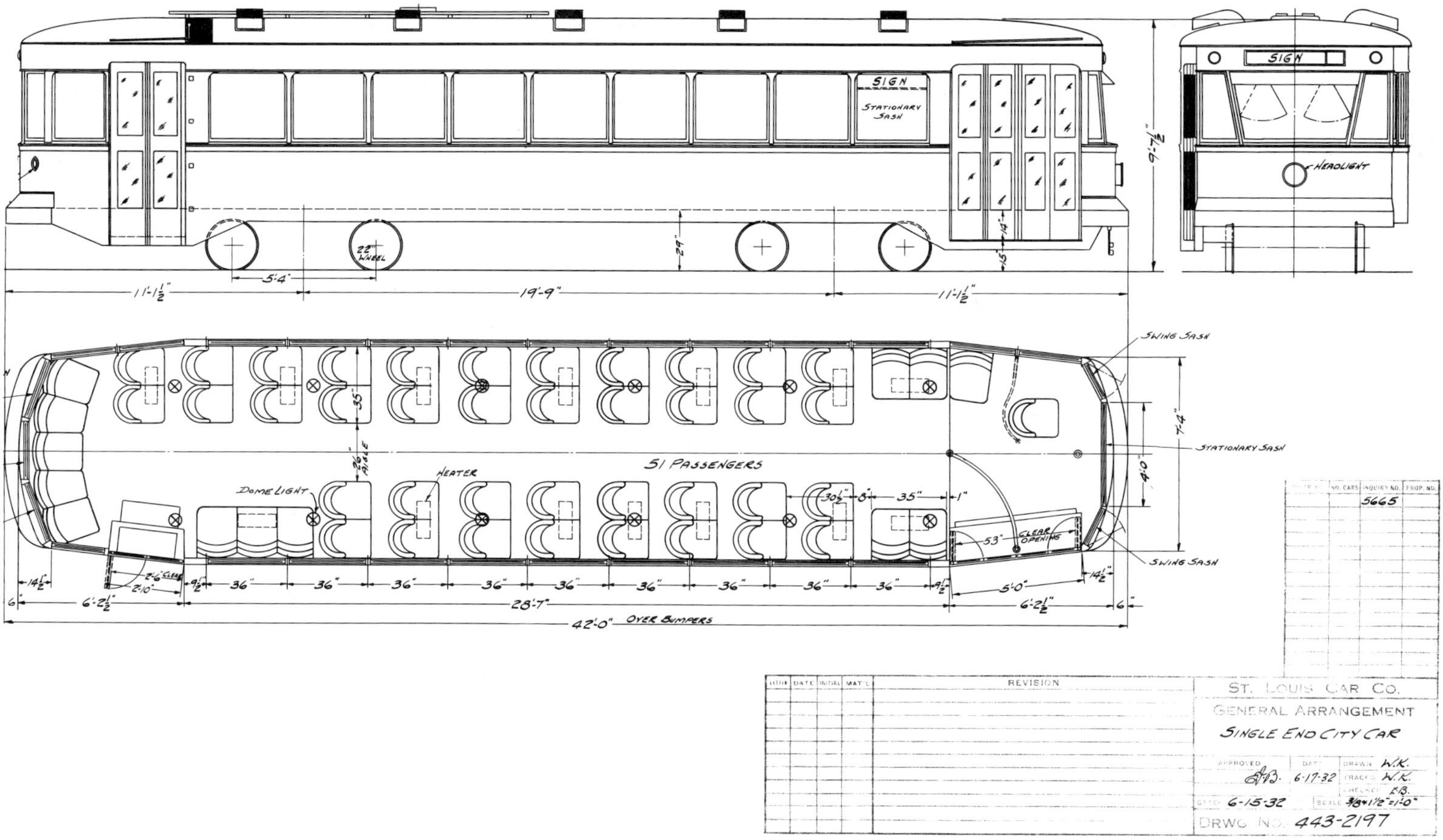

Proposed single end city car for Honolulu, 1932.

been unable to purchase it outright, and now "experts" considered it valueless. In the middle of 1917, at the time the capital reduction proceedings were occurring, he was offered an executive position at a large local chemical plant, and he seriously considered accepting. But his conscience was troubled by the ethics of working with a firm which among other things manufactured explosives, and he eventually decided to stay with the Car Company. He gradually regained his old self-assurance and poise, and a large aircraft contract was the result.[5]

Storeroom, plant #2 of St. Louis
Aircraft Co. Note young boys at work.

CHAPTER 13

WHEN THE U.S.A. entered the war in April 1917, there were only twelve firms in the country capable of manufacturing aircraft in quantity. Indeed prior to the war, less than 1,000 planes had been built. Only one factory was totally devoted to aircraft production; that of Glenn Curtiss in Hammondsport, New York,[1] while the U.S. army's aviation section had only 131 pilots, student aviators and non-flying administrative officers, and 1087 enlisted men.[2] Notwithstanding, enormous allocations were made for airplane manufacture once the country went to war. Under the direction of Major Benjamin Foulis, a program was drafted which called for the manufacture of 22,625 airplanes, 44,000 aircraft engines, and complete replacement parts for an additional 17,600 airplanes.[3] In retrospect, such a projection of needs seems absurd, for except for Curtiss and his associates, no firm had any experience in large-scale airplane manufacture, and as it turned out, though numerous types of fighters and trainers were produced, only the Curtiss-Wright JN4D was built in quantity.

This plane, commonly known as the "Jenny" had been designed by B. Douglas Thomas, an English aeronautical engineer under contract to Curtiss. Designed as a training and reconaissance plane, the JN4D was the first U.S. plane to be employed in combat by American forces when in 1916 General Pershing used it as an aerial spotter on the Mexican border when pursuing Pancho Villa. Though Glenn Curtiss was the principal contractor for the planes during the war, his plants in Hammondsport and Buffalo were unable to cope with the large orders placed, and other manufacturers sub-contracted to build the plane.

Meissner, always ready to try something new if it had commercial possibilities, was one of the successful bidders, receiving an order for 450 planes early in 1918. It was not his intention to make St. Louis a major aircraft production center. The planes were instead viewed as a way of helping the war effort, and to that extent were a source of great pride to the staff, and a symbol of the company's patriotism; very important in a plant with a high proportion of workers who were either German in origin, or by descent. There is practically no written record of this particular order, and very few photographs. Defense work was shrouded in secrecy and much of the material that survived the war has since been destroyed. However, William Fitzgerald, later the company's chief purchasing agent, was with the Car Company during the First World War, and saw the whole airplane project at close quarters, being involved in materials procurement for it.

To undertake the work, a new company was formed, and Fitzgerald attended its first meeting.

> The St. Louis Aircraft Corporation was formed one night at the Missouri Athletic Club with the executives of the Huttig Sash and Door (Company), Mr. Segal, his son Ralph, Mr. Meissner and myself. It was decided that Huttig Sash and Door would manufacture all of the wood parts, and the Car Company would manufacture all of the metal parts, and assemble the planes . . . Building No. 1 was converted, and many women and girls were employed (for this job) as well as whatever men could be found at that time . . . There was a great deal of cloth used in those planes . . .[4]

Indeed there was, and it was the use of large quantities of cloth that led to the hiring of women for the first time in the company's history. But bringing women into a hitherto all-male preserve, and at short notice, presented many problems. Particularly acute were the social problems. It was not that the men and women didn't get on together at work, rather it was that they got on too well.

> We had to ready (the) shop in a hurry in order to get production started, so washrooms for both men and women were built off the (shop) floor, and the men and women were thrown together very much during this time

Construction of JN4D warplanes: wire inspection and splicing.

Wire soldering and wrapping.

FUSELAGE TRUEING

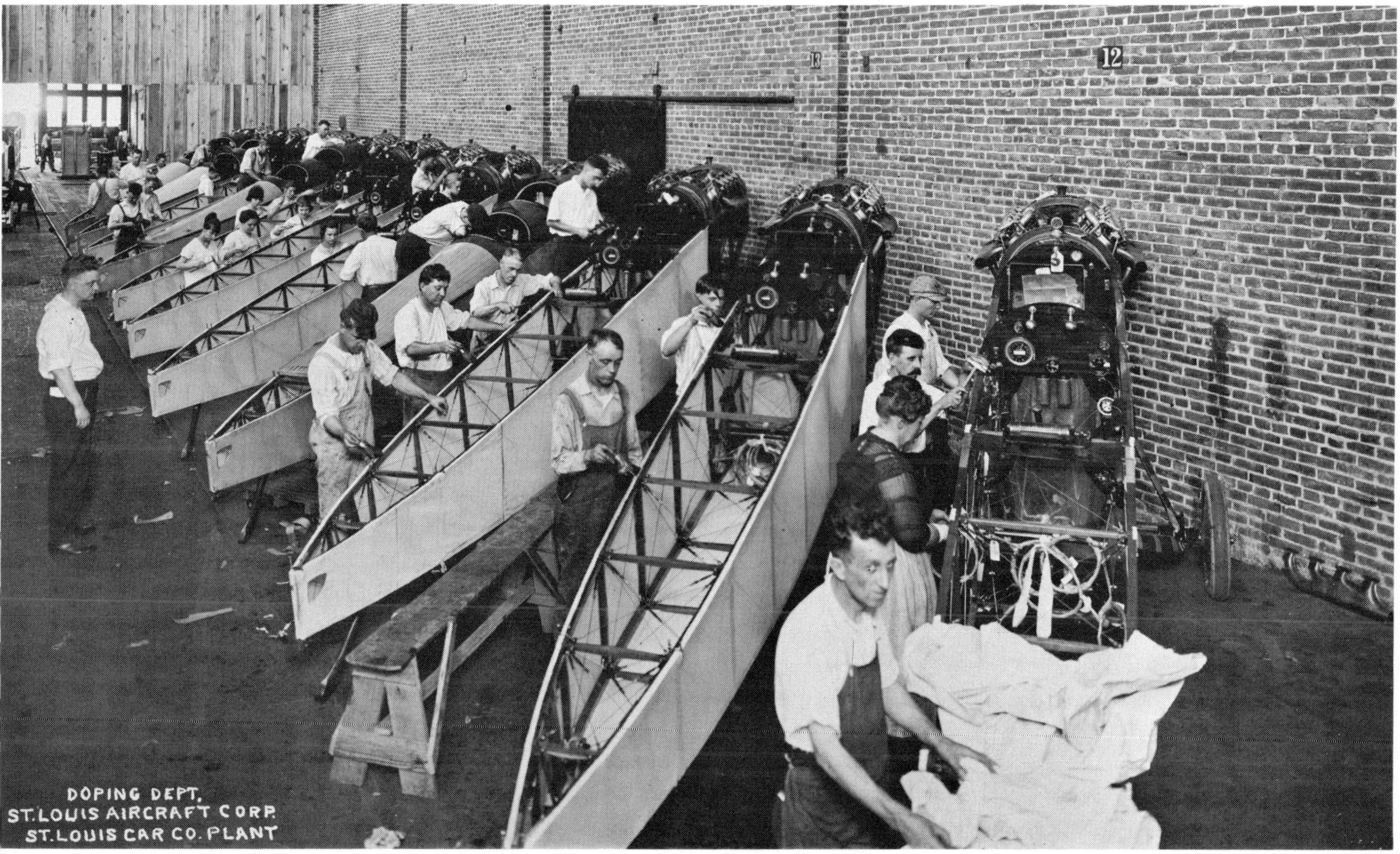

DOPING DEPT,
ST. LOUIS AIRCRAFT CORP.
ST. LOUIS CAR CO. PLANT

Propellor manufacture.

Covering Department.

Meissner, seated in the cockpit of a finished plane.

. . . so much so that many of them were discharged for being "over active"![5]

To keep contact between the sexes to a minimum, the women worked on different assembly lines, even when doing the same work as the men. The women's primary task on the airplane project was assembly, for the task involved the stretching and sewing of canvas over the frames, an operation considered to be women's work. Once assembled, the planes were sealed with a waterproof dope, the motors were fitted, tested, boxed and shipped to England.

The wages of the women were lower than those for the men, even when both sexes performed the same task, but men's wages themselves were quite low at the time. Severin Merz, later the company treasurer was the son of a Car Company upholsterer who was transferred to airplane assembly in 1918 at a wage of 17¢ an hour! The average wage of a skilled mechanic at this time was but 25¢ an hour, and it was not uncommon to be expected to work 55 or 60 hours a week.[6] This was a particularly low rate of pay for war work, and other St. Louis plants with defense contracts paid considerably more.

This quickly led to difficulties at the Car Company, and on April 27, 1918, a major strike was called, involving approximately 700 of the 900 workers. Encouraged by outside union organizers, the strikers demanded a 10% salary increase, a decrease in working hours, and a recognition of union organizing and bargaining rights. Despite the willingness of the company to accept these demands, the strikers refused to honor the settlement, though it appeared fully to comply with their original demands. The strike thus came under government arbitration, and was not settled for another month, regular work being resumed on 25 May 1918. The men and women did get their 10% increase, and it was agreed to refer all future disputes to the National War Labor Board.[7]

The airplane contract was the most exotic received by the Car Company during World War I, but many unusual products were manufactured. The metric machinery left over from the American Mors was put to good use when the Car Company became one of two streetcar manufacturers to take part in an otherwise exclusively mainline railroad car builders' contract for 100,000 box cars to be used by the Army in France. The Car Company's share of the order was 1000 vehicles.[8]

During the war the Car Company built tens of thousands of machine-gun carts, gun carriages, ammunition boxes and portable (mobile) blacksmith's shops. Before awarding such contracts, the Army had prospective companies build samples, which then were taken to Washington for tests. Meissner later told Fitzgerald of the acceptance test conducted in Washington on the Car Company's sample gun cart.

Machine gun carts were produced in great quantity during 1918

. . . and the plant was at times covered with acres of wheels.

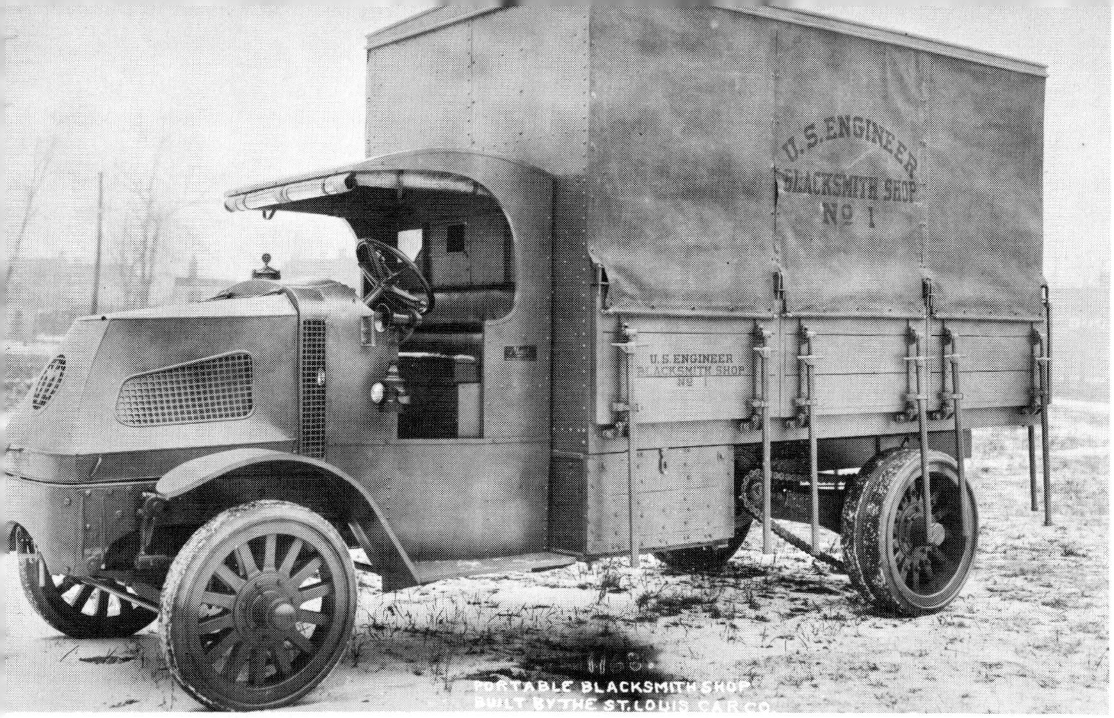

Portable blacksmith shop on a Mack truck chassis.

Transport bodies under construction.

Completed transport body.

Civilian equipment manufacture was allowed during the war, but production delays were frequent and lengthy. Car #163 of the Danville Street Railway Co.

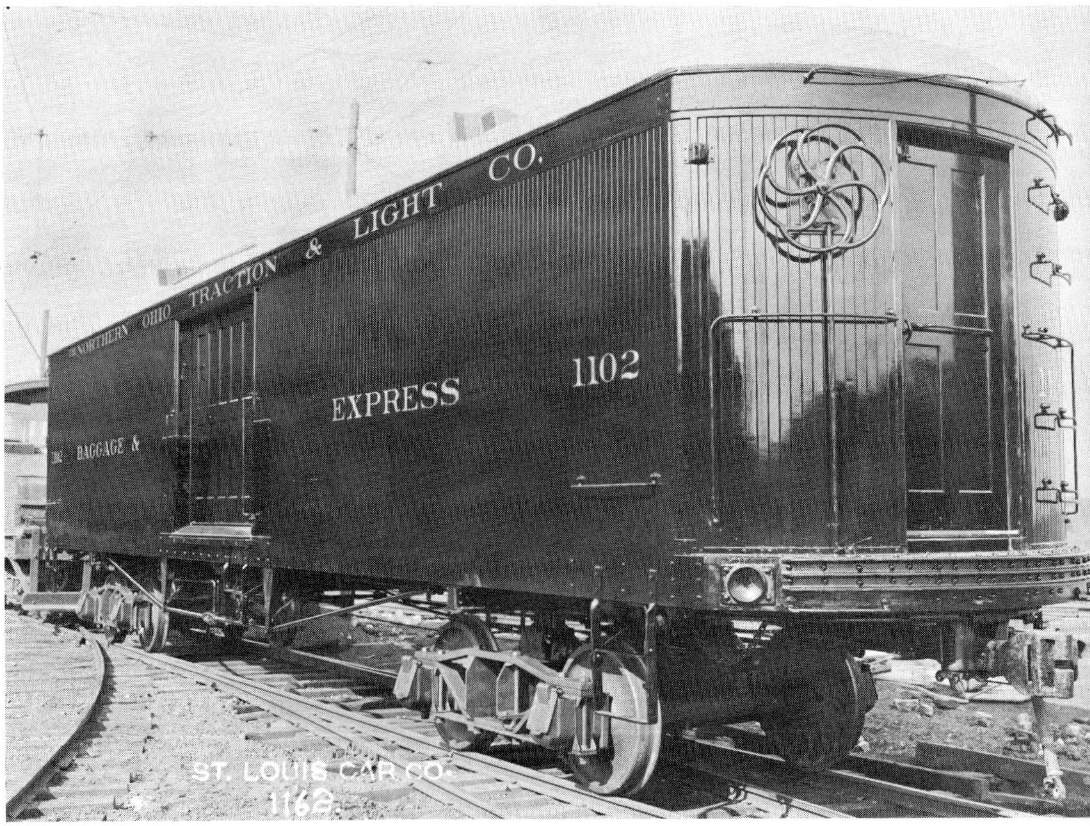

Baggage express car for the Northern Ohio Traction & Light Co., built in 1917.

Chicago, Ottawa & Peoria safety car #200, on a St. Louis #121 truck, and photographed on July 26, 1918.

City car #114 for the same company.

One-man, near-side safety car, mounted on St. Louis #113C truck for the Fort Wayne and Northern Indiana Traction Co. in 1919.

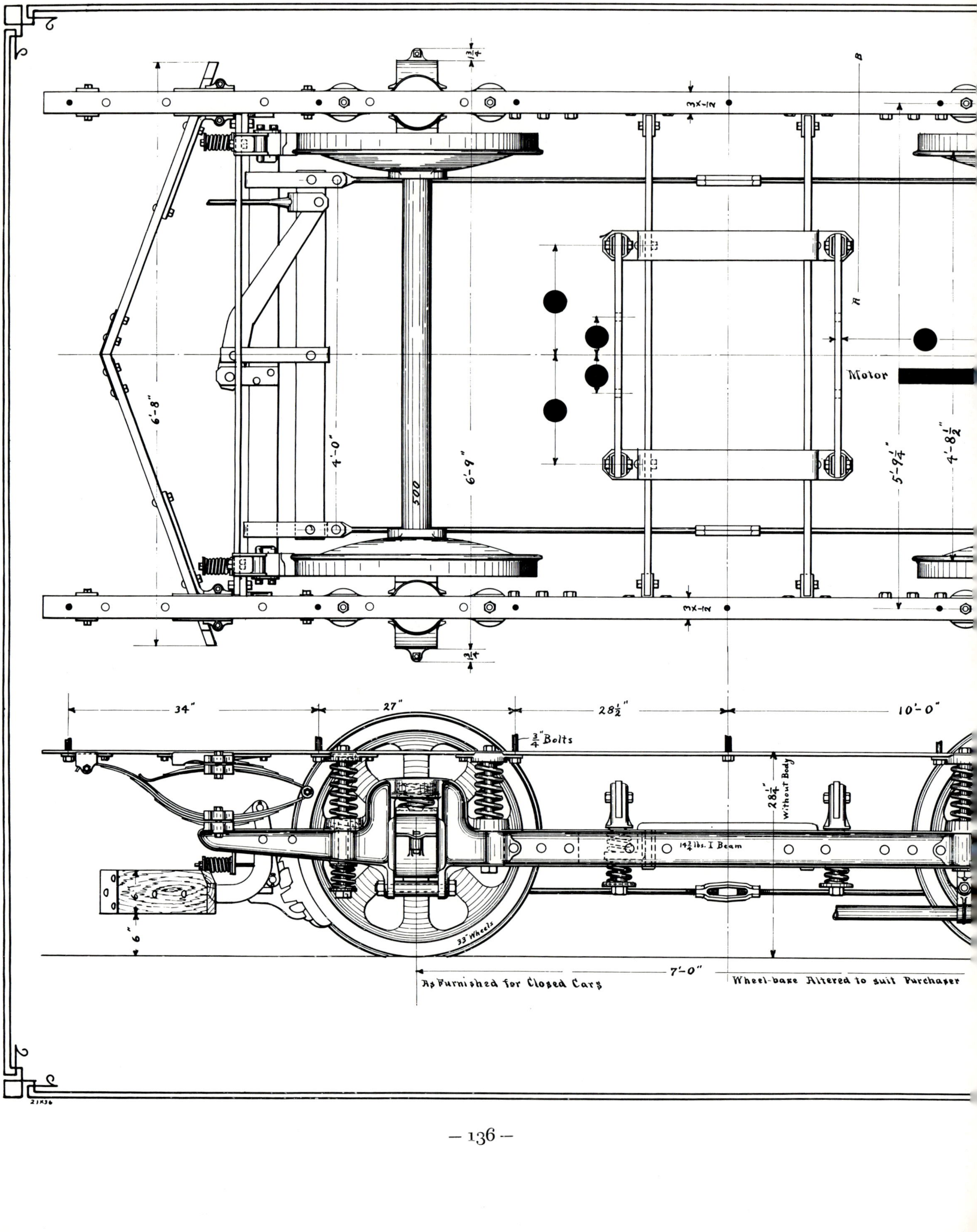

Motor
6'-8"
4'-0"
6'-9"
500
5'-9¼"
4'-8½"
3x-½
34"
27"
28½"
10'-0"
¾"Bolts
28¼" Without Body
14¾ lbs. I Beam
6"
33" Wheels
7'-0"
As Furnished for Closed Cars
Wheel-base Altered to suit Purchaser
21K36

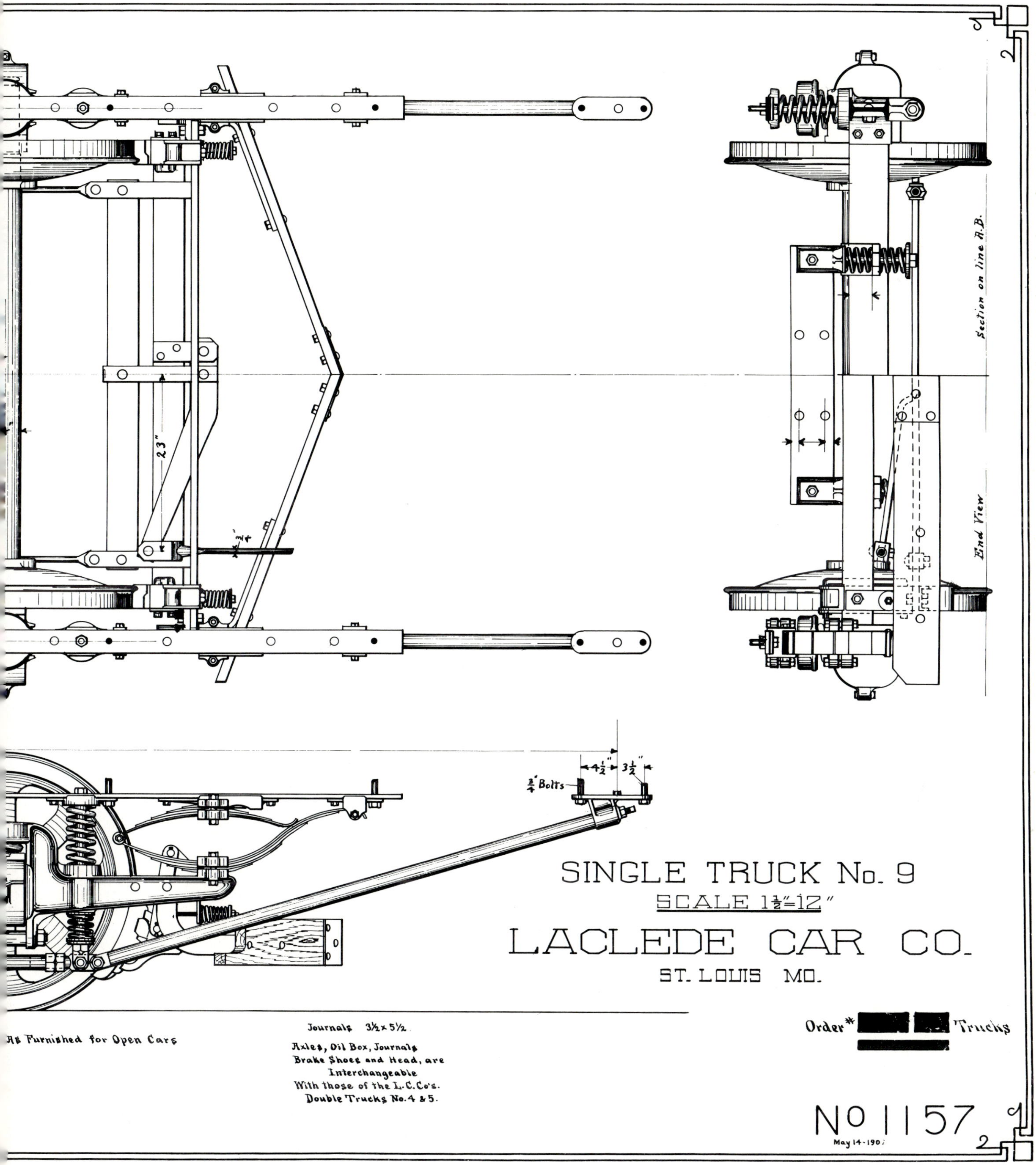

Laclede Car Co. truck #9, drawn May 14, 1902. This reproduction is not to scale.

15 cars of a 25 car order for the Los Angeles Railway, ready for shipment in 1920. The interior, below, was as spartan as ever.

> To test it . . . the Colonel in charge threw it out of the window, and it held up![9]

The woodworking section of the plant, in decline since steel cars became a commercial success was revived by war contracts, and for some years thereafter was very busy. One strange contract was for a standardized casket. In the Fall and Winter of 1918, there had been a nationwide epidemic of a killer flu, with a corresponding rise in the death rate. Great quantities of caskets were needed quickly, and the Car Company supplied a great number at $18.00 each. When the epidemic was over, a contract was signed with the Columbia Phonograph Co. in October 1919 to build 37,000 wooden cabinets for that company's Grafanola.

The year 1919 and the first half of 1920 continued profitable. While defense contracts had been phased out, the boom was still on, and the Car Company was busy filling a backlog of orders for the Birney Safety cars, and the first of the "Peter Witt" city cars. Thus a fire which razed the entire east side of the plant on October 12, 1920 was a major setback for the company. Caused by an explosion in an acetylene tank, the fire completely destroyed the pneumatic tool, steel car, wheel and axle and truck departments, the machine shop, power plant, steel and forging plants, planing mill and the pattern and storage warehouses.

Meissner and his wife were in Atlantic City at the time of the fire. Throughout his career he rarely permitted himself vacations, but as compensation almost always travelled with his wife when he took trips to the more attractive cities of the country. On this occasion, he was attending the American Electric Railway Association Convention, and the news of the fire came to him in the middle of the night. They took a train back to St. Louis immediately, and once there, he went straight to the plant to survey the ruins. What he might have had in mind was the subject of uneasy speculation before his return; it was clear after all that the company need not continue in business if neither Meissner nor Beggs had any interest in it. No indication was given whether layoffs would be made or exactly what was to be the immediate future. An apocryphal story dating from that time suggests that Meissner on his arrival stared long and hard at the ruins for quite some time, and then turned to his staff with the terse remark "Let's get to work." And that is what was done, with commendable speed and thoroughness.

Everything lost in the fire that had any insurance value was tabulated, and at the same time, anything that could be rehabilitated was salvaged from the ruins. But for some time thereafter, the loss of production facilities was a major problem. The shops had only recently been re-arranged to produce Birney Safety cars on a large scale. Before 1920, the Car Company had built Safety cars in lots of fifty, keeping them in stock until they could be sold by distributors. This was not the normal way to sell streetcars, but for a time, it does seem to have been the usual way to sell the Safety car. In late 1919 a new Safety car distribution company had been established in St. Louis by George Tontrup, previously of the American Car Co. After contracting with St. Louis Car Co. to distribute a number of Safety cars, Tontrup's National Safety Car and Equipment Co. had persuaded Nic Le Grand, for many year's St. Louis Car Co.'s general sales agent, to join them, much to Meissner's annoyance.

Thus when the Car Company had completed its contractual obligations to Tontrup, it did no further business with him, and returned to the old method of selling cars directly to the customer. By January 1920, the necessary shop conversion was complete, ensuring a production rate of five Safety cars a day, and more if necessary. In addition, the sales staff was augmented, and an all-out effort was made during the year to obtain new orders and offer more speedy delivery on all equipment. At one point during the war, there had been a six-month delay between placing an order, and delivery of the first vehicle, and it had been expected the new arrangements would substantially improve on that figure. The fire destroyed any hope of that.

The Car Company had the additional misfortune of losing its very able Secretary and Treasurer, Arthur Diekmann, shortly before the fire. He had filled that position since the strange departure of his predecessor in office, John Little, with more than $40,000 of the company payroll in January 1920. Diekmann was only 38 years old and had

The Skelton Car Looks Good—

BECAUSE THERE is sweeping grace in its every line. The body dimensions are generous, the upholstery deep and high grade, the appointments much finer than you would expect in a car of its price class. The owner of a Skelton car will take just pride in the eye appeal that his car inspires, for nowhere in its field is found an automobile of such striking beauty.

THIS automobile proves absolutely that a car may be superlatively good looking and still be marketed at a moderate price.

The Skelton Car is As Good As it Looks—

BECAUSE NO detail of its mechanical make-up has been slighted or compromised to meet a predetermined price. Through simplicity in design, the use of the finest grade units has been made possible in a car of moderate cost. The motor, the starting and lighting system, the full-floating rear axle and large steering wheel are typical of the elements that go to make up a Skelton car.

THE Skelton is rugged and proves in service that it is basically sound, truly good and trustworthy throughout.

THE SKELTON

A Car That Looks Good and Is As Good As It Looks

Advertisement for the Skelton, 1920.
Below is the Skelton 5-passenger tourer.

The Skelton tourer's elegantly simple dashboard.

died as the result of an operation. Thus the latter half of 1920 was a very bad period for the company, and Meissner made every possible effort to get the company back to work after the fire.

Limited production recommenced on October 23, 1920 on three 8-hour shifts, but delays in completing new car orders were inevitable. United Railways of St. Louis was particularly unfortunate. Fifty trailer cars had been ordered to replace vehicles damaged by fire on their own property, and United Railways was anxious for speedy delivery. The parts for all fifty cars were ready to be assembled at the time of the fire, but were totally destroyed in the blaze, and it was another six months before new ones could be completed.

It was fortunate that throughout his career, Meissner never skimped on insurance coverage. The entire plant was covered, and the total claim when it was finally settled 18 months later was over $3 million, the largest single insurance claim to be settled in St. Louis up to that time. The 50 trailers alone had been valued at $8,412 each.[10] The $3 million was augmented by a further $300,000 business interruption insurance payment, compensating the Car Company for lost production time.[11]

Most of the buildings destroyed were relatively new, housing modern equipment, but practically all the machinery was salvaged and renovated locally during 1921. On reinstallation the machines were regarded as practically new. However the temporary loss of such a great quantity of machinery together with the 1921 slump adversely affected the company's financial performance during 1921 and 1922, normal production and profits not being attained again until 1923.

The most surprising manufacturing decision made in the immediate postwar period was to reenter automobile production. An agreement was signed with S. L. Skelton a wealthy Oklahoma physician and businessman with a financial interest in a prototype automobile designed by Reed and Glaser of Indianapolis. The Skelton had a four-cylinder Lycoming motor, was built over an ash frame, and sported a walnut dashboard. The proposed selling price was $1145, though this had increased by the time production began. The car was double the price of a Model "T" Ford, and was therefore a high-priced vehicle, though not in the luxury class.

Meissner himself took out a dealership to sell the car in the St. Louis area, and had great hopes for the Skelton's success.

> Our vision for the Skelton is ambitious, just as the car itself is qualified to attain a reputation above and beyond anything in its class. With our 57 acre plant, equipped with the latest type of modern machinery at our disposal and with a product that is surprisingly good, we confidently expect and affirm that this car will shortly become known not only as one of the greatest values in the field, but also as one of the largest in the standpoint of numbers.[12]

Dr. Skelton possessed distributorships for the car all over the country, and it was felt to be wisest to contract with him for production lots, rather than with the designer or dealers. When the contract was signed in 1919, 3000 cars were called for with the expectation that up to 30,000 would be needed. The first vehicles were ready by early 1920, but only after substantial alterations had been made at the Baden plant. Fitzgerald remembered remodeling

> shop No. 5 to build the cars, installing a baking oven for the bodies, and buying all of the parts from . . . outside contractors. After we built five or six hundred cars, it was decided that we would purchase materials for an additional 3000 cars, and everything seemed to be rolling right along all right until the Depression came in 1921 . . . We had cars all over the country . . . All our dealers being broke, refused to accept the cars, which (had been) shipped sight draft against bill of lading. Many of these cars were thus sold for whatever we could get for them . . . four or five hundred dollars . . . material alone (had cost) $720. After production ceased, we then had the job of canceling orders and settling whatever claims we could.[13]

This was extremely bad luck. Unlike Kobusch's forays into automobile manufacture, the company had a good product, competitively priced, ample supplies of capital, and a well laid out plant. Moreover there was a ready-made distribution network with the capacity to absorb all the vehicles it had intended to make.

To further complicate matters, Dr. Skelton had died at the beginning of the 1921 depression, and the legal tangles which ensued when his estate came to be settled made matters considerably worse. The Car Company lost nearly $2 million on the Skelton, and almost went bankrupt. Creditors had to be stalled as long as possible, though sometimes exceptions had to be made. Fitzgerald remembered one bill for transmissions supplied by the Muncie Gear Works of Muncie, Indiana which

> we did not settle . . . as promptly as (the creditor) thought we should, and he filed suit against us through Bill Igoe, a prominent St. Louis attorney who was then a congressman in Washington. Mr. Meissner said "This is one we do settle right away," which we did.[14]

How Beggs reacted to this debacle is not recorded. It was obvious that Meissner, whatever his mistakes, was still trusted by Beggs to keep the company (and therefore his investment) solvent, and Meissner was thus largely left alone. Consequently when Beggs did put in an appearance at the Car Company, it was something of a state occasion. Fitzgerald, at that time working in the order department, recalled those visits vividly.

> He'd come down to the Car Company about twice a month when he'd come (to St. Louis) for (various) board meetings . . . About 8:30 or 9 o'clock, the chauffeur would pick him up at the train (and) he'd come in with his swallow-tail coat green . . . with wear . . . Sometimes he didn't go to his desk, he'd go out in the shop . . . He had . . . one old guy out there (that) he used to get the gossip from (named) Martin Russerman. The main part of a car . . . is . . . the (steel) center sills . . . and one day he saw a pile of steel beams about eight inches long on the floor . . . He (continued) walking through the shop and he (saw) . . . that they'd cut off some steel beams eight inches to fit a center sill. "What the hell goes here? Why did we order them long?" And of course old Martin down there said "We got them (that way) from the Order Department." Beggs took that beam up to the office and said to us "If that was cut off your pecker, you'd soon know about it." He was a tough old guy.[15]

Beggs was an arbitrary man, with an intolerance for idleness, smoking or drinking. He had a reputation for being exceptionally careful with money, aside from satisfying his rather lavish personal requirements, and apocryphal stories are told of Beggs' insistence on eating only 15¢ breakfasts, or his saving of 5¢ at lunch by not eating dessert, on the grounds that 5¢ saved in one minute was the equivalent of the money earned by one of his dollars in a year. Having succeeded in a hard school unaided, he saw no reason to give others a helping hand, and could never be persuaded to make charitable contributions.[16] These defects in his social character did not diminish his reputation as an impeccably honest businessman, and he was

The Skelton roadster.

Fine workmanship was apparent in the upholstery.

still a powerful figure in St. Louis and Milwaukee. Moreover by 1920 he had through a series of tactical moves regained the presidency of TMERL, and his position of authority in North American.[17] As a financier with a national reputation, his regaining of power in the companies with which he had previously been most closely associated was regarded as something to be expected from so astute a man, and thus he was largely forgiven his social eccentricities. His presence continued to be sought everywhere in St. Louis except by those who worked at the Car Company.

Some self-propelled rail vehicles were built at Baden before 1924. There were five gas-electric cars for the Missouri, Oklahoma and Gulf Railroad in 1912.

Three gasoline railcars for the Nebraska, Kansas and Gulf Railroad, shipped in 1916. Notice the coupled chain drive on the rear truck, and the drive shaft from the motor.

It is not known for whom this 1919 Bowen Motor Railway car was built. The car body is in its essentials a standard Birney safety car.

CHAPTER

14

After twelve years at the Car Company, Meissner's management style was well established. His prime concern was the financial health and profitability of the company in its main field of operation, the manufacture and sale of electric rail vehicles. But the company was not exclusively limited to this work, and the airplanes, the Skelton, the caskets and the new steel-bodied Birney motor bus of 1924 were all experimental projects which could use existing labor and facilities without adversely affecting the company's main business. Indeed so careful was Meissner to protect his major customers, the streetcar operators, that he refused to manufacture motor bus bodies except for sale to those companies. Some projects were profitable, some not, and while Meissner hoped to make money from them all, failure did not automatically jeopardize the Company, except when he was exceptionally unlucky, as in the case of the Skelton.

As it turned out, some payment was eventually made on the Skelton. The debts of the dealers were absorbed into Dr. Skelton's estate; he had after all controlled almost all the dealerships. When the estate was settled in 1927, $58,000 was paid to the Car Company as a final payment on the debt, leaving $230,000 still outstanding. Meissner never lost his interest in new schemes with possible commercial application, and he was usually able to help an otherwise penniless inventor raise money to finance production.

One typical action on Meissner's part occurred in 1923 with a lightweight gas-electric powered railcar project. The Car Company (and others) had been interested in the development of self-propelled rail vehicles for many years, but with the exception of the Kobusch-Wagenhals steam car experiment, and a handful of gasoline-powered cars for the Missouri, Oklahoma and Gulf Railroad in 1912, it was left to other companies to build such cars. Since 1910, Brill, McKeen and the Hall-Scott Co. had built self-propelled rail vehicles in commercial quantities, but they were heavy, slow and in the early days unreliable.

In 1923, the Car Company had begun to produce Sykes mechanical railcars, but this type of unit was not as powerful or capacious as the railroads required. Their urgent need was for a vehicle light enough to run on branch lines, yet powerful enough to pull a passenger car trailer or freight cars in emergency. Existing designs could not satisfy such service requirements without wearing out at an early age. But in that year Meissner was approached by H. L. Hamilton with an idea for just such a vehicle.

Hamilton and his colleague Turner had been working on the design since 1920 and had succeeded in interesting General Electric engineers in the gas-electric propulsion unit. The next step was to interest a car builder in the lightweight body. In 1922, they had formed the Electro-Motive Engineering Co., and then approached all the carbuilders to negotiate the building of a prototype. The design was intriguing and radical, for the complete car was to weigh 35 tons ready for the rail, about half the weight of previous units. When first approached by Hamilton, Meissner was somewhat skeptical, but was persuaded to back the project by the enthusiasm of his new Chief Engineer Seelar, who was impressed with the ingenuity of the lightweight car body design. A contract for one car was signed in November 1923, but the Electro-Motive Co. was very weak financially, and before the car was completed, Meissner had put much of his own money into the project.

Technically, however, the new car was very promising, and a buyer for the prototype was quickly found, though the conditions under which they would accept the car were exceedingly onerous. They insisted that the car run 30 days in regular service upon delivery, with no more than two fifteen minute delays in the whole of that time for mechanical failure. Owing to the inaccurate fitting of certain wiring, at the car's first run on the Car Company's test track there was an anxious moment when the wheels of one truck were seen

Cars for the Four Wheel Drive Co. (above) to be used on the Oklahoma and Southwestern Railroad.

The front end of a Sykes railcar was exceedingly plain. This belongs to one of 11 built for the New Haven Railroad in 1924.

A typical 1924 Sykes unit (below) for the New York Central.

An EMD gas-electric for National of Mexico. Meissner is fourth from the right.

Some of the first EMD gas-electric cars under construction in 1925.

A classic early EMD gas-electric. Great Northern #2310 being tested on the St. Louis Waterworks line in 1925.

Rock Island #9000, hauling a train of completed gas-electric cars for that railway along the Wabash right of way, and passing De Baliviere station, St. Louis in 1928.

to be rotating in one direction, and the wheels of the other truck in the opposite direction! But matters were quickly put right, the car successfully fulfilled its obligations and commercial production of gas-electric railcars for Electro-Motive started in 1924. Rather than purchase Hamilton and Turner's interest in Electro-Motive, and sell the design himself, Meissner preferred to continue contracting with Electro-Motive whenever cars had to be built. Once their first car was a success, Electro-Motive began to place orders for their cars with every car builder, not St. Louis Car Company exclusively and, as a result, instead of a runaway financial success, the Car Company built only 171 cars, until they became obsolete in 1932. Essentially Meissner's failure to invest in Electro-Motive was a lapse of judgment on his part, for by 1929, it had become strong enough to attract a take-over by General Motors. As their Electro-Motive Division, they were subsequently responsible for the diesel-electric revolution on the world's railways.[1]

In fairness to Meissner, however, 1924 was not a year in which his close attention to long-term investment possibilities was to be expected. Beggs was once more in a position of supremacy at North American and TMERL and his interest in St. Louis Car Co. had dwindled to nothing. Moreover, Beggs was reinvesting his personal moneys away from utilities into oil and Florida land. The Car Company had always been a personal investment, and the wearisome details of running a company whose business was largely peripheral to his main spheres of activity, constructing materials for an industry whose profitability was in doubt, was no longer attractive to him. Now over 75 years of age, he had neither the strength nor the energy to continue indefinitely his close watch on the Car Company, nor his regular commuting between Milwaukee, St. Louis and New York. Yet so close and uncommunicative a man was he that his decision to promote Meissner to the presidency of the Car Company came as a complete surprise, not only to Meissner, but to Beggs' own TMERL colleagues, with whom he worked daily. In addition, Beggs revived for himself the position of Chairman of the Board, a post vacated since Kobusch's resignation in 1913.

Meissner and his family were elated at his promotion, and the local press was quick to compare Meissner's career with the Horatio Alger stories (as they had done with Beggs years before). They did, however, point out that Meissner had surpassed most of Alger's fictional creations by having gone from messenger boy to company president in less than 25 years, and before the age of 40. Moreover, by his exertions, he had been able to keep his

The all-metal Birney bus was added to the Car Company's product line at the end of 1923. It boasted almost all the safety features of the Birney safety car. This vehicle is thought to be the first to leave the Baden plant early in 1924, and was sold to Yellow Coach.

Shortly afterwards, the same bus (below) appeared in the fleet of St. Louis' People's Motor Bus Co.

Birney bus body for Houston, 1924.

Head-end view of a completed East St. Louis Mack bus. Notice the air-springs under the headlamps.

Completed body shell of an East St. Louis Mack bus in 1925.

Four buses for United Railways, St. Louis, delivered in 1925.

Provided the customer was an electric railway operator, Meissner would gladly custom-build any type of bus body. Eighteen double-deck buses were thus shipped to the Kansas City Railways late in 1925. This same operator ordered five palatial "parlor" buses (below) in the same year.

The Birney bus sold quite well for a period.
New Orleans #1121 was photographed in 1927.

mother's family together during his years in St. Louis, and had managed to put a brother through law school. Thus of all the letters of congratulation he received, his mother's letter thanking him for what he had done is the most touching.

Beggs had explained his action by noting that Meissner's work with the company over the preceding years had been of exceptional service in building up the business, and Meissner's friends in the industry were quick to agree. The following letter is typical:

> St. Louis, February 8, 1924. My dear Ed, I just returned yesterday from New York, and leave again for a few days in Indiana tonight. I wish to congratulate you on your well-deserved election as President of the Car Company. Of course, I know you have been the real "boss" for many years, ever since the time we used to have, working around with "renewal notes" . . . and you *did* all *that heavy work* and more too. I know it as well or better than anyone else, so that you are surely entitled to all the salary and glory that the new office may bring. I have always said that you and our good friend George Kippenberger were responsible for the Car Company's remarkable success. Again, permit me to congratulate you.[2]

A similar telegram from Bosenbury of Illinois Traction prompted this response from Meissner:

> (no date) My dear Bosy, Thank you very much for your telegram conveying congratulations. May I say at this time that I feel you have been helpful in my accomplishments here, so that I owe you a vote of thanks for your constant cooperation and goodwill.[3]

By 1924 then, Meissner had gone as high as he could go in the Car Company. In view of Beggs' continued lack of interest, and his own hard work, he had begun to look upon the rejuvenated company as essentially his own creation, and almost as his personal property. If he wanted to stay at the Car Company he would somehow have to buy Beggs' interest, and himself become the company's sole owner.

CHAPTER 15

It is not known whether Beggs and Meissner had any agreement concerning first refusal in case of Beggs' sale of the company. In view of the close working relationship between the two over the past 25 years, and Meissner's known desire to buy Beggs' Car Company stock, one might have expected an unofficial agreement of the sort to have existed. But Beggs was not that kind of man. He was cold and uncharitable, with a reputation for ruthlessness which in old age had not deserted him. He was honest certainly, and he was very able; his whole career was a monument to those qualities. But where there was sufficient profit to be had, he was quite capable of ignoring old business ties, and after his promotion of Meissner to the presidency, he might well have felt he had fulfilled any obligations he owed Meissner.

Late in 1924, a Car Company telephone operator overheard part of a conversation between Beggs and the Stone and Webster Corporation, Birney's employer, and an important Car Company customer. Stone and Webster had until recent years designed and built many of their own streetcars, and was now investigating the possibility of purchasing a car builder. Beggs, without informing any other member of the Car Company board had tentatively entered into an agreement with Stone and Webster for sale to them of the St. Louis Car Co. Worse yet, he had verbally agreed to make over, at a specified price, company stock held by Meissner over which he (Beggs) had no control whatever. Beggs had wrongly assumed Meissner would go along with the sale, and when he found out he was mistaken, the affair became a matter for the lawyers.[1]

Meissner did not want to sell his stock under any circumstances. Indeed since 1916, he had been buying stock in small amounts to augment his own holdings. While Beggs still had absolute financial control, Meissner was by 1925 in a far stronger bargaining position than he had been in 1916, and Beggs realizing the seriousness of his mistake was thus compelled to be more accommodating to Meissner than he had been previously. Though he was not prepared to entertain a bid lower than that made by Stone and Webster, he did allow Meissner time to raise sufficient money to match their bid, and in October 1925, Meissner became the sole owner of the St. Louis Car Co. By a strange coincidence, Beggs unexpectedly died in the middle of the transaction, and the final details of the sale were handled through his estate.

Beggs died a multi-millionaire, the probate of his will being made in the sum of $30 million. Beggs was not only the last of the original electric traction tycoons to survive, he was one of the very few who died without losing the millions he had earned. In addition, his investment sense had been extremely sound, and by the time his estate was finally settled in 1930, its value had grown to $54 million.

Meissner was jubilant at getting the Car Company and so were his senior staff. The following exchange of letters is typical:

> San Francisco November 6, 1925. My dear Ed. In the first place, I want to congratulate you on the success of putting over the deal as you expected and I sincerely wish you all the good luck in the world with the success of your great undertaking. I am also pleased that you were able to give that d - - - - - - (sic) hold-up squad a complete knockout which perhaps they did not expect . . . Gus Koch.[2]
>
> St. Louis, November 11, 1925. Dear Gus . . . I sincerely appreciate your congratulations. We paid the Beggs Estate their money yesterday—$2,350,000—so that I can now say to you that I personally own the control of the Car Company. My success is due to the fine ability, loyalty and co-operation of your good self and many others who are associated with me in this business, and I sincerely trust our relationship will continue for all time with the same material, personal and business satisfaction derived therefrom so far. EBM [3]

Indiana Service Corp. #440, one of a special batch of 15 drop-platform, near-side safety cars built in 1922 for ISC's Fort Wayne lines. The truck is a St. Louis #113D.

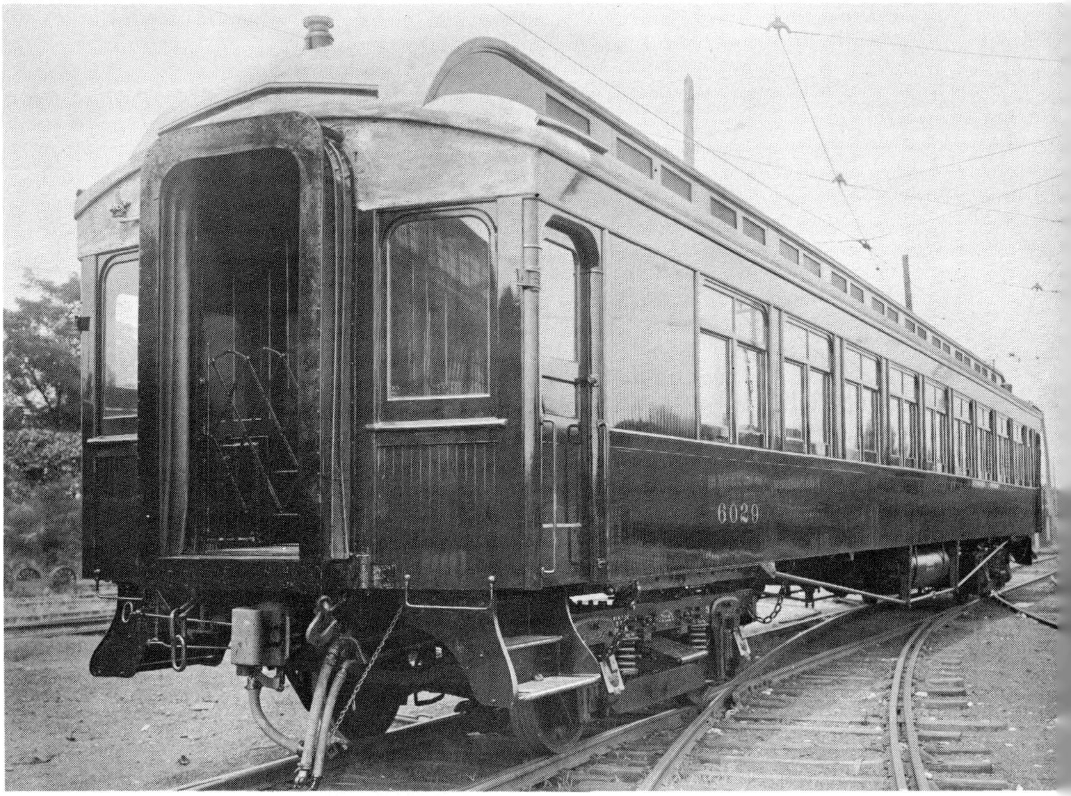

Once the phonograph cabinet contract was completed, the woodworking department turned its attention to a substantial repair contract for the Missouri Pacific Railroad. These two photographs give some idea of the quality of the work done on cars #6029 and #8014.

The big steel interurban was still being ordered during the 1920s. Indiana Service Corp. #325, built in 1923.

Fifty cars for Pacific Electric. Cars Nos. 652, 653 and 654 receive final adjustments on the loading ramp.

Los Angeles experimental car #2501. Many new cars of the 1920s looked like the old cars they were intended to replace. Notice the wood slat seats, still considered adequate for passenger service in 1924.

The Liquidating Car Co. was incorporated on October 25, 1925, one week after Beggs died, with authorized capital of $3 million divided into 20,000 shares of preferred stock at $1000 a share, and $100,000 shares of common stock with a value of $10 a share. Meissner himself owned 10,400 shares of preferred stock and 9480 shares of common stock, while the total paid-up capital of the company was reported to be $1,990,000, a sum equal to its reported assets.[4] The practical changes were however minimal. Orders continued to be placed, and the plant was working fulltime.

Once the Liquidating Car Co. had dealt with the formalities of the change of ownership, a new St. Louis Car Co. was quickly formed and incorporated. The directors of the new company were as follows: Meissner, H. Luedinghaus (President of St. Louis Malleable Castings Co. and of the Luedinghaus Wagon Co.) George Raterman (President of Raterman Construction Co.) Sears Lehmann, (Car Company attorney) George Kippenberger (Car Company Vice President and Assistant General Manager in his 25th year with the company) and Arnold G. Stifel (Vice President of Stifel-Nildaus and Co.). Despite this formidable array of business expertise at his disposal, there was no doubt that Meissner was the man in charge.

What had he gotten for his money? The plant at Baden (47 acres), the old Laclede plant, and the old automobile factory located on the west side of Wabash right of way at Withers Avenue. He had also come into sole charge of 650 employees, many of whom were stockholders in the old company. Many owned their own homes, something unusual for the time, as was the length of service some could boast, up to 35 years in some cases. In 1925 the plan operated on the "open shop" basis, and worked a fifty-hour week, conditions that prevailed until 1937. While full-time work was being done, the plant could have been busier at the time of the take-over. It was estimated that the work force should have been 1200 men, with whose aid the plant could manufacture the equivalent of five passenger cars or fifteen box cars per working day, 300 days of the year.[5]

Once loaded on flatcars, the plant's electric switcher assembled the units for shipping into a complete train and backed it onto the tracks of the St. Louis Terminal Railroad Assoc. who would then pick up the train, and transfer it to a main-line railroad for shipment.

Southern Pacific interurban car under construction in the mid 1920s. These cars were of more striking appearance than those normally built at the time.

Lightweight car for the Illinois Traction Co.'s Illinois Valley line.

The well-established practise of calling regular executive meetings continued when Meissner took charge. Sunday morning was felt to be the best time for such conferences, there was no telephone to interfere with their deliberations, and no other disturbances which could prevent the company's officers from getting their desks cleared, ready for Monday morning. The conference room was the usual meeting place, and in that room practically everything was open to discussion—policy in general, new business, data to better price new bids, and reviews of new design techniques.

There was a period of concern later when the old stock was called in to be re-issued. The problems arose over stock bought by Kobusch in 1911 which unexpectedly began to be cashed in. For years, Kobusch had been paying his personal debts by assigning shares in the Car Company to his various creditors. This stock was of almost no worth to them, since he had also borrowed large sums from the company which had never been repaid. Under Car Company bylaws, stock held by any person in debt to the company was automatically transferred back to the company should the debt remain unpaid. It was Kobusch himself who was responsible for this bylaw, and he had successfully used it against Vogel's stock when the Danville Car Co. became financially troubled and attracted a take-over by Brill.[6]

Complications had developed when a William O'Herin notified the Car Company that in June 1927, he had bought at a sheriff's sale 117 shares of Kobusch stock for $2000, with a face value of $95,000, on which he wanted payment. The company naturally refused to pay, and O'Herin filed suit. Records were then produced by the company which showed that between 1911 and 1922, Kobusch had incurred a continuing debt with the company totalling $90,000. This meant that while O'Herin possessed stock with a face value of $95,000, only $5000 of it had any value at all.

Lehmann explained to Meissner that if O'Herin acquired "only the Kobusch interest at the Sheriff's sale, he acquired nothing."[7] The affair was thus settled out-of-court, and O'Herin got his $5000 plus costs, in other words the balance of the Kobusch account, for which he had paid a mere $2000.[8] Kobusch himself died on November 8, 1927, at a relatively young age, but there were no problems for the company over the settlement of his estate, and the reorganization and consolidation of the St. Louis Car Co. under Meissner's personal ownership and control could now be called complete.

Car #3200, the first of 30 lightweight interurban cars for Detroit United Railways, delivered at the end of 1924.

CHAPTER 16

The period of the change of ownership was not an easy time and the chaotic relationship between the company's top two executives had been reflected by feelings of unease among the other staff. Until the final change of ownership, Meissner had been a tense and anxious man, devoting less time than usual to the everyday affairs of the company. This air of unease had spread to the company's clients and for a period there had been a reluctance to place orders. Thus, once Meissner gained full control, he made a determined attempt to show that not only was the company still very much in business, but also that his style of management was for the good of both the company and the transit industry.

Meissner's obvious release from pressure after 1925 had its effect on the company also. The plant consisted of a happy, working team of men, but the camaraderie and the somewhat paternalistic approach of the management to labor relations could not make up for the poor physical conditions and the lack of "fringe benefits" offered by the company. There were no eating facilities, and the washing and cleaning arrangements were very poor. The main erecting shops were large, but they were bitterly cold in winter, owing to an inadequate heating system, and were insufferably hot in summer. Practically none of the shop floors were paved and the lighting was inadequate. Accidents were a frequent occurrence and while Meissner, of course, would invariably pay all the medical bills of a man injured at his work, this could not always make up for the lack of more formal welfare benefits such as hospital insurance. Indeed the company had no pension plan until as late as 1960!

Such defects in the personnel policies of the company were largely of no importance in normal times, and it could be argued that what was lacking in formal benefits was made up in other respects. Many officers of the company have testified that it made no difference to Meissner what sort of education a man possessed; if he did his job well and showed any ability, there was practically no job that was closed to him in the company. It was all a question of attitude. If one liked working at St. Louis Car Co., then it really didn't matter what the job was, so long as one had the aptitude for it. William Kamman, later Chief Engineer, had no formal training as an engineer when in 1922 he first went to the company's drawing offices, and indeed regarded himself as very fortunate to be taken on without an engineering degree. He learned his profession on the job, and in night school. Severin Merz, later the company Treasurer, told the same story; hired in 1917 straight out of high school, he never took an accountant's examination in his life, yet managed to learn his business on the job and through extra courses. If one enjoyed working at the company, among cranes, machinery and rail vehicles (and it must be assumed that was a powerful attraction for many who worked there), then it must also be assumed that such men would not be perturbed at working on any job in the plant. Merz was eventually the company's treasurer, but had done so many other things around the plant by that time, that in a crisis he could put his hand to most jobs, apart from skilled shop floor or engineering work. At one point he was both treasurer and joint traffic manager with Kamman, responsible for arranging shipment with the railroads, and occasionally, in an emergency, he could be found switching vehicles in the yard.[1]

It was this cohesion among those who had worked in the plant for any length of time that was the most attractive feature of employment at the Car Company, and overrode most of the disadvantages of long hours and frequent weekend work. Indeed, there were those who commuted very long distances daily to continue working at the company; a number lived in St. Charles, Missouri, and one man came from as far as Crystal City, Missouri. In the main, however, the bulk of the employees lived in the St. Louis area, and in the early days were largely from Baden, the German immigrant suburb in which the plant was located. This made for a culturally homogeneous group of men, and during Kobusch's time, there was definite glamour in working in a young and growing industry, under a man with the charm, dynamism and flamboyance that Kobusch possessed. By the 1920s, while there no longer were so many Germans among the workers, long service employees were a major proportion of the company's work force, and continued to be so up to the time the company finally went out of business. The mood of the "boss" was all-important in determining the mood of the men, and thus the quality of work. Meissner's relaxation once the take-over was successfully accomplished was thus immediately reflected in the plant.

Many old work customs were practiced, possibly because of the continuing German influence in the wood and cabinet making departments. Especially strange to the present-day reader was the manner in which beer seemed to flow like water during working hours, at least until Prohibition. Any excuse was sufficient, the completion of an order, the first car of a new order, perhaps even the signing of a new order. Whatever the reason, the custom was to hold a beer party, frequently at the company's expense, and many kegs of beer would be disposed of quite quickly. Beggs, who thoroughly disapproved of drinking, was unable to stop this custom, although his equal distaste for tobacco more than made up for his powerlessness over alcohol. When Beggs would visit, there would be a considerable amount of apprehension, for if he were to catch the smell of tobacco smoke, he would fire the man concerned on the spot. A considerable amount of behind-the-scenes activity, from top management downwards, was always necessary when Beggs came to the plant.[2]

Beggs' final cessation of interest in the company was thus a relief for everybody. Age had not mellowed him, and he could be exceedingly arbitrary if irritated. Merz recalled an occasion when Beggs, standing in his office, and looking out across the transfer table, got highly annoyed at seeing a man sitting down while waiting for the table to arrive so he could take his load across. The man was sacked for idling and within the hour was out of the plant.[3] For Beggs, everything had to run smoothly, and if not, trouble would ensue. Virtually no excuse was acceptable. Even Meissner was, on occasion, so intimidated that he would practice small deceptions in order to keep the peace. One such occasion occurred in the 1920s when, for some reason, a large shipment of cars was running behind scheduled completion time. Knowing that Beggs would want to fire someone if the truth were known, Meissner arranged for the incomplete cars to be taken to the shipping tracks, and covered with the company's usual shipping tarpaulins. When Beggs arrived and wanted to know "why in the hell the cars are still standing there," he was given the story that the cars were complete, but the railroad hadn't yet brought in its flatcars to ship them out. Beggs was hardly a fool, and must have seen through many of these deceptions, but on this occasion chose to accept the explanation, and the matter was closed.[4]

Meissner was a totally different kind of man. Whereas Beggs would appear at best once every two weeks, Meissner was always visible on the shop floor, and always accessible. Moreover, he let it be known by both his attitude and his actions that although he was in control, he was neither arbitrary nor ruthless.

There were times when his understandable desire to be in sole control of everything and everybody could lead to problems. It was always recognized that he was boss and that whatever else happened, it was he alone who made the decisions, and had to live with them. Although not formally trained in car construction practices, he knew his business thoroughly. Being an intelligent and alert man, he had, during his time at the company, picked up most of the detailed knowledge that was of importance. Unfortunately, for many years he refused to delegate his work, and this, coupled with his very real knowledge of the work of every department, could lead to major altercations with his staff, with its accompanying depressive effect on morale, when he and a department chief disagreed over some detail of engineering practice or shop construction method.

Kamman felt that:

> It was uncanny what he did know . . . He would really surprise you. You had better not be talking to him and assume he was

just stupid about something . . . he'd trip you up real fast. . . . It might be something that's mechanical that you would think, "Well, after all, he's the president, he doesn't know anything." . . . Really he didn't, but he was pretty sharp (and) . . . could pick up things rather fast. At one time he was over (in the drafting room) when I was working on the board (and) he was tearing the chief draughtsman apart . . . And I thought to myself . . . "That's awful, if ever I get in charge of this, I'll put a stop to that" . . . He was a wild man . . . When he would get into a place, he would tear it apart (and) the whole damn place would be disrupted for a couple of days. He would really shake them up . . . He was a pretty good-sized fellow, so he could . . . throw his weight around . . .[5]

Kamman was appointed Chief Engineer in 1935, but by that time Meissner had finally washed his hands of the entire engineering and tool design elements of the plant, for these departments were now run by Meissner's own trained men whom he trusted.[6] Consequently, in later years these departments ran without as much daily interference from Meissner as before. Initially Kamman had tried to keep Meissner out of the engineering shop by reporting to him in his own office, and by keeping detailed reports of the problems in his department largely to himself. He felt that if anything did go wrong, he should take the blame personally for he had total responsibility for his department. In that way harmony was maintained in the engineering department, and a few other crucial sections after 1934. However, Meissner continued his practice of personal inspection of the shop throughout his entire career, with the inevitable friction.

Meissner's chief abilities lay in another direction. Most of his commercial success stemmed from from his ability as a buyer, willing to work hard for long hours, and his natural gifts as a salesman, willing to go anywhere and talk with anyone in order to sell his company's expertise.

> He was a shrewd buyer. When there were big contracts to be placed, he would enter into it . . . He would talk to the salesmen, and the purchasing department who were handling it, but (of course) he was too . . . and knew everything that was going on . . . And I got the impression through the years that he didn't want that company to get too large, because he would not be able to keep his finger on everything.[7]

It was this personal touch which was Meissner's hallmark. Theories of modern management seemingly had little place at the Car Company. While there was a rudimentary departmental structure and a hierarchy of executive officers, the company remained essentially a successful one-man owner-manager operation, and by its success defied conventional business wisdom. At a time when other car manufacturers were going out of business or developing a recognizable corporate hierarchy, St. Louis Car Co. remained a successful anachronism.

This vehicle was built by the Betzwood Film Co. of Pennsylvania for making movies based on the Fontaine Fox "Toonerville Trolley" cartoons. It was exhibited at the American Electric Railroad Association's convention in October 1923, and this photograph shows the AERA's exhibits committee with the car. These men were trying to kill the Toonerville image of the industry and were responsible for arranging the exhibition of new cars and equipment at the convention. The battered trolley was their way of showing the progress made in equipment design since the turn of the century. Meissner is peeping out of the saloon door next to the right-hand platform.

CHAPTER 17

THE MID-1920s WAS a trying time for the transit industry. Profitability had been restored to the major urban systems, but it was becoming increasingly obvious that the industry, still streetcar oriented in 1924, was stagnating; there was little influx of new blood or new ideas, and all too frequently the new and dynamic techniques of 1895 or 1900 were still being utilized over a quarter of a century later. Long-term profitability was being threatened as passengers continued to desert the streetcar in large numbers in favor of competing bus lines (where these existed) and the private automobile. The automobile gave its owner greater mobility than the streetcar could offer, and this mobility aided the already sustained growth of the new city suburbs. Their development was not usually followed by extension of existing streetcar lines to serve them and as a result, the commuting population, who still depended on the city for their livelihood, were totally lost to the streetcar operators. In later years, operating franchises were modified so that buses or trolley buses could be run as well as streetcars. In such cases, operating companies generally received a new lease on life that carried them through to the early 1950s by being able to serve the suburbs cheaply with these vehicles, unhampered by the large fixed costs of a streetcar line, which otherwise could have swallowed up the profits of these lightly travelled routes.

But in the mid-1920s, neither the bus nor the trolleybus could yet compete with the streetcar in terms of capacity or performance. The streetcar had become an exceptionally reliable and capacious vehicle, well able to handle the largest crowds without fuss. It was, however, noisy, slow, heavy, and extremely uncomfortable. The bus could offer upholstery and a smoother ride on its rubber tires, while the automobile could offer speed, mobility and privacy.

The transit industry thought of solutions to streetcar competition (and the restoration of profitability) strictly in terms of producing modern streetcars which could outperform their competition in service, speed, comfort and cost. This essentially had been the thinking used to combat the Jitney ten years previously albeit modified slightly in the light of operating experience. The Birney Safety car had been the result of the Jitney experience, at least on the smaller systems. By 1924, the Birney car's steeply declining sales showed it was no longer an adequate answer to the industry's problems, but its previous successes blinded those who were examining the nature of transit malaise. Modernization to defeat automobile competition in big cities and small towns alike should have included not just the cars, but ancillary equipment, track, power supply and corporate finance, all of which were badly in need of attention. "Across the board" modernization of this sort had been proved successful in winning back passengers and profitability in certain areas. Though not strictly a street railway, the Chicago, North Shore and Milwaukee line had won the Charles Coffin prize for modernization and quality of service in the early 1920s by completing just such a program, and its commuter service between both cities was a model of what public transport could do (and remained a model until the day the line closed in 1963). There were too, isolated examples of total modernization schemes in other large cities: Detroit, San Francisco and Los Angeles in the U.S.A., and Toronto, Montreal and Vancouver in Canada, but such examples only served to further emphasize the general lack of initiative, and the half-hearted attempts to solve the industry's problems.

This half-heartedness was exemplified by the artificial limitation of the debate solely to the question of new car design. Why satisfactory car design rather than overall system modernization should have been regarded as the universal panacea has never been explained. Yet that was the case, and agreement that this was the correct approach was practically universal in the industry. Modernization simply meant new cars.

Despite the excitement surrounding the appearance of the prize-winning Grand Rapids car, it was not radically different from anything previously built at Baden, as can be seen in this 1924 construction view.

Nor was the interior of the car so greatly different, except in comparison with the Birney safety car, or other vehicles with austere passenger fittings.

Light weight was a crucial element in saving operating costs, and the new St. Louis EIB 64 lightweight truck series (below) demonstrated that for the first time light car weight was not incompatible with good riding qualities.

The real difference in the design lay in the imaginative use of color to create an impression of lightness, speed and grace. This impression was intended to be made by day and night. The interior illumination was brighter than previously used, and taken altogether these features created a favorable psychological climate. The car was proof that well-tried body designs of proven reliability could be up-dated with astonishingly good results.

Interurban car design too was becoming lighter. Cars #378 and #390 of Indiana Service Corp.'s Indiana Central lines in 1926. *(William J. Clouser collection)*

The production series of cars for Grand Rapids had better interior finish, but unfortunately, the exterior was not exciting.

However, the Grand Rapids cars were more stylish than their contemporaries in overall appearance. South Jacksonville #110 of 1926 (left), Muskegon Traction #121 of 1926 (below), San Francisco #195 of 1927 shown at left below.

With the exception of these 32 cars for Memphis, built in 1926, there was a gap of two years between the placing of the Grand Rapids order in 1925, and the next order for thoroughly modern cars.

Unfortunately, agreement did not extend to the design of such cars. In the absence of a coordinated research and development program, or even an industry-wide forum for debate, this was hardly surprising. All that could be agreed upon were the general design criteria, which did not differ substantially from those of the safety car a decade previously. The new car types were to possess all the safety cars' advantages of light weight, speed, cheapness and safety, with none of their disadvantages of small size, spartan comfort and rough ride. The body design was to emulate contemporary automobile styling and color, while in speed and comfort it was to offer standards high enough to entice those who now regularly commuted to the city by automobile (not all of which were weatherproof in 1924) back to the superior comfort, service and all-weather protection to be offered by the transit operators' new streetcars. Profits would be thus made once more, and the transit industry's dynamism, lacking since 1914, would be restored.

That was the theory. Unfortunately, with existing designs of commercially available equipment, even these limited design criteria could not be met. For a period during 1924 and 1925, there was an acrimonious debate between the operators, who accused the manufacturers of not marketing any new or radical designs for them to try, and the manufacturers, who accused the operators of not allowing them to introduce such designs, except at their own expense and risk. While this argument was raging, new car purchase was at an all-time low, itself a worrisome phenomenon.

The log-jam was finally broken, not by a big city operator, but by the medium-size Grand Rapids Co. of Michigan. Suffering greatly from bus and automobile competition, it needed new cars badly. Being unimpressed with the designs currently available, and subscribing to the industry's car modernization theory, it ordered three sample cars from three manufacturers in 1924, the design specifications of which were left entirely in the hands of those manufacturers. The three cars were to be tested in operating service over a period of months, and a single design would then be chosen for the main order. Because this was the first attempt that had been made to solicit the manufacturers for radically new car designs, the Grand Rapids experiment attracted industry attention, and the success of the St. Louis Car Co.'s design, which was chosen at the conclusion of the trials, was of great and tangible benefit to the company's street railway sales over the next few years. The modern and stylish appearance of the cars, their use of new types of trucks and controls, the relatively large size of the order, and the fact that more orders for similar vehicles were being received by the company thus assured Meissner of a respectful hearing whenever he or his staff

Much of the intervening period was spent by the Car Company in investigating new manufacturing projects. One of the most bizarre was a feasibility study made of the market potential for an armored police wagon, to be known as the "Flying Fortress." Meissner must have been very hopeful for the success of this project, for he was always interested in police affairs, and later in life was a St. Louis police commissioner. But this fearsomely equipped vehicle, akin to an early riot truck, was the only one built by the Car Company.

subsequently delivered papers on the topic of new car design.

Meissner was exceptionally visible in the industry at this time. He was a member of the American Electric Railway Association, serving on both the Manufacturers Committee and the Executive Committee. In these capacities he presented a number of papers at the Association conventions during the mid- and late twenties, in addition to looking after his own company's exhibits at such gatherings. He encouraged his senior staff to follow suit, and the papers prepared by these men represent what might be termed the "Meissner philosophy" of car building during the difficult times of the mid-1920s.

George Kippenberger, the company vice-president, summed up the transit industry's problem from the Car Company's point of view in June, 1925, shortly after the delivery of the first of the Grand Rapids cars. While praising Grand Rapids for its courage in ordering an untried design, he emphasized how unusual this was in the car building industry.

> (Normally) we contract to build on specifications — the master mechanic's specifications, and the result is a master mechanic's car; well built if you please, from a maintenance standpoint, and efficient for handling passengers . . . (But) we sense that in this day and age, passengers want something more than being safely handled. Were it possible for the car builder to merchandise his car, his standard car if we dare mention the word standard . . . the builder would have opportunity and incentive constantly to improve and develop style and design . . . Building his standard car under his own specifications, he would be free to put quality in his work and place the stamp of individuality on his product . . .[1]

Of course, this was exactly the point; the car builder was not normally free to do any such thing, except at his own expense, and in the St. Louis Car Co. at least, there never had been money for sustained development projects of this nature. Moreover, in an age where the conservatism of the master mechanic continued to dominate streetcar design it was equally clear that even should such a line of vehicles be developed, operating companies would still be reluctant to purchase. Yet the public was now demanding higher design standards than in the past. There were constant improvements in the design and appearance of public buildings and other artifacts in this period, largely corresponding to the shifts and developments of public taste in city and industrial design, while the average streetcar, built in a more utilitarian age, was perceived to be more of an eyesore the older it became.

Meissner gave an extended interview on this subject to Charles Gordon of the *Electric Railway Review* in February, 1926. He made the point that modernization of equipment was a way of better merchandising the transit operator's product — rides in a streetcar. Such an investment was good public relations, which could bring long-term benefits to the operating company.

> The public reacts favorably to visible evidence of progress and improvement. Improved equipment offers the opportunity of winning a more friendly attitude from both the public and its representatives . . . Visible evidence of the desire to effect improvement which is afforded by new and attractive equipment will lend additional impetus to the present tendency to relieve railways from unfair restrictive regulatory and taxation burdens.[2]

He believed that new methods of deferred payment through equipment trusts were a satisfactory method of obtaining new rolling stock for a company otherwise unable to spend large capital sums on renewals.

> . . . Properties in reasonably good standing can purchase cars on a basis of a small percent down payment, with the balance spread over a period of from three to five years . . . at a cost very little above the cash price. Interest rates on such paper are reasonable because car trust paper is recognized in banking circles as one of the best investment securities.[3]

While he fully recognized the problems, he also realized that as a manufacturer and therefore one of the electric railway industry's leaders, he had a responsibility to that industry to be optimistic about its future, and he expressed that optimism in unequivocal terms:

> There is apparently a new spirit in the electric railway industry . . . a renewed confidence. The public is awakening to its own needs . . . and the industry is becoming alert to the possibilities.[4]

Charles Gordon attached great importance to Meissner's having granted him the interview, for Meissner possessed

> . . . the characteristic reticence of electric railway men toward talking for publication which has sometimes been a handicap to the exchange of ideas in the industry . . . To Mr. Meissner's energy and faith, is largely attributable the Company's survival and progress. Thus his expression of confidence in the electric railway industry (is) . . . amply supported by the record of his own contact with it.[5]

Quite true. Unfortunately, the number of orders in hand for new streetcars at the company did not yet fully justify the optimism expressed in this interview, but this did not prevent Meissner from taking the point further later in the year. In a paper to the American Electric Railway Association, bluntly entitled "The car; show window of the Industry," he again put forward the view that the entire vexed question of car design was essentially a merchandising problem. The transit operating company is in business to sell seats (or rides) and is in competition with others selling the same product. To sell effectively, the streetcar operator therefore has to draw attention to his vehicle.

> Your own city is your show window, and the cars you operate are your display . . . Your display (your cars) are in attraction, design, safety, speed (and) comfort whatever you make them, which prompts the question whether you have kept your display in condition to attract trade. Fashions in electric railway equipment as in clothes, have changed. The up-to-date management keeps its cars . . . clean, light and airy, with safety appliances installed . . . comfortable seats . . . well maintained . . . attractively painted . . . and quiet, thus merchandising their service, and by doing so increasing their net earnings . . .[6]

Obviously Meissner wholeheartedly subscribed to the industry's erroneous car modernization theory, but to his credit most of the few really modern cars commercially built during the mid-twenties were his, and his success prompted other manufacturers to follow suit. In terms of radical design change however, the Car Company vehicles were unquestionably ahead: the Grand Rapids cars, the later cars for Houston, East St. Louis, Louisville, Memphis, Oklahoma City, and the most interesting and radical new car of all, the New Birney of 1928.

Regrettably, after all this design experimentation, it still proved as difficult to commit operators to large-scale modern car purchase at the end of 1928 as it had five years earlier. A token showing of new cars could not disguise an operator's reluctance to purchase, and thus public reaction to new cars was short-term interest and long term scepticism. Transit continued to be seen as a choice between the family automobile and the streetcar, and on that kind of showing, the family automobile was an easy victor.

East St. Louis was an excellent example of "tokenism." During 1927, five old cars were reconditioned at the Car Company to contemporary standards and five brand new vehicles ordered. When delivered, public reaction had been positive. The five new cars had been paraded around the town, and a few days later, free rides were given amid a blaze of publicity.[7]

But that was all. No further new cars followed, and the system never considered modernizing other parts of its physical plant. The new cars failed, for they did not win back the automobile commuters to the streetcar. Yet they were all the transit industry (and Meissner) said modern cars should be in design. Their external appearance was eye-catching, leaning heavily on the best of contemporary automobile styling, while their interior was airy and comfortable, with an uncluttered appearance achieved by enclosing all control equipment in neat cabinets. The cars were quiet and their powerful new motors gave much better performance than the cars they replaced. Indeed

The new steel erecting shop #6 was opened in 1926, enabling the company to manufacture full-size railroad cars profitably for the first time. Wabash car #611, ready for shipment in early 1928.

The Grand Rapids influence was first seen in these 10 double-end cars ordered by the Northern Texas Traction Co. of Fort Worth in 1927.

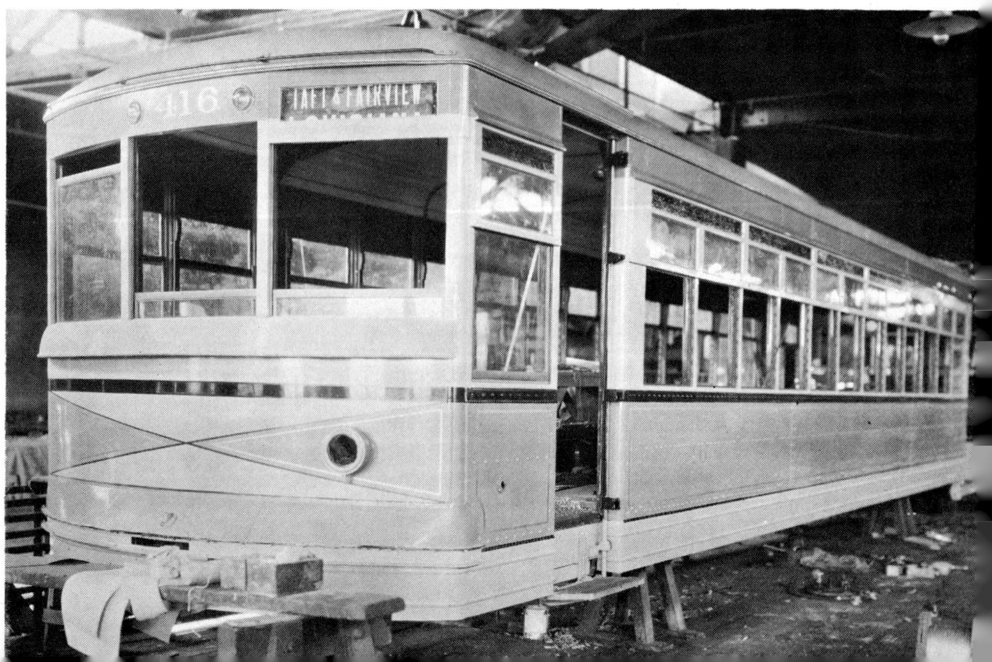

One of twenty very similar single-ended cars for the Houston Electric Co.

Detroit Peter Witt car #3727 of 1927.

Pittsburgh #3814, one of fifteen lightweight interurban cars built in 1928 for the Washington and Charleroi lines.

The New Birney of 1928 was in every way the most radical of all the cars produced during the "new car" movement of the 1920s. The body was uncompromisingly modern, and its truck design was unique. Unfortuately the truck proved to be the car's weakest element. Picture at right shows the striking frontal appearance. Below is the light and spacious interior. At right, top of page is the complete car.

All-steel cars of the 1920s were imposing but attractive looking vehicles. St. Louis Car Co. built New Orleans 1013, which is shown shortly after delivery in 1928, on one of that city's famed "neutral ground" tracks. This was one of the few cities to modernize its fleet on a large scale in the 1920s, though the St. Louis Car Co. received orders for only 10 of the new cars. Almost identical cars (built by other manufacturers) run to this day in New Orleans. *(Teunisson photo, Edwin J. Klasky collection)*

The vast majority of operators remained skeptical of modern cars, and TMERL was a good example of that attitude. This superbly run and excellently maintained system was one of the few still to pin its faith to the trolley and interurban. It had built many new extensions to city lines during the early 1920s, and later in the decade built a heavily-engineered, high-speed cutoff route for its interurbans. By doing so it created an embryonic rapid transit system for Milwaukee. It had bought many hundreds of cars to run on these new lines. But even their latest one-man cars built in 1928 and 1929, exhibited conservatism in equipment and body design. This is TMERL #985, on exhibit at an AERA convention in Atlantic City in 1929; a car built to a basic design at least ten years old.

they were given the nickname "Rail Sedans," a not-very-subtle way of suggesting that they could do all the family automobile could do, and more. But with only five cars, it was impossible to completely equip more than one line and while the riding figures on that line were satisfactory for some time after their introduction, it is probable this was as much due to the car's novelty as to any more tangible attraction they might have offered. In short, the riding public was not convinced, and until it could be, it was not prepared to give up its automobiles. The only way to convince them a company meant business was system-wide modernization which could offer service superior to the automobile on all counts. Yet by artificially limiting the debate to new cars only, the transit industry appeared utterly oblivious to this verdict. After all (they said) there was not much point in spending money on new cars if they were to run noisily on worn-out tracks at slow speed, and who had the money to fix the tracks, let alone buy new cars?

This negative rationalization was typical of the industry's mood, and so far as Meissner was concerned that mood meant few new car orders. By the end of 1928, new car purchase was rapidly declining, and in the meantime the modern car debate was becoming further limited. No longer was the concept of total system modernization for profit, as opposed to new car purchase for profit, the point at issue. Now the question was whether to buy any type of new cars, immediately, or wait for further modern designs to appear before purchasing. Most operating companies were prepared to wait, oblivious to the declining passenger counts.

By 1928, the motor bus or electric trolley bus was becoming a practical solution to the streetcar profitability issue, and many operators were beginning to investigate the economics of change-over. Where such changes were made, results were immediately beneficial. Here were new vehicles and a modernized transit system, and the public almost invariably responded. But such action, if it became a universal trend, threatened to leave the car building industry with no market whatever, and as they already seemed to have little market left, cooperation in research and development for new transit modes to compete effectively with the automobile was urgently needed.

In this atmosphere of near panic were held the private conferences which led to the establishment in December 1929 of the first industry-wide research and development group, the Electric Railway Presidents' Conference Committee. It is a measure of the industry's unimaginative approach that despite the urgency of the situation, this committee's research program was from the first restricted to an investigation of the desirable characteristics of modern streetcars. The idea of investigating all transit modes, and designing vehicles best suited for the different service conditions encountered on the properties of the participating companies, had occurred to no one.

The transit industry had grown in an unplanned and haphazard manner, a creature created by the forces of a totally free market. The streetcar had been the instrument of that growth, and had brought the industry its largest measure of commercial success by filling a need which until then had been impossible to satisfy. Only recently had the term "transit industry" been coined, and it was quite apparent that most industry officials still felt themselves in an exclusively street railway industry with a monopoly on public transit. To such men, it was axiomatic that the streetcar could move the largest number of people of any vehicle using the streets, and as that remained in their view what urban transit was all about there was therefore no need to investigate other modes. Nor did there seem to be any reason to investigate the merits of totally modernizing existing street railway properties. The car was the thing, and nothing else seemed to matter.

The PCC was thus "hamstrung" from the outset, in being confined in its research to investigating only the modern streetcar. But for the highly conservative men of the transit industry, setting up the PCC was a radical action, forced upon them by the gravity of the industry's financial situation, and therefore, under the circumstances a highly commendable action.

A few customers purchased modern interurban cars in the 1920s, although by then the trend was against the interurban as a mode of transit. Indiana Railways #375 of 1926 stands in the Indianapolis interurban train shed. It is posed with a US mail truck, shortly before inaugurating a new interurban mail service to Peru, Indiana *(Edwin J. Klasky collection)*

Illinois Central gas-electric locomotive of 1929. This vehicle could also operate as a straight electric using either its own on-board traction batteries, or electrified sections of the railroad.

Gas-electric cars for the Rock Island under construction in 1928. These were updated models of 800 hp.

Modern city car for the Oklahoma City Railway, 1929. The slogan on the car side reads "Service with a smile."

CHAPTER 18

By 1928 the reorganized Car Company had completely reestablished itself commercially and from then until the war, new projects were continually investigated, and the most promising led to the creation of subsidiary companies to better exploit them. The St. Louis Lift and Equipment Co. established in 1934, manufactured and sold hydraulic lifts for use in automobile garages and service stations, while the St. Louis Cottonpicker Co. manufactured and sold a small mechanical cottonpicker in the late 1930s. This last-named product was very unsuccessful on the market, however; it was estimated that a good human cottonpicker could outperform the machine with ease. The most spectacular product for which a new company was created, and perhaps the least successful, was that formed to market another St. Louis Car Co. venture into the airplane business, the Cardinal airplane. First built in 1929, the Cardinal was a single wing aircraft, similar to the early Piper Cub. This single engined business or sport plane was intended to sell for under $4,000 and was equipped with a LeBlond-85 engine. The plane anticipated the enormous interest in private flying that was to develop after the Second World War, but regrettably the plane was first put on the market just prior to the Depression, and as a result its market quickly disappeared. The experience with the Cardinal, however, did provide the Company with important design and manufacturing experience that helped to open up markets in the aviation field for them at the beginning of the Second World War.

What was of major concern to Meissner during this period, however, was the continued poor sales of streetcars. While the company was sufficiently diversified by this time to counteract slow streetcar sales, it remained a prime cause of concern, and Meissner was prepared to do practically anything necessary to make substantial increases in streetcar sales. Yet new streetcars seating between 50 and 60 passengers, and fitted with "sales appeal" extras such as leather upholstered seats, electric heating, composition floors and good lighting, could cost over $16,000 each by 1929, and although for four years the industry had continually stated that modernization of cars was the solution to their problems, financing of sales had to be made, usually on the installment plan, otherwise no sales of streetcars would have been made at all.

The Car Company stayed clear of finance houses, and instead used a five year payment plan of a type approved for use within the industry. Purchasing customers would be given installment notes each month for five years at 6% interest, and these notes would be met out of revenue. Once in the hands of the Car Company, the notes would be turned over at a discount to a bank, and the security of the notes would be a first lien on the revenues of the customer's car operations. This method of financing, while somewhat cumbersome, worked with reasonable efficiency until the Depression, but as most of the company's sales were being made in this fashion by 1929, the Depression found the company in a relatively unprepared state to meet it. While there was a considerable surplus which could help carry the company for a year or more, there were no contingency plans for carrying on through a more extended slump.

The transit industry in general first considered the Depression a minor irritant, one that would hardly affect so basic an industry. Transit was felt to be an essential part of the lives of an urban population which, like food, would be given up only as a last resort. To a certain extent this was true; the first few years of the Depression saw very little change in revenue or riding, and much of the cost-cutting that occurred was of non-essential services. The real slump and the associated financial problems did not hit the industry until 1932.

However, certain sections felt the slump much earlier. The interurban operators, always financially weak, were in a poor way by 1930, and continued financial problems lead to the demise of a considerable number of properties, either by out-

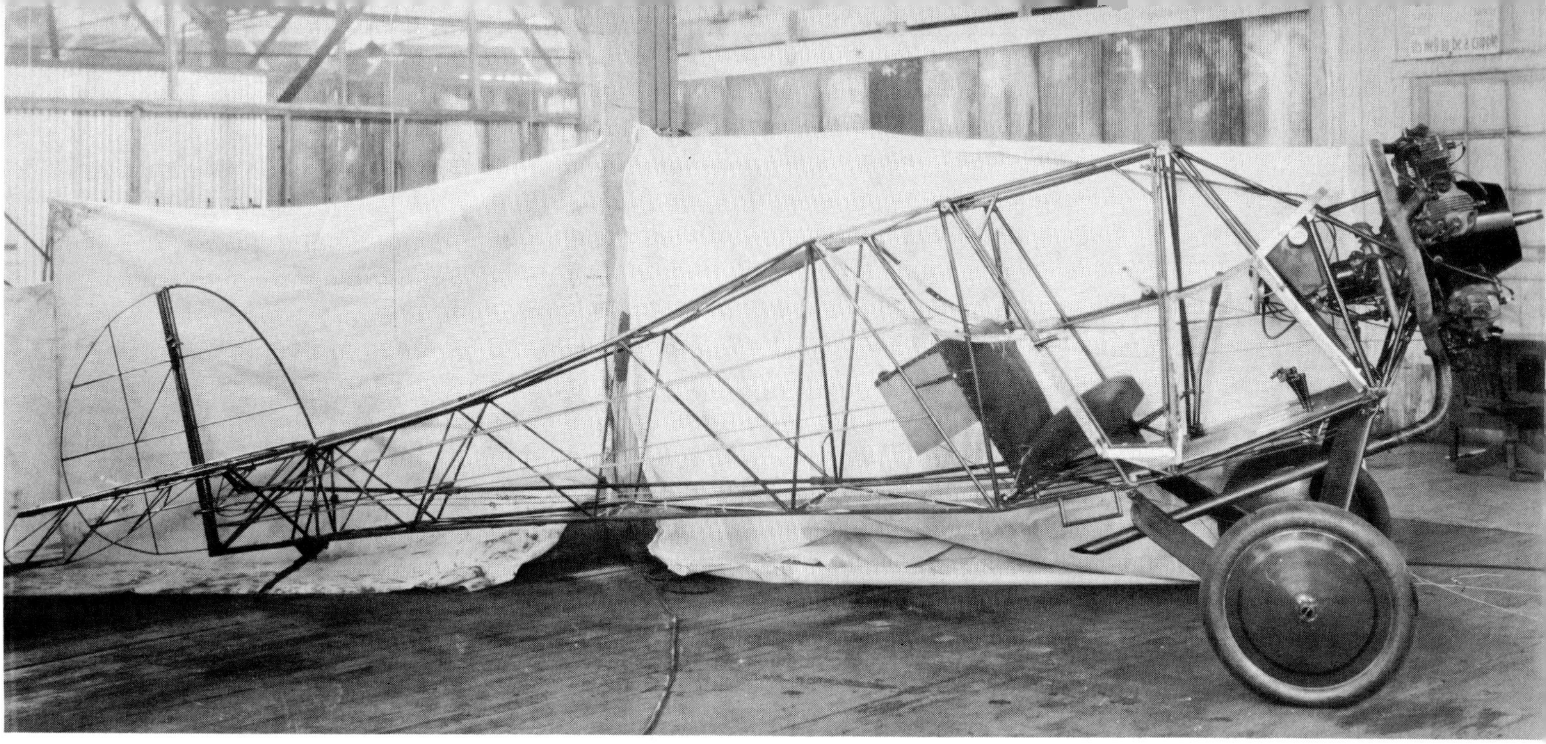

The Cardinal airplane sold at a price of $3000. It was of light and simple construction and was intended to make flying a private plane as simple as owning and driving an automobile. The cockpit was surprisingly uncomplicated, even by the standards of the day, and the plane's ability to carry two people with baggage made it directly competitive with the two-seat automobile. Though the Depression killed the Cardinal project, one model is still preserved in flying condition by a private owner.

CARDINAL

ST. LOUIS AIRCRAFT CORPORATION

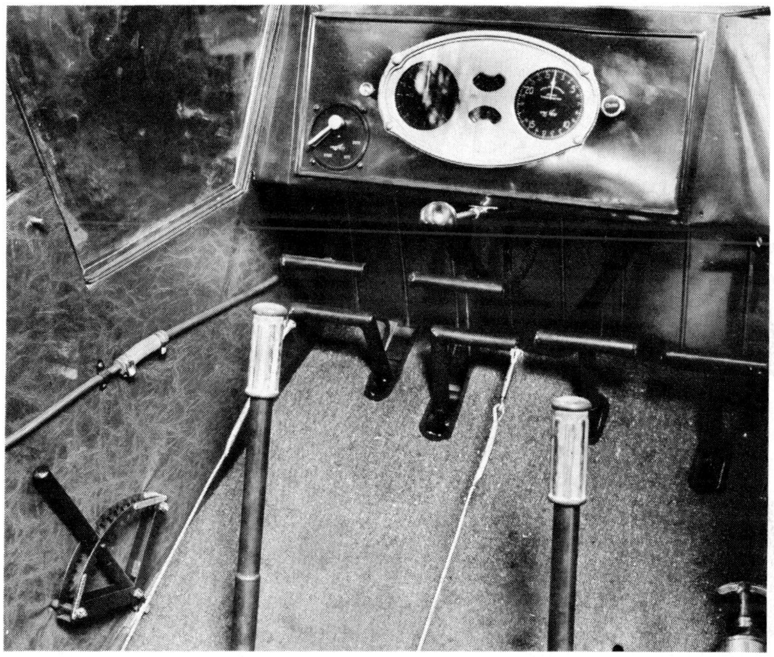

TMERL bought ten two-car articulated trains in 1930, of more modern appearance than their predecessors. Interior is shown below.

Los Angeles #2601, one of two experimental cars built in 1930, intended as prototypes for a new fleet which the Depression prevented from being built.

There were 130 Peter Witt cars built for Detroit during 1930 and 1931. Car #3965 illustrated here is one of twenty mounted on the experimental Timken trucks shown below.

St. Louis Car Company shipping tracks on December 12, 1930, almost the last time they were full in the early 1930s. From left to right can be seen a transformer-well car for Union Electric Co., cars for the North Western Pacific Railroads, a gas electric locomotive for the Illinois Terminal, Detroit car #3961 and Pacific Electric city car #108.

right abandonment and liquidation, or by merger and conversion to bus traction. But it was the manufacturing side of the industry that was both the earliest, and the worst affected by the Depression.

This could be seen in early 1930, as operators, in an attempt to reduce capital expenditure almost totally ceased to place orders. In 1929 it had seemed that the new car movement had finally got underway. More than 1400 units of new equipment had been bought in that year and the initial feeling at the beginning of the slump was new car purchase would continue to increase, making 1930 at least as good a year as 1929. This was not the case for only 620 streetcars and interurbans were ordered that year, St. Louis Car Co. building nearly 30% of the total.[1]

As a result, all the manufacturing companies did badly in 1930, and Meissner did well to secure from Detroit an order for 130 cars in the face of very stiff competition. Much jealousy ensued.[2]

The new contract was worth $1,744,000 and the bidding on the job had been so desperate that rumors of Meissner's involvement in a bribery scheme had begun to circulate. Meissner denied the rumors and explained the procedure by which the contract had been awarded in some detail. The bid had been submitted to the Detroit Common Council on April 11, 1930, and rejected as being too high. On April 15, copper prices were reduced, and Meissner lowered his bid accordingly, resubmitting a tender, which was accepted on April 29, 1930.[3] This was the simple explanation and the industry was satisfied.

The rumors persisted, however, and early in May matters came to a head when Meissner was contacted by a St. Louis man through a friend in Detroit who said he could so arrange matters that the Car Company would receive a favorable vote from the Common Council on their bid. As the contract was already his, Meissner was perturbed, and at the same time, curious to see what this was about.

> (I) suspected at once that this was an effort of someone to thrust themselves upon us for employment, and I lost no time and spared no words in letting the man at the telephone know that he and his Detroit friends would get themselves into serious trouble if they attempted to block the award to which our company was entitled.[4]

Yet the bribery attempt continued, and subsequently a "Mr. Carrol" made an appointment to see Meissner. Careful plans were made to deal with him in order to protect both the company and Meissner.

> I placed a stenographer and a witness, both employees of my firm, in a back room of my

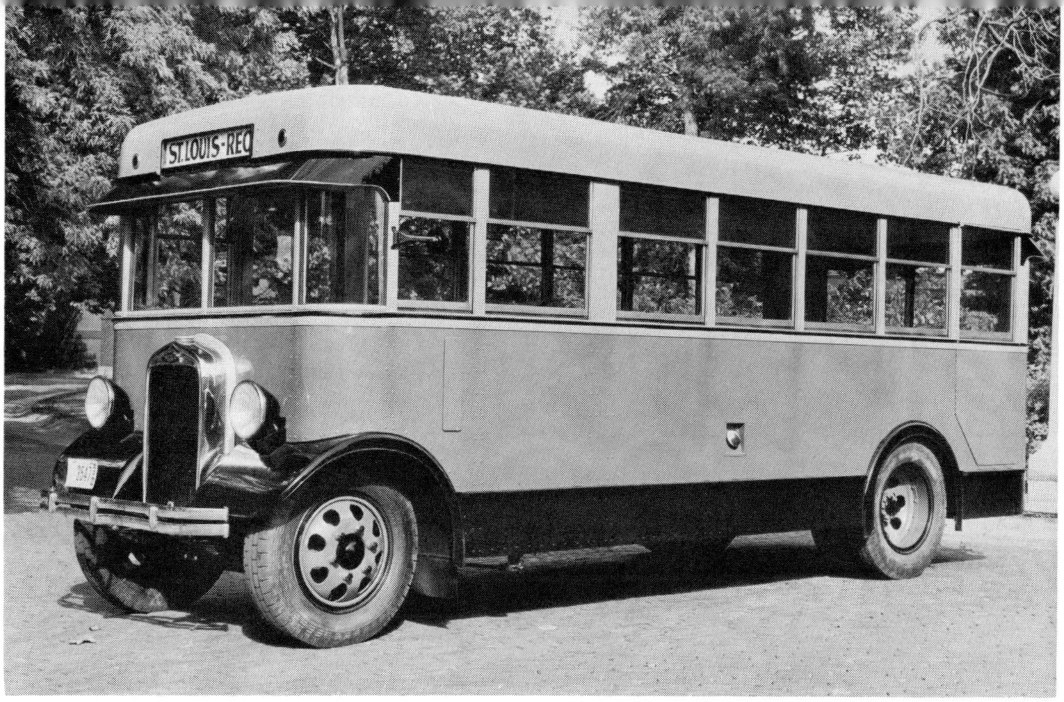

One of the experimental lightweight bus bodies built in conjunction with the Reo Company in 1933.

> office, and concealed a photographer, also in my employ, nearby, and instructed the telephone girl and a secretary to take a good look at a man I expected, so that they could later identify him.[5]

In due course "Mr. Carrol" arrived and made his offer: $32,500 to help secure the Detroit contract. Without letting him know the contract had already been legitimately awarded the company some weeks earlier, Meissner made it quite clear he was not the least interested in such a scheme and showed his unwelcome guest to the door, where the company photographer was waiting to take a picture. Unfortunately, the flash powder failed to ignite, and realizing that "Mr. Carrol" was about to get away without a photograph being taken, Meissner grabbed him around the waist and held on tightly until the photographer was finally able to take the picture. The photograph was then given to the St. Louis newspapers and published, together with an explanation of the incident. "Mr. Carrol" was soon identified as John J. Casey, a New York man who over the years had been involved in the street railway business as a manufacturer's agent. The newspaper took up the story.

> A few months ago, Casey was employed as an agent for a firm which wanted to bid on the contract for 130 streetcars. "Mr. Carrol" did not get his bid in, because he was ten minutes late in getting over to the Water Board building where the bids were opened. He blamed a delay in getting from the station on a cab . . . "Mr. Carrol" wanted the bids readvertised so his company could bid. There was no readvertisement . . . Since he could not get a bid in, he (thought) he might as well try to make some money some other way. He knew as every Detroit official and newspaper knew the contract was to go to the St. Louis Car Co. He thought maybe Mr. Meissner didn't know, so he went down to St. Louis to try to get over a fast one and collect $30,000 (sic) from Meissner for putting through a contract which had already, to all intents and purposes, been put through.[6]

With that, the matter was laid to rest. Casey's subsequent fate is unknown.

Without the Detroit order, the company would not have survived the Depression. This large order, together with smaller orders of cars for Oklahoma City and Pacific Electric, and a handful of orders for railroad equipment and gas-electric cars, enabled the plant to remain in full-time operation until almost midway through 1931, at which time layoffs became unavoidable. The remainder of the year was very bad, with no street railway work forthcoming and very little other work to keep the plant in business. The profit for the year was less than $10,000.[7] In the following year there were no orders whatever for street railway equipment, and in the whole of 1933, the

The dredge pontoon order of 1934 was the most unusual order to be executed in any year prior to 1941. Here forty of the pontoons are being cast off from the St. Louis waterfront in July 1934, in charge of a Mississippi stern-wheeler.

only work done was the construction of two buses, two steel derrick boats, a transformer car and twenty demountable truck bodies. Another subsidiary company known as the St. Louis Plowshare Edge Co., was formed at this time to manufacture replaceable steel-tip plowshares and by contrast did very well.

The Car Company's desperate need for work of any sort is graphically illustrated by the astonishing number of design proposals which still survive from this period, drawn up for every conceivable type of vehicle, including gas-electric cars, buses (with which, in association with the Reo Co., St. Louis Car Co. hoped to capture a new market) and trolley coaches.

Streetcars, too, were proposed for innumerable operators who appeared likely to need new vehicles. But no orders materialized, and this was a more disturbing fact for the Car Company than the failure of other manufacturing projects, since streetcars had up to that time provided the company's main source of income.

By early 1933, it was clear that the company would be unable to pay interest on its outstanding bonds and might have to liquidate. To avoid this, Meissner took a great personal risk by directly requesting the bondholders of the company (against legal advice) to agree to allow the company to waive interest and sinking fund payments until October 31, 1935, and that they also be allowed to extend the bond issue maturity date from 1935 to 1945. In a letter to the bondholders written in April, 1933, Meissner explained that

> . . . all we are seeking is relief during the present period of industrial inactivity, with a pledge to continue interest and principal payoff at the later date suggested.[8]

Of the original $1,560,000 of the 6% bonds issued in 1925, $1,123,100 were still outstanding. Under the conditions of the mortgage, 4% of the outstanding bonds had to be retired each year. Since there had been no profits during the Depression, this was obviously impossible. The company, in an attempt to cut expenditure to an absolute minimum, had, by 1933, laid off nearly all the workers, with the exception of supervisors and shop foremen. The salaries of those few who remained were drastically reduced, being kept at a level just sufficient to keep the individual and his family free from want. Not all the staff who could have remained agreed to this arrangement, and the company lost many people at this time, most important of whom was Chief Engineer Seelar.

The early lightweight bus body was later refined into an up-to-date streamlined design of nice interior appearance and finish, but almost none could be sold.

As a result, almost any work that could be procured was now the subject of bids. Twenty demountable truck bodies were built on a 1933 order.

General Motors took over EMD in 1929, but relations with the St. Louis Car Co. were not completely broken. In 1934, EMD ordered two self-propelled streamlined mail baggage cars for use on the Boston & Maine Railroad. In addition, two body shells were ordered for a pair of 1800hp mainline diesel-electric locomotive, to be used on the Atchison, Topeka & Santa Fe. These units (below) are seen here under the trolley wires of the St. Louis Waterworks line at Baden in 1935.

Details of the coupling arrangement be. tween the two units are shown at left.

Economies had to be made in the maintenance of the physical plant also, and Kamman, the new Chief Engineer, and Fitzgerald, both recall how the roofs began to leak in various buildings and that it became necessary to carry umbrellas when walking through parts of the plant in rainy weather.

Total sales for 1933 amounted to $99,842, as compared with $404,272 in 1932.[9] By contrast, 1923 net sales had been $3,559,389, which yielded a profit of $607,607, practically all of which had been earned through the sale of streetcars.[10] Thus Meissner now had to seek any kind of business that could keep the company functioning, and as a result 1934 found the plant engaged in building 70 dredge pontoons for the U.S. Army Corps of Engineers. The contract price for this order alone was more than the entire 1933 earnings at $114,985,[11] and, in addition, the company managed to get an order for 26 passenger and mail express cars for the Chesapeake and Ohio Railway Co. But still a loss of $28,881 was incurred in that year.

There were continuing problems with the bondholders. Although 98% had responded favorably to Meissner's suggestion of deferring payments and increasing bond maturity dates, there were a few who were not only dissatisfied, but were prepared to file suit for liquidation of the company, to enforce interest payments on bonds worth a mere $8,000. Suit was indeed eventually filed, and it became evident the bondholders concerned were prepared to see the other bondholders lose their money in a liquidation, provided their own debts were paid. Fortunately, the suit was dismissed, and by that time the company had weathered the worst of the Depression, but as the affair had dragged on for some years, it was one more nagging and worrisome problem for Meissner.

The St. Louis cotton pickers, also built by the Car Company.

Though only a small subsidiary, the St. Louis Aircraft Corp. began to do quite well towards the end of the Depression, and played a part in helping the parent company over the fiscal crisis. Among other items the Aircraft Corp. built during the 1930s, the most significant (shown here and on the following page) were the bomber plane training targets, two different types of dirigible airship gondolas, and complete primary training planes of Fairchild design, the one illustrated below being a PT1-W.

The worst of the problems in those years, however, were largely personal. It is not easy to make a decision whose consequence is the laying off of hundreds whose sole source of support is working in one's factory, but Meissner had to make such a decision. Indeed, at one point he was so desperate to keep the company solvent that he was mortgaging his own personal securities, including his life insurance to pay the fixed costs of the empty plant. Inevitably there was personal tragedy during the Depression and the staff of the St. Louis Car Company was unfortunately not immune from it.

George G. Scruggs was secretary and treasurer of the company in the year 1930, and had filled that position since the death of Arthur Dieckmann in 1920. Scruggs was paid an extremely high salary, and used his income and his contacts within the business over the years to build a large portfolio of real estate holdings. Unfortunately, he had no capital funds with which to buy them outright and had bought practically everything on a down payment basis. By 1930 a considerable amount of the purchase price of these properties was still outstanding, despite his having obtained 2,000 shares of common stock in the Car Company from Meissner to help him secure some loans. Scruggs then had a run of extremely bad luck. The Depression started, many of his properties were foreclosed, and the sellers of the others began to call on him for the remainder of the money. Much of his property was uninsured, and was badly damaged by windstorms in the winter of 1929-1930 and the worry so broke his health that he was unable to attend to his office duties for six months.

Eventually a security company wrote to Meissner asking to be relieved of its liability on Scruggs' bond, and Scruggs had to resign. It also led to a final reckoning on Scruggs' account with the Car Company. An arrangement had previously been made whereby Scruggs would pay $200 a month to meet his loan debts out of his salary, but with his resignation, that was no longer possible. Meissner, of course, needed the money once the Depression had started, but Scruggs was not in a position to pay and from 1932 to 1937 there was exchanged between the two men a long series of somewhat sad letters; Scruggs attempting to excuse his inability to pay, and Meissner, not wishing to pursue the matter through the Courts, pressuring Scruggs continually to pay even just a little. The matter was never resolved, and Meissner did not recover the money. Scruggs was as much the victim of the Depression as his own folly, and Meissner himself, a far more capable businessman, was very close to bankruptcy in the Depression through no fault of his own. It would not have been seemly to pursue the matter further, nor would it have been loyal. Meissner was always loyal to those who had been loyal to him, and Scruggs had been so, until his difficulties overwhelmed him.[12]

Business remained very poor in the mid-1930s. The Reo bus project was a commercial failure, as was an agreement with Ingersoll-Rand to produce the bodies for diesel-electric cars and locomotives.[13] It was not until the end of 1935 that prospects began to improve when the company decided to seek orders for manufacturing the new "million dollar" streetcar which the industry had been developing since 1929—the PCC car.

"Now a Reality – the PCC car" reads the caption to this 1936 promotional folder. In styling, both the car and the associated advertising literature were very much of the 1930s.

Head-end of the first production PCC car for Brooklyn in 1936.

Streamlined pre-PCC car under construction for Washington in 1935.

CHAPTER 19

By 1927 the question of new car design had become an almost exclusive preoccupation of the transit industry. Between 1927 and 1929 many other manufacturers had followed St. Louis Car Co.'s example in catering to this industry preoccupation, largely at their own expense, by producing sample vehicles of various designs with which the industry could prove (or disprove) its theories as to the tangible benefits to be derived from large-scale car modernization.

But there had been no coordination between customer needs and manufacturer abilities, and practically every design, while an engineering success, was a commercial failure. The only new vehicles to achieve a modicum of industry acceptance in this period were some of the "Master Unit" series of vehicles, introduced by Brill in early 1929, after the success of prototypes in Wilmington, Delaware. These cars, however, were merely the traditional streetcar in lightweight form, with modernized body styling. With the exception of their standardized appearance they incorporated little that radically departed from previously accepted practice. On the other hand, the St. Louis Car Co.'s "New Birney" car, and the three sample Twin Coach streetcars, the most radical of all the new designs, were never further evolved, and their promising new features, many borrowed from automobile technology were pronounced impracticable and therefore unsaleable.[1]

The major problem continued to be the lack of an industry-wide forum in which discussion could be centralized and brought to a focus. Moreover, because new car design was so major a preoccupation, the continuing lack of agreement on suitable design led to an ever greater reluctance to place large orders for new vehicles, which might shortly become obsolete. In this climate of uncertainty, the manufacturers declined to continue building sample cars, and while there were a few large city properties that could afford to finance their own research and development laboratories, and therefore confidently order new designs of car, generally it seemed as if the modern car movement was about to fade away.[2]

It was at this point that the *Electric Railway Journal*, under the guidance of its publishers, the McGraw-Hill Publishing Co., commenced an active "Buy cars now!" campaign, at meetings of the American Electric Railway Association, of which they were members. At the same time, it increased the intensity of its editorial exhortations to its readers in the transit industry to buy new cars. In this way the magazine was able to create a climate of "crisis" throughout the latter half of 1928, and the first half of 1929.[3] This in turn enabled the Association to set up a series of regional conferences between executives of member transit companies with some hope of a successful outcome.

The first of these meetings was held in December, 1928, later described as an attempt to discuss industry problems in a "frank and open manner." The secrecy with which the meeting was shrouded and the total lack of any written record of its deliberations, even after half a century, suggests that frank and open discussion between such men must have been a new and unnerving experience. Yet a series of similar regional meetings was successfully arranged throughout the country during the first half of 1929, and the results reported to the October 1929 AERA conference. The conference appointed a small committee to consider the reports and act upon them, and in due course this committee called together 25 street railway company presidents to deal with the specific problems raised by the regional reports. The first meeting of this group took place in December, 1929, and the committee quickly became known as the Electric Railway President's Conference Committee, later more commonly known as the PCC.

In January, 1930, the immediate prospects for the industry had appeared favorable. The previous year had been a comparatively good one, and although ridership had declined slightly, more than 1400 units of new equipment had been

The initial body design proposals for the PCC car were developed from the 1934 Kuhler/Brill pre-PCC car for Chicago. The development work was undertaken as a joint venture between the TRC and the St. Louis Car Co. and these wooden body mock-ups were used in the process.

The PCC car interior was comfortable, uncluttered and functional.

The entrance was steep and congested.

The opening of the PCC production lines prompted the throwing of a party.

While similar in appearance to the standard model, the Chicago PCC cars (below) were very different in detail.

It is not generally appreciated that although Pittsburgh #100 was ordered after the Brooklyn, Baltimore and Chicago cars, it was in fact the very first PCC car to be completed, delivered and put into service. Finished in June 1936, it was running in Pittsburgh a few days later, over four months before the Brooklyn cars went into traffic.

bought in the U.S.A. and Canada, a 50% increase over 1928. This in itself was felt to be an indication that the new Committee's work would be successful, and it was hoped that 1929's favorable trends would continue into 1930, thus stimulating both a new purchasing climate and the coordinated research into car design which the PCC had quickly decided was to be its main task.[4]

The chairman of the PCC was Dr. Thomas Conway, Jr., head of a number of traction companies already committed to large-scale purchase of modern equipment. For many years he had had a reputation as a man with a gift for making unremunerative transit companies profitable. During the first few months of the Committee's existence he was responsible for most of the work done, including the setting up of a research and development department, and the hiring of men to work in it.

The PCC was financed by industry-wide contributions, and St. Louis Car Co. was among those who paid their dues to the new Committee. The money was spent in the new research and development department and in paying high quality staff to conduct the experimental work. The most important task of all was the recruitment of a capable head of research, and ultimately Dr. C. J. Hirshfeld, research head of the Detroit Edison Co., was selected. He was man of unquestioned ability and moreover one with no street railway experience whatever; a decided advantage, for he brought to the project no preconceptions which could prejudice the research.

By the time of his appointment in June, 1930, the PCC's program had been unofficially outlined. In brief, the PCC was to coordinate an industry-wide cooperative effort to evolve an ideal car design which could be used without modification on practically every property. The Committee did not intend itself to build the car since it did not wish to compete with any manufacturer. Instead it was hoped that industry-wide financing of "worthwhile" experiments, and subsequent testing of the results for commercial practicability would produce a vehicle acceptable to the industry, at which point the manufacturers would themselves be able to carry the project forward.

It was particularly unfortunate that this unofficial outline of the PCC's work should have been circulated, for it gave the definite impression that the Committee was to attempt to design the "universal" streetcar. Meissner, with thirty years' experience of streetcar manufacture behind him, had very strong views as to the practicability of such an exercise, and with the Depression daily becoming more serious, he was not about to waste more money on the PCC if, as he believed, they were wasting their time investigating a totally impracticable idea. Yet his attitude was based on a total misunderstanding of the true nature of the PCC's work. As it had taken some time for the PCC to find a field laboratory in which to conduct

The Pittsburgh seating arrangement was slightly different from the PCC specifications, but was soon added to the official design as an option.

The driver of the PCC had a seat, and all controls were readily to hand.

its experiments, it had not seen fit to explain officially exactly what it intended to accomplish in the design of a finished product, nor did it deny the unofficial outline or the estimate as to the time needed to do the work. In the absence of an official estimate, individual members of the PCC had been wont to give their own in the name of the PCC. The erroneous impression given by these men was that the PCC not only intended to develop a standard streetcar, but to do the job in less than two years. This misunderstanding of the PCC's program and the estimated time for its completion formed the basis of Meissner's decision to withdraw the St. Louis Car Co. from the project in 1931.

In his view, and that of his engineers, the attempt to produce a truly universal streetcar, which could run without substantial modification on all properties, was a futile task in a manufacturing industry whose very nature demanded the custom-building of vehicles to customer specifications. As an example of the kind of intractable problems involved in formulating a completely standard full-size streetcar design,[5] Meissner and his engineers would point to the streetcar system in Washington, D.C., which possessed a repair shop in which the distance between support posts restricted the length of the transfer table and therefore the length of car which could be ordered. Differences in gauge, variations in the degree of curvature, clearance problems and weight restrictions were found not only on different systems, but quite frequently on individual routes on the same system. Meissner thus refused to involve the company in the PCC's work until they dropped the notion that they could design a standard car.

While it is true that Dr. Hirshfeld (and individual committee members) emphasized the standard car concept rather more strongly in the initial phases of the PCC's work than later, Dr. Hirshfeld was never as rigid in his attitude as Meissner believed and consequently, Meissner's views were not generally shared in the industry. It was fortunate for the PCC project that they were not. Thanks to the generosity of the Brooklyn and Queens Transit Corp., that company's small research department was turned over to the PCC together with office facilities. The management and technical personnel of the Brooklyn Co. were highly enthusiastic about the PCC, while their streetcar system was ideal for the proposed test program, having both paved and unpaved tracks situated so that field research could be conducted without interfering with regular operations. An added advantage was the availability of shop and storage space for test equipment, and the presence of many commercial laboratories and precision instrument makers close by.

After three and one-half years and many tests and experiments, the concepts of the new car had been developed and in October, 1933, the first complete car was service tested at the Brooklyn laboratory.[6] The first results were astonishing, demonstrating a level of performance unexpected even by the research team. The riding comfort and silence of travel were unsurpassed. Dr. Conway, as a result of this demonstration, went so far as to predict

> . . . that it should be possible greatly to decrease the investment in track structures and to prolong the life of existing structures . . . The new cars should change the existing economic balance as between surface railway and automotive common carrier, presaging the continued operation of railway service over many routes.[7]

Dr. Hirshfeld commented that the successful conclusion of the rigorous tests of these new components were proof of his claim that the PCC had not only developed basic design guidelines for streetcars, but had tested them successfully on full-size cars in service.

> If the principles are accepted, we, the operators, and the manufacturers can certainly bring the various pieces of equipment to commercially accepted form and price.[8]

The publication of tangible results after more than three years of experiment sent a considerable flurry through the industry. Chicago Surface Lines was the first operating company to express a desire to prove the results for themselves, and ordered two experimental cars incorporating Hirshfeld principles, to make their own demonstration of the PCC's claims. An extraordinary feature of the order, in an industry where custom-building cars to operator specifications was almost the invariable rule, was the giving of a free hand in design to the manufacturers.

The first of the Chicago cars was delivered from Brill in March, 1934, attracting enormous public attention. The response of the industry, however, was not as enthusiastic as that of the public. The Brill car, and its Pullman-Standard partner delivered in June, had cost $40,000 each, a very high figure for the period. Moreover, although the cars did follow Hirshfeld principles in many respects, they did not precisely correspond to the PCC's specifications for the "ideal" car, so that their operating costs could not be matched exactly to those estimated by the PCC. Nonetheless, the improved performance over the ordinary streetcar was impressive. There was a 30% increase in speed, a smooth and rapid start due to the use of a newly-designed multi-notch remote control mechanism, and a startling reduction of noise due to the extensive use of rubber throughout the car.

A third car ultimately intended for Brooklyn was delivered to Chicago in August, 1934. At the time of its presentation, Dr. Hirshfeld remarked that even this car was not the last word in the design, for since its completion his team had found they could reduce car weight by a further 2,000 lbs. In his opinion, the major significance of the third car was that it was the first built entirely to PCC specifications.[9] The car body of this vehicle was the first to use the new Cor-Ten alloy steel; a lightweight material with great strength, subsequently in almost universal use for steel car production.

The vehicles were shipped to Cleveland for the 1934 American Transit Association's convention,[10] and they were the main attraction of the gathering. Relieved speeches were made, mostly making the point that these new cars represented the first major advances in street railway design in over 50 years, and now it had proved possible to build them, the time had come to make them marketable by simplifying the design and reducing first costs, without sacrificing any of the essential performance characteristics. The PCC suggested that this be left to the manufacturers.

At this conference too Dr. Hirshfeld officially abandoned his position concerning the PCC's adherence to the principle of designing a completely standard car. While he maintained it would still be perfectly possible to do so, individual manufacturers had custom-made vehicles for so long to oblige their customers, that it was perhaps desirable that this tradition continue with the new car.

As a result of this convention, and the demonstration of the new cars, the new Capital Transit Co. of Washington made it known that it wanted to try the Hirshfeld car in considerable quantity, indeed, wanted to operate an entire line with it. Now that the PCC car was not to be a completely standardized vehicle so far as its dimensions were concerned, the Washington company felt it would be able to order the rather shorter vehicles it required to fit its transfer table. The PCC specification had called for a 46′ long vehicle, while Washington could only accommodate one of 44′6″.

Capital Transit, in an attempt to reduce first cost, specified non-PCC cars, vehicles with the same performance and appearance as the PCC car certainly, but of simpler design. As detailed specifications were once again to be left to the manufacturers, and as the PCC had now abandoned its stand concerning the standard car, Meissner, desperate for work, decided to re-enter the PCC project financially and at the same time put in a bid on the Washington cars. As it turned out, the order was split, with Brill building ten cars and St. Louis Car Co. building the other ten. Both companies designed a car which closely corresponded with the PCC's concepts of modern styling. In physical appearance, the cars were not very different from the first Brill prototype for Chicago.

Yet Washington's order remained the only tangible prospect in sight for the manufacturers. Car ordering was to a certain extent being hampered by the terms of the newly-passed National Recovery Act, which for the first time had made the coordination of pricing between manufacturers (price-fixing) not only legal, but compulsory. An agreement on PCC car manufacture and price had to be arranged between Brill, Pullman-Standard, St. Louis Car Co., Clark equipment, Westinghouse and General Electric, as the principle manufacturers. It had been the PCC's intention to encourage a cooperative buying movement among the opera-

Welding the body panels.

Wiring the switchgear.

Installing the floor coverings.

General view of the erecting shop in late

(below) Adjusting pneumatic door engines.

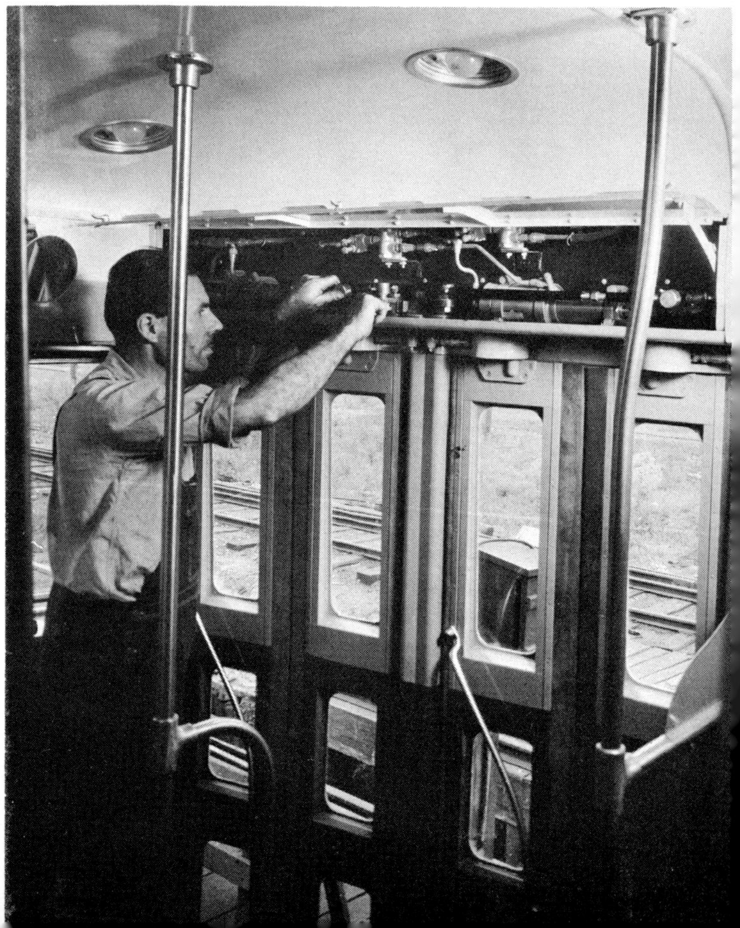

owing PCC cars under construction for San Diego.

(below) Fitting window frames.

Fitting interior body panels.

Rubber suspension spring, developed by the Goodrich Tire Co. This was the heart of the PCC's suspension, and the key to the car's good riding qualities. Note the tubular metal portion of the truck, and the brake rigging for the air-applied clasp wheel brakes, one of which is visible on the left by the wheel. This rigging was omitted when an all-electric braking system was developed in 1941.

Curving steel panels.

From the erecting shop, cars went to the paint and trim line. Here painters are spraying on a gray undercoat.

An underside view showing the truck frame, resilient wheel and track brake.

Installation of the trucks. The double hoists were made by the St. Louis Lift and Equipment Co., another successful Car Company subsidiary of the 1930s.

(below) Batteries for the low tension electrical circuits.

(below at right) Final tightening ensured the cars stayed in place on the flatcar during shipping.

Sign painters finishing detail work. In contrast, the three pictures to the right are examples of an earlier style of decoration and are drawn from a Laclede Car Co. painters' work book assembled in the 1890s. Applying such decorative flourishes could take weeks, while detail work on a PCC car's paint job took only a few hours.

(National Museum of Transport)

Philadelphia #2001, shortly after entering service in 1938.

Canadian PCC cars were built in Canada, except for the body shell and trucks. The body was built at Baden, fitted to the trucks, and then shipped to Canadian Car Co. for the work to be completed.

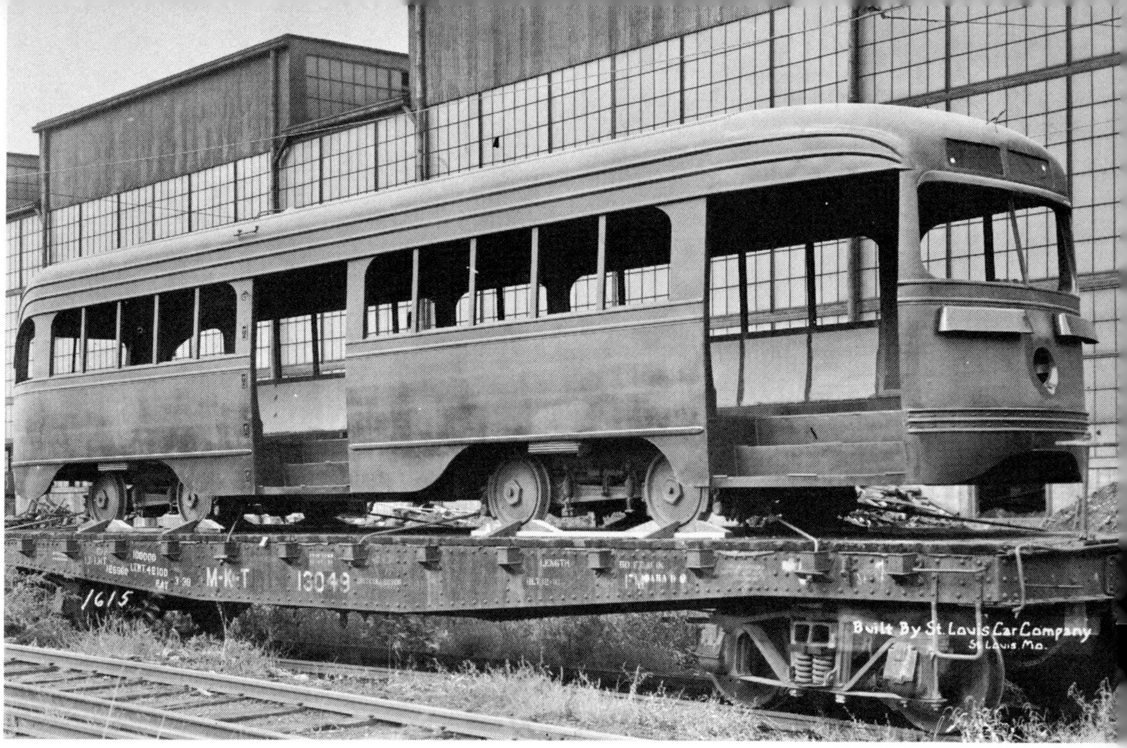

tors in response to the need to buy the PCC car. Such a cooperative would be able to order large quantities of the car from a manufacturer, keeping the manufacturer's unit cost per car down, and thus the price to the customer. The issuing in March, 1935, of bids on 100, 300 and 500 new PCC cars by the Brooklyn and Queens Co. was an attempt to put purchasing cooperation into practice, but the price-fixing agreement between the manufacturers prevented the scheme from working exactly as it had been envisaged.

The bids were issued to coincide with the publication of final PCC car specifications. The car, as finally developed for quantity production in 1936, was to be of lightweight double truck type, one-man operated and single-ended, with front and center doorways and a body made of welded Cor-Ten steel. This would achieve the PCC's objective of producing a car of modern appearance, greatly improved performance and safety, at a price which would make extensive car replacement economically advantageous. The excellent performance of the Washington cars delivered later that summer was very helpful in generating orders for the new car.

Kamman, as Chief Engineer, was sent to New York to participate in the writing of a joint proposal of the manufacturers to be submitted to the Brooklyn company. The proposal was not accepted.

> I was one of the people that was at the Astor Hotel in New York when the proposal . . . was written by the . . . car builders to take over the Brooklyn . . . and I went over to Brooklyn with the group. When . . . the head of the Brooklyn property, Mr. Menden (saw the bid), well, he just rejected the thing, said "Aw, no that's ridiculous, such prices . . . much too high."[11]

Mr. Menden was quite emphatic in his dislike of the proposal; he tore it up and threw the pieces out of the window, at which point the startled delegation left the office, made their farewells and departed. However,

> George Kippenberger and I, we said goodbye, but we didn't leave right then . . . we stayed and then we turned around and went back upstairs . . .[12]

The discussion that ensued resulted in an informal agreement between Brooklyn and the St. Louis Car Co., that the St. Louis firm bid on a car similar in design but not identical to the PCC car for which the combined manufacturing group had quoted a price. This would technically let the company out of its agreement with the other manufacturers on PCC car price. Within a few days of this agreement, formal approval was obtained and Meissner hurried to New York to finalize the contract, only to find on the morning of his arrival that the Supreme Court decision in the Shechter case, made the day previously, had once more made price-fixing illegal. This formally nullified the agreement between the manufacturers, and as St. Louis Car Co. had already been let out of its agreement with the other manufacturers by the subterfuge of bidding on a modified PCC car (Meissner's reason for being in New York), there suddenly existed an unrivalled opportunity to be first to make a low bid on the genuine PCC design, without running into legal difficulties with the other manufacturers. Meissner thus went straight to the Brooklyn office, bid on the genuine PCC design and had the satisfaction some few days later of receiving the order for 500 vehicles. The Brooklyn company was to take the first 99, and was to be responsible for finding customers for the remainder.

Was this sharp practice or not? Kamman didn't think so.

> When we made the proposal and it was thrown out . . . our agreement was done with . . . They didn't like it . . . they called us bastards and everything else I suppose after that . . . but remember this was in the Depression . . . and the plant was empty, absolutely no work whatsoever . . . When you walked through the buildings . . . there were sparrows flying around and . . . you could hear the buildings crack . . . because you were the only one in there. Probably they were a bit peeved at our taking that order at such low figures . . . (but) we had to get back in business again, and at the time I think it was a question of "do we throw the key away today or tomorrow?"[13]

It was not just a question of being in the right place at the right time to submit a lower bid. Meissner's personal relationship with many of his customers was such that he would take the Car Company out of its way to accommodate one whose requirements were somewhat unusual, without necessarily being difficult when it came to modifying an already agreed price. Sometimes this policy could backfire, and the company would lose money on a contract. On the other hand, this approach could pay off handsomely in the form of increased or repeat orders. It is probable that because of their attitude towards the Brooklyn Company in the past (Meissner and Menden had been doing business for more than twenty years), Menden was prepared to do Meissner a good turn at a particularly difficult time in the Car Company's existence. Certainly it would seem so when the terms of the bid are examined closely. In order to have the company reach an acceptably low price on the vehicles to be supplied, Brooklyn was unofficially prepared to accept delivery of the cars in something less than their usual degree of completeness.

Briefly, St. Louis Car Co. was to supply the car body but the customer was to furnish the seats, the trucks and the other "specialty" items, normally delivered with the vehicle. The final price of the car was based on these unusual terms. Brooklyn received its cars at the acceptable low price, while the Car Company received its money for the other items normally included in the car body price, through a separate series of transactions. The Car Company's final Brooklyn bid was thus at the very low figure of $5,000 per car body, but on a firm order of 500 cars, the company was able to raise sufficient working capital to tool up for quantity production and establish a healthy cash flow for the first time since 1930.[14]

In 1935 a long-simmering legal battle with the J. G. Brill Company was renewed over the right to market a type of semi-convertible car. St. Louis Car Co. held a 1902 patent on a particular design of semi-convertible car which they had not manufactured, but which Brill had in considerable quantity, thus infringing the patent. The case had dragged on for many years prior to this and was not finally settled until 1937, in favor of St. Louis Car Co. But it had the immediate result of convincing Brill that the conflict with St. Louis Car Co. and the granting to them of the PCC order under such extraordinary circumstances was less than "fair play" and Brill left the PCC project altogether to concentrate on the development and marketing of its own modern trolley car to be sold as a rival to the PCC's new car.[15]

This left but two car body manufacturers prepared to build the new car; a situation much to the advantage of St. Louis Car Co., for the Pullman-Standard Co., the other manufacturer, had neither the inclination nor the orders to produce PCC cars until the beginning of 1938. Thus, for a crucial two years, St. Louis Car Co. had an effective monopoly on the building of the PCC car.

Although Brooklyn was the first to call for bids, Chicago was not far behind and true to the traditions of the industry, required a custom-built car to a design not covered by the PCC's specifications. All PCC cars built for Chicago had 50′ bodies, three doorways and were fitted for two-man operation, as opposed to the PCC concept of a 46′ body with two doorways for one-man operation. The standard seating capacity of 50 was raised to 59 in the larger Chicago car. Fortunately for the Car Company, the non-standard nature of the Chicago car meant that the 83 vehicles required had to be built on a separate contract from that agreed with Brooklyn for 500 standard PCC cars, and consequently a more realistic purchase price of $15,000 per car was quoted. By 1937, the prices of a normal PCC car without trucks had settled down to $13,500, and with the exhaustion of the 500 cars to be distributed by Brooklyn, the company went back to soliciting orders in the old manner.

With more than 500 cars on order before the end of 1936, the company took it upon itself to alter radically its traditional production methods, so that from the first, these new cars could be built on an assembly line basis. While not a true line in the sense understood by automotive manufacturers, nonetheless the car now moved to the workers, rather than the workers to the car. Up until the PCC program, cars had been traditionally assembled on the spot in every car manufacturer's plant.

> But when we entered the PCC program, it was determined that we should develop line production in order to build cars at the lowest cost . . . Assembly fixtures were built for the sides, the ends, the underframes and the various small assemblies going into these larger assemblies. The work of making the sub-assemblies was essentially line production. When the sub-assemblies required for the main structure of the car were in sufficient quantity, the steel shop line was started and carframes were assembled on the basis of one or two frames a day . . . The steel shop work was not done on a moving line. Each frame was mounted on shop supports and remained in that position until it was completed. From there it was mounted on trucks and moved into the building shop . . . where the different types of work were set out for the various stations and the cars were moved once or twice a day, depending whether one car a day was being built or two . . . The materials required on a station would be located at that position so that they were available for the mechanics with as little delay as possible. The car moved through some twenty-odd positions, which completed the basic work on the car. From there it would go to the paint shop. At that time such items as the sash were not installed and probably not the doors themselves, but the mechanism would be in place. The cars would be moved through a short painting line . . . then moved to the trim line . . . (and) the seats would be installed . . . the doors . . . the stanchions, other items inside the car and the floor covering. After these approximately eight positions, the car would then be completely finished except for . . . testing.[16]

The drawings and the patents on the car were the property of the PCC. These were transferred to a new PCC corporation, known as the Transit Research Corporation, on November 22, 1935. The engineers of the TRC worked very closely with the St. Louis Car Co. throughout the entire production run of the PCC car (and with the other manufacturers) as modifications to the basic design were evolved and introduced. As a result, a situation developed whereby Transit Research Co. engineers would work with Westinghouse and General Electric in developing new braking equipment, Pullman-Standard and St. Louis Car Co. for changes in body designs and fittings, and with Clark Equipment and St. Louis Car Co. for changes to the trucks. Many of these changes were minor, but some substantial modifications were made to the methods of braking and in the design of the trucks. In some cases the development of these modified pieces of equipment took almost as long as the evolution of the original PCC car; the St. Louis Car Co. B3 truck, for example, was first

Toronto #4002, on August 21, 1938, shortly after delivery.

produced as an experimental model in 1939, but did not go into quantity production until 1947, after innumerable modifications.[17]

Once the first flush of enthusiasm for the PCC car had died away, and the operating results were shown to be less conclusive than had been originally hoped for, sales became somewhat slow, and remained so until wartime restrictions on automobile production and use artificially increased the utilization of public transit and new cars were required in large numbers. In consequence, from 1941 to 1949, sales of the car were excellent, and a number of cities changed over to exclusive PCC car operation in base services, and the PCC car, by becoming a steady seller in the early 1940s, laid the foundations for the company's renewed prosperity.

Like all the modern car designs that preceded it, the PCC car could not, and did not, restore profitability to financially troubled operators by winning back extra passengers from the automobile and bus. Indeed in being designed to solve a transit problem twenty years old, the car was in a sense obsolete before it ever turned a wheel! What success it had was due to artificial factors, such as the war, and its sheer novelty as a new car among so many old cars. It was a beautifully engineered car, and its purchasers were well satisfied.

CHAPTER 20

BETWEEN 1936 AND the end of 1941, business improved considerably. While there was a minor slump in PCC car sales during 1938 and 1939, and profits remained low until the war, there was no doubt the Car Company had weathered the Depression. A sizeable proportion of the new orders were for mainline railroad equipment, a market Meissner had turned to when urban transit operators failed him. A small number of streamlined and semi-streamlined diesel-electric power car bodies were produced in the 1930s, as well as diesel-electric locomotive bodyshells. The best known of these units were ordered by EMD, for the Santa Fe railroad's "*Super Chief*" Chicago-Los Angeles train, undergoing diesel-electric trials. The Boston & Maine Railroad also bought some diesel-electric units with Car Company built bodies during the 1930s. Drovers' cabooses were built for several railroads, new designs of lightweight streamlined passenger cars were supplied to the Missouri Pacific, and a number of steel subway trailer cars of conventional design were sold to New York's IRT subway. The most interesting subway car order was that for five sets of lightweight articulated subway cars (incorporating many PCC features) for New York's BMT subway.

But three projects stand out in this period apart from the PCC car; the resumption of trolleybus manufacture, the streamlined diesel cars for the Southern Railroad, and the Electroliners for the Chicago, North Shore and Milwaukee.

Trolleybus construction had begun in 1922, with the completion of an experimental vehicle, later sold to the Windsor, Ontario Hydro-Electric Board. A repeat order for four more vehicles was placed, but no more were built until the beginning of the Depression when Chicago became the first major U.S. city to experiment with trolleybuses on a large scale. The Car Company participated in Chicago's first trolleybus order in the early 1930s, and from then until the war, orders for trolleybuses were steady, if small in numbers, the company gaining a reputation as a quality builder. Meissner regarded all trolleybus work done before 1932 as experimental. The lightweight trolleybuses, made during 1931 for the Wisconsin Power and Light Co. for use in Kenosha, Wisconsin, were a typical experimental trolleybus project, and their design weight of 17,500 pounds was exceptionally light for such a vehicle. This order was shared with another manufacturer, and both sets of vehicles experienced metal fatigue, with failure of side post and other framing members after a short time in service. It is not clear whether this failure was due solely to their light weight, or whether the use of an all-aluminum framing structure was to blame, but the Car Company subsequently had to send men to Kenosha to reinforce the side posts with steel.[1]

The design of the weight-bearing sections of the trolleybus chassis too had undergone considerable change. Kamman explained the nature of these changes.

> The early trolleybuses had underframes with cross members, which were known as outriggers, and this construction was (also used on) . . . buses. At that time the thinking was evidently unclear as to how loads were carried on a bus, so the deflection of the sides, as related to the deflection of the longitudinal underframe center sills and the side members, fatiguing the . . . outriggers. . . . To eliminate this, we changed the construction . . . completely, designing the buses as "side carrying" units . . .[2]

Deep cross members took the springs, and by this means the load was transferred into the side member of the body structure.

> There was a heavy member at each end of the elliptic springs at the front and rear of the bus. The letterboard . . . was carried up into the roof in order to increase the depth of the side . . . and permit the side to carry the loads with minimum deflection. . . . After this construction was put into use, failures were completely eliminated in the . . . bodies.[3]

From 1937, the body styling of St. Louis Car Co.

Articulated subway train for New York's BMT lines, 1936.

A finished Southern Railway locomotive and car.

Interior of a Southern Railway car.

Chicago, North Shore & Milwaukee Electroliner being built in 1940.

Electroliner #802 in 1941.

Electroliner tavern car.

Electroliner passenger car interior. Notice the decorative motifs.

Convention booth used to commemorate the Car Company's 50th anniversary in 1937.

The first experimental trolleybus was built at Baden in 1921, and later the same year an order for four more was placed by the Hydro Electric Railway of Windsor, Ontario.

Little is known of this 1929 integrally constructed one-man vehicle, except that it could operate as an electric trolleybus, or a gas-electric motor bus.

trolleybuses was redesigned to more closely conform to the profile of the PCC cars then being built. An extremely attractive vehicle resulted. Milwaukee purchased a large fleet of these in the late 1930s, as did the Georgia Power and Light Co. of Atlanta.

The Southern Railroad diesel-electric cars and the "Electroliners" seem to bear more than a passing resemblance to each other in their outward appearance. This similarity however is deceptive for the two sets of vehicles were entirely dissimilar, built to solve different transit problems. The Southern Railroad required their new cars to make up six new high speed, lightweight, air-conditioned trains. New departures in railway vehicle design and construction were utilized in the production of these vehicles, most notable of which were the provision of sound-proofing, insulation and indirect lighting. The power unit in the motor car was a Fairbanks-Morse 750hp 8″ x 10″ model 38D8 Diesel railway engine, which provided power for Westinghouse 366 traction motors. The motor and trailer cars were intended to form part of four new Southern express passenger trains: two sets for the *Vulcan* which ran between Chattanooga, Tennessee, and Meridian, Mississippi, one set for the *Golden Rod* running between Selma and Mobile, Alabama, one set for the *Joe Wheeler*, running between Chattanooga and Tuscumbia, Alabama, and two sets for the *Cracker* running between Atlanta and Brunswick, Georgia.

The Electroliners were designed for high-speed electric operation between Chicago and Milwaukee on every type of track, from streetcar lines in city streets to high-speed open railroad track. These cars presented one of the most difficult design problems that the company had faced up to that time. A maximum speed in excess of 80mph was specified, yet the units had to negotiate the tightest curves in the Chicago Loop. There was also a severe width restriction, overcome by the design of a fish-belly cross-section that bulged out above the platform level. These vehicles were also the first air-conditioned electric units to be built by the Car Company.

The decorations used in the cars were novel, in combinations of blue, coral and silver, scarlet and grey or apricot and turquoise. There was a "tavern lounge" on board, which in service became one of the train's most popular spots. The initial inquiry for these cars had been made in 1937, but it was not until 1940 that the design had been fully developed and the units were not delivered until early in 1941.

The company's normal accounting and bookkeeping procedures were recommenced in 1937, when depreciation and "unabsorbed manufacturing costs" were once more reflected in the

A closer view of the experimental trolleybus of 1921. The motor and switchgear were placed under the hood.

This vehicle was an experimental Birney trolleybus.

balance sheet. Sales for 1936 had been $1,622,181, yielding a profit of $61,000, and for 1937 sales totaled $4,367,427, with a profit of $69,836. The following year was somewhat poorer, with a profit of only $58,694.[4] The fact that the company was once again making a small profit was not however a reflection of the financial state of the operating industry. Many contracts were being placed by customers whom it was known would have difficulty in paying on time. Even the Detroit order, placed in 1930, had a proportion of the purchase price still outstanding at the end of 1936. But the fact that the volume of business was once more increasing meant that plant maintenance and improvement could be recommenced. New concrete floors were installed in shop No. 2 for the first time, and pits were dug in 1936 to aid work on the new PCC car lines. By having men work underneath the car in these pits, the cars themselves could remain on their own wheels at rail level, and thus roll from station to station with the minimum of inconvenience.

The return of large-scale business brought the company its first major labor problems since 1918. Unionization was occurring on a large scale, and in March, 1937, a strike was called by company employees seeking recognition of the bargaining rights of local 1055 of the Amalgamated Association of Iron, Steel and Tin workers, under the leadership of Ralph Shaw. Approximately 700 men were involved in the walkout, and not only was this the first strike against the company by organized labor, but the first strike of significance in the campaign of steel workers to organize St. Louis area plants. In addition to union recognition, a $5 a day minimum wage was sought, together with a 40-hour working week. The company's first offer to the men was based on a reduction of the then current 50 hour week to 44 hours, together with a recognition of the union. This offer was rejected, and the plant remained closed for 35 days, with pickets patrolling each of the company's six gates. Meissner's son, Bud, had by then started to work part time in the plant, and remembered that at the time

> Dad and I used to drive to work together . . . and every morning we drove through that picket line. . . . There was a little guy . . . Ralph Shaw . . . the union organizer who called the strike . . . (always present) . . . He was also one of the organizers of the Communist party in the state of Missouri, which didn't endear him to us very much. . . . When we'd drive through the picket line, he'd . . .

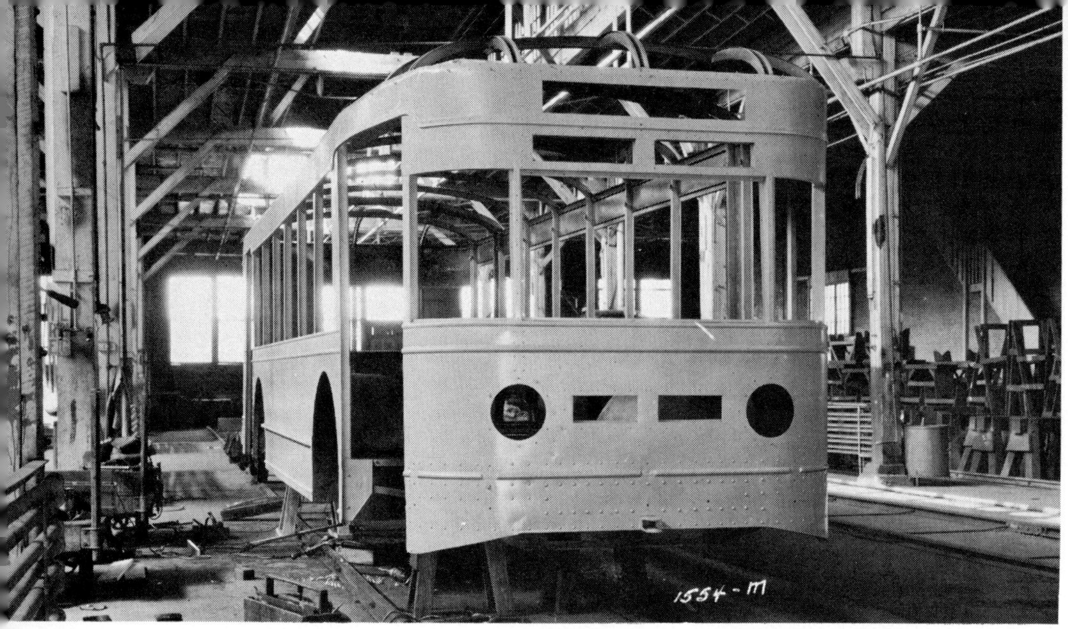

The first modern trolleybuses built at Baden were sold to Chicago, Kenosha and Memphis. This construction view shows Memphis vehicles in 1932.

Memphis #109 in 1935.

Kenosha #17 in 1932.

Chicago #172 in 1936.

Semi-streamlined trolleybus for Milwaukee.

(below) Lightweight streamlined cars for the Missouri Pacific, 1941.

Missouri Pacific E M D diesel electric #7100, and two of the new cars, 1941.

> nod and tip his hat to my father . . . a sarcastic sort of gesture, and dad used to growl. . . . It really burned him up . . . I think he would have run over him if he had gotten in front of the car! . . . It was a very difficult adjustment for my father to have the men, many of whom he raised and brought in and taught all they knew, all of a sudden to tell him how . . . he should run the company. . . . He wasn't of a mind to take that too readily.[5]

The strike was eventually settled by compromise. A forty-hour work week was instituted, but the raise was a mere 8¢ an hour, making a minimum shop wage of 50¢ an hour. This was not quite so poor a wage as might appear, for most jobs were paid by the piece, and generally a good working team of men in the shop could earn a considerable amount. A further increase to 52½¢ per hour was made in 1939.

Normally, however, there were few labor problems. Contracts, while bitterly fought over, were generally signed amicably and promptly. Frequently a peaceful signing of a new contract was an excuse for a celebration. A Meissner testimonial dinner to the men and their union, given in a local Baden hotel in March of 1940 was typical of normal practice, and in a sense was a continuation of the older tradition of the giving of dinners and beer parties by the management for the staff and employees.

Meissner's son joined the company full-time in 1940, but he had been familiar with the plant and many of its operations since early childhood.

> . . . My first job was during spring vacation from St. Louis Country Day School . . . and I remember I had a week off and was given the job of assistant to the office boy. . . . The office boy was getting $40 a month, and since I was his assistant, my father gave me $30 (a month) . . . I worked there a week. . . . I must say I was never forced to go into it . . . (but) I always loved the business . . . starting from my visits there when I was a young boy. . . . In the days when we had a brass foundry . . . it was a fascinating experience to get out and watch them pour castings. . . . Then of course I knew a lot of the workmen and I loved the excitement of the traveling cranes and the transfer tables, the welding equipment and rivet hammers. You know, it's a pretty glamorous thing, and knowing that this was something that would be a part of my life, I took a deep interest in it . . .[6]

Bud Meissner finished college in 1940, a time when the war in Europe had already broken out. He was of draft age and had a relatively low number. At that time there was a provision for draft exemption if one volunteered for a year's tour of duty. It was felt that it would better serve the company's interests if, rather than wait for

Train of IRT trailers, ready for shipment in 1939 with cars #5660 and #5662 in the lead.

Money collection car #66 for the New York subway, 1940.

his number to be called, he volunteer immediately and thus dispose of his military obligations. His army service commenced in February, 1941, and because of the war, he did not return to the company until 1946, except for short periods of leave. His father, however, was reluctant to have his son totally ignorant of company affairs during this enforced absence and sent him copies of every major piece of correspondence going in or out of the company.

By 1941 the company had already become involved with defense work, after a considerable amount of solicitation for the business on Meissner's part. With the beginning of the war in December, 1941, defense work became the company's principal concern. It was the sheer size, volume and variety of these contracts which set the company back on a sound financial basis. The work done more than compensated for the extremely tight government regulations which limited the production of civilian vehicles at precisely the time when restrictions on gasoline and automobile use were sending millions of passengers back to the transit systems.

The first PCC car to be delivered to St. Louis, adrift in a sea of humanity awaiting the ceremonial unveiling by St. Louis' mayor, June 18, 1940.

The mayor did his duty, and the obligatory "staged" photos were taken.

(below at right) St. Louis PCC cars, had two-pedal control.

CHAPTER 21

National wartime restrictions on automobile use had a major impact on public transport, and by early 1942 there were not sufficient serviceable transit vehicles to cope with demand. Various manufacturing companies were allowed to keep a number of production lines devoted to civilian vehicle manufacture, and both St. Louis Car Co. and Pullman-Standard continued to produce PCC cars. Development and improvement of the PCC car had continued before and during the war. In 1941 an all-electric braking system had been developed to replace the previous electric and air system, which had proved troublesome in winter due to freezing air lines. First introduced on an order of 100 cars for the St. Louis Public Service Co., this new feature was at first an optional extra, but later became the standard method of braking for the PCC car. The next group of St. Louis Public Service cars also saw major modifications to the body design. A sloped-back windshield, experimentally fitted to the previous group of 100 cars was a standard fitting on the new fleet. Each seat was for the first time placed next to an opening window, and "standee windows" were fitted, windows whose function was to provide eye-level vision for standing passengers.

During the war, the TRC and the company, after assessing the results of the experimental use of these features, began work on formulating a design for a "post-war" PCC car, and a number of wooden mock-ups were prepared. In addition to body and electrical design alterations, the post-war car was to feature major truck design changes, and new methods of ventilation, utilizing thermostatic control and fans providing for a forced-air blast. All these changes were incorporated in Pittsburgh 1600, a car built on job 1646, which was heavily advertised as the "1945" model PCC car. The B3 trucks for the new vehicle, designed to provide more stability on long, high-speed runs along open or railroad-type track, were still not satisfactorily developed and were not used on this car.

Military contracts naturally dominated the Car Company's wartime activities. The first contract had been a $744,600 order for the War Department, for all-steel ammunition cars. This was similar to the work the company had done in the First World War. In 1942, however, the company began to build amphibious assault craft for the Navy—an entirely new venture.

Serious American interest in amphibious vehicles had begun during the mid-'20s when Donald Roebling, a wealthy Florida businessman, became interested in developing a tractor, known as the "Alligator," capable of rescue work in the Everglades. The patents for the vehicle produced were turned over to the government just before the outbreak of war, and Meissner's earnest solicitations to be allowed to participate in defense work (sent to every defense department) were followed up by the Navy Department, who wanted to use such craft. As a result, early in 1942 Kamman went to Washington, D.C. to meet with Homer Gruenther, the company's Washington representative and prepare for a conference with Navy officials. An agreement was made for the company to build ten amphibious vehicles on a trial basis to assess the feasibility of line production on a large scale. A test model was delivered to the Company a little later and the ten units ordered were successfully produced, and spectacularly tested in Spanish Lake, a large body of water a few miles northwest of the Baden plant. These vehicles became more familiarly known as "Water Buffaloes" and at one point during the war over eight a day were being turned out by the plant. By war's end over 2,600 had been built by the Car Company—a significant percentage of the 18,000 such vehicles built for the Navy during the war.

The early vehicles were made of steel, and lacked armour plate, although later versions of the craft were armoured. During the Korean war, the company resumed amphibious production, and several hundred more were made, until the increasing use of aircraft, especially helicopters, made landing craft obsolete.

1939 wooden mock-up for PCC car body changes. The most important were the slope-back windshield, and the operator's shadow curtain. December 1939.

The new "serve-yourself" fare-taking turntable was a failure, and was quickly removed.

The modifications were first applied to 100 cars for St. Louis Public Service, delivered during the spring and summer of 1940.

More revisions to the body design were made in 1940, and the styling was made more closely to conform to the new General Motors bus design. St. Louis Public Service #1585 outside 39th and Park shops, fitted with card mock-ups showing the revisions. 1940.

1941 PCC cars for St. Louis incorporated all the styling changes, and in addition were wider than normal.

It was intended that the St. Louis modifications should become standard on future PCC cars. But with the U.S. fighting a war, civilian vehicle production was curtailed and brought under the control of the Office of Defense Transportation, who allowed only the pre-war design to be built. This 1942 Philadelphia car had a modified windshield.

Framework of the first experimental St. Louis B3 PCC car truck, 1939.

Complete experimental B3 truck on the transfer table in 1939.

Test of the Alligator by the military, at Spanish Lake, St. Louis.

Alligators ready for shipment in 1943.

Alligator as part of St. Louis Navy Day parade, October 29, 1942.

Driver's view from the Alligator.

(below) Alligators in action, somewhere in the Pacific.

The first Russian mobile power station under construction in 1943.

With such ambitious new contracts coming in, Meissner had to expand the shop space extremely quickly. Unable to get the necessary steel which he required for constructing new buildings, he was at a loss how to proceed until he was told that the old Curtiss-Wright aircraft buildings at St. Louis Lambert airfield were to be demolished to make way for new buildings, and immediately he decided that these old buildings might serve his purpose. Bud Meissner, on leave, went with his father

> . . . to (buy) the contract from the man who had already contracted to scrap the buildings. His job was to . . . remove all the debris and have the site cleared within a very short time . . . so that the contractors could come in and build (a) new plant. . . . Dad bought (the) guy's contract, and I think he paid $6,500 for it, then arranged to get (the building) dismantled piece by piece, put on railroad cars (at) . . . a Wabash siding (out) there and . . . hauled . . . into our plant. We increased our floor space by about 35% on that transaction . . . so . . . we really (had) bought a secondhand plant. . . . It was very expensive (in that) . . . (we) had to pay the labor to take it down and the labor to put it back up. But there really wasn't any alternative because (we) couldn't get permission to build any buildings (and we) couldn't get steel. . . . (However) being wartime, we got the privilege . . . of a five-year write-off of the expense. So it cost a lot of money to put them up, but we got a rapid amortization of the expense under tax rulings.[1]

Materials for civilian building were strictly allocated during the war and nothing could be bought, built or sold without specific authorization. This could lead to a situation where an order for vehicles existed, together with enough material and labor on hand to build them, but no government authorization, and these regulations caused continual problems in trying to complete work. Fitzgerald, as company purchasing agent, was the "front man" for the company when such problems occurred and he was in difficulty many times with the authorities after exercising his ingenuity to obtain material and get the jobs completed for which the company was responsible. At one point during the war, the company was short of welding equipment. Standard procedures for acquiring this equipment frequently entailed long delays and the

Loading a mobile power station onto a ship in Portland, Oregon in 1944.

unnecessary idling of other equipment at the plant. To avoid this, Fitzgerald located the necessary equipment locally, installed it and did the work, at the same time as the correct applications for the materials were made through the appropriate government agencies. In due course an inspector came to the plant to see if the request for the materials was justified, and finding the requested equipment already in unauthorized operation, had Fitzgerald prosecuted for violation of wartime operating procedures. Although the charges were eventually dropped, this was a nasty shock for Fitzgerald, and a sharp reminder to the company.

Among the most interesting contracts the company received during the Second World War was an order to build portable self-contained power plants for Russia, as part of a Lend-Lease agreement. These complete electrical generating plants were built on railroad trucks of Russian gauge and were intended for quick transfer to a war area that had lost its power supply. Once at the site, they could quickly be connected into what remained of the local grid. These units generated 400 volts at 50 cycles AC, and came in sizes ranging from 300KW to 800KW.

As usual, the customer was to design the vehicle, and the Company was simply to build it, but as it happened, it did not occur that way. The first intimation that such a project was under consideration was given in a telephone call to Meissner from Washington early in the war asking him whether the company would be prepared to build this kind of vehicle. Meissner, never a man to refuse business, immediately said yes, delegating Kamman to take care of the details. Kamman went to Washington to talk with the Russian engineers assigned to the project to assess its feasibility. After reviewing the design plan he declared his unease with the concept.

> I was sitting in the Russian headquarters . . . in Washington talking to their engineers through an interpretor. The engineer was sitting in back of me, so I couldn't see him directly and as the day went on, things became a bit cool between us. I had been telling them . . . (that) the details as they had been specified were not at all satisfactory for what they were trying to do. (What) I didn't know (was) that I was talking to the man that had developed those details. About four o'clock in the afternoon, we adjourned the meeting for the day and it was agreed that I should come back early the next morning and continue. The next morning when I arrived, they were waiting at the door with their hand out. . . . (They) were (suddenly) most friendly and the man who couldn't speak English the day before could now speak English very fluently! Evidently he had overnight checked what I had told them the day before and was satisfied that I was right. From then on we were friends.[2]

Kamman was thus able to return to St. Louis, write a specification, and prepare a general arrangement drawing. These were taken back to Washington, discussed with the Lend-Lease officials and the Russians, and approval was given to make an estimate and proposal. This was done, the order was received and construction began.

The power generator was driven by a large diesel engine, fueled by an extremely thick, relatively unrefined crude oil. This, in combination with the severity of the Russian winters, meant that special arrangements had to be made to get the oil thin enough to ignite, and so a special boiler was also included in the unit to heat the oil to a consistency thin enough for effective ignition. More than 150 of these 80-ton units were built by the Car Company under the Lend-Lease agreement.

Tank production was also undertaken, in fairly high volume, but there were very few untoward incidents with those vehicles and while production was not without some hitches, it was largely uneventful, the biggest problem being found during shipping, when their caterpillar treads (and those of the "Water Buffaloes") continually pounded the company's concrete-paved yards into rubble.

Aircraft too were built in considerable quantity during the war. The St. Louis Aircraft Co. had been largely dormant since the relative failure of the Cardinal, but Meissner was unwilling to wind up the aircraft subsidiary company and the name continued to be registered through the Depression. During the late 1930s, however, a certain amount of profitable work had been undertaken in con-

Framework of XCG 111 glider in 1942.

(below) The completed glider.

Glider ready for shipment, 1942.

Aircraft erecting shop, 1943.

(above) A St. Louis Aircraft-built Fairchild PT 23 in flight.

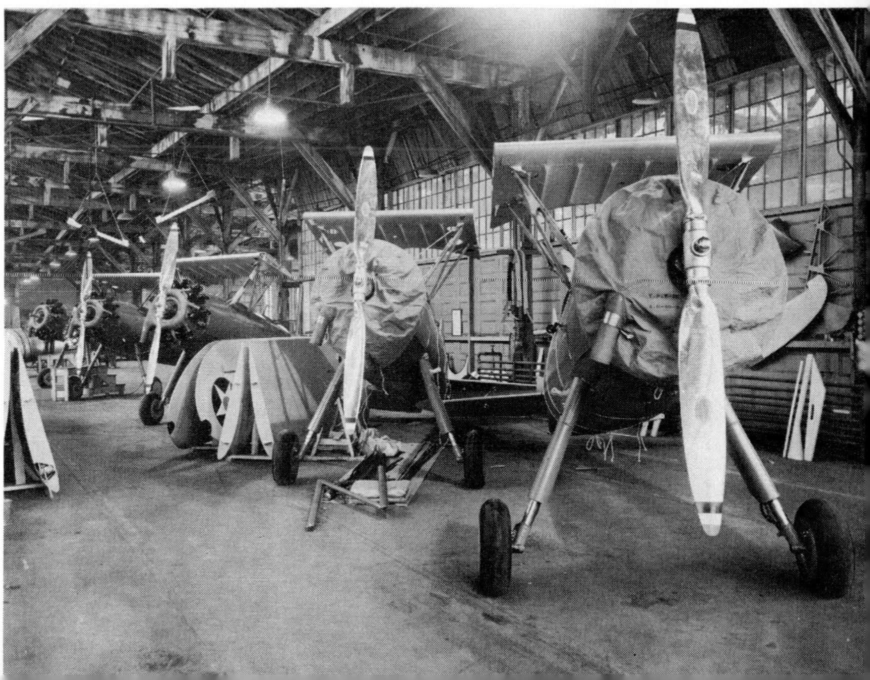

YPT 15 primary training aircraft ready for shipment in 1943.

structing a few training planes, and control gondolas for army balloons. A little other work was also done, primarily in the design and construction of skis to be fitted to aircraft landing gear, but it was not until the war started that the company began to build complete planes in quantity once more. Specializing on Fairchild designs, the aircraft company, using shops 6, 7, 8 and 9, built large quantities of PT19 and PT 23 primary training planes, as well as smaller amounts of other Fairchild designs and some experimental high-capacity gliders. New machinery had to be procured for the aircraft work; the first new machinery the company had used for over a quarter of a century.

The glider project came about as a result not only of the company's aircraft experience, but also because it had before the war built some secret new designs of bombing plane instruction mock-ups. It was thus selected to build an experimental glider, known as the XCG 111, a huge, cargo-carrying vehicle designed to carry both men and materials needed for the invasion of enemy territory. To ensure lightness of weight at a time of great scarcity of aluminum, the glider was built of wood, and so secret was the project that the construction work was arranged in such a way that most men working on it did not know exactly what it was they were building. Merz recalled that the biggest problem was to ship the completed glider from St. Louis to Dayton without its being recognized, and with much difficulty it was so shipped, only for Merz to have the galling experience of having a man come out of the hanger at Dayton, look at the heavily-wrapped shape on the railroad car, and then ask Merz in a loud voice if that wasn't the glider which had been expected.[3]

The hanger at Dayton was the site at which the extremely rigorous tests were carried out, tests largely concerned with crushing the glider to the point of collapse. All the tests were successfully completed, but the plans for invasion changed, and the glider was not put into production.

Chester Bleikamp was the man whom Meissner generally delegated to negotiate the details of government contracts, and he was usually away from St. Louis for long periods of time doing such work. It was Bleikamp who was responsible for St. Louis Car Co. obtaining one of the more unusual orders of the war—radar antenna mounts. While on one of his trips, Bleikamp had heard a rumor that the authorities were dissatisfied with the quality of work on mobile radar mounts then being delivered. Knowing that Meissner would unquestionably want to bid on any work that could be found, he had to find a way of getting some kind of sketch of the mount, which was top-secret. It is not known how he did it, but he succeeded, and mailed a copy of the sketch to Meissner, subsequently managing to find out what the other companies had bid on the contract. With this information, Meissner submitted a lower bid, got the contract, and put the mounts into production for the Signal Corps, at one point making two per day.

Wooden mock-up of the 1945 PCC car, photographed in 1943. Notice the alternative window arrangements available, and the deck roof in which thermostatically controlled fans were to be fitted.

Pittsburgh #1600, the 1945 model PCC car. This photograph has been heavily retouched.

The Baden plant was too crowded for these vehicles, and so they were constructed at what had been the automobile plant, which stayed in active use by the Car Company throughout the war.[4]

The company became profitable in a spectacular manner during the war. Over $6¼ million in sales were made in 1942, yielding a profit of $308,000, but in 1943 sales exceeded $18 million with after-tax profit of over $1 million. Even the aircraft company did well, with $2 million of sales in 1942 and a profit of $40,000. Sales in 1944 for the parent company were $44 million, $7 million was paid in taxes and the new profit was $1½ million, bringing the company surplus over the $1½ million mark for the first time since 1930. In 1945, despite large-scale cancellation of defense contracts results were almost as good, with total sales of over $40 million, and a net profit of $870,000 after payment of $2.65 million in taxes. By war's end the company surplus had grown to $2.26 million and the book value of the company $15 million.[5] What was even more encouraging, although somewhat ignored in the other statistics, was that despite government controls, streetcar production throughout the war had exceeded $6 million in value, and at war's end there was a backlog of orders for streetcars and trolleybuses that promised to give the company at least four years of solid work.

With the company working at such pressure during the war, it is surprising that there were not more labor disputes than the handful that did

Antenna mounts ready for shipment.

occur. In May, 1944, for example, there was a half-day strike over a contract dispute. The two major items in dispute related to employment discrimination, and grievance procedures. The men were not prepared to recognize President Roosevelt's executive order prohibiting discrimination in employment, and they were also not prepared to recognize the company's demand that the company be allowed to file grievances against the union in the same manner that the union could against the company. In the matter of discrimination, however, Meissner was ahead of his time, and obviously ahead of his workforce. Meissner had always been extremely active in social and civic affairs in St. Louis, and by this time was known to be a vocal supporter of civil rights and desegregation activities. However, the discrimination problem was not a real issue in this temporary stoppage, and the matter was quickly settled.[6]

More serious was a twelve day strike in August of the same year. A dispute over piece-work resulted in the walkout of the entire workforce, and Meissner was powerless to stop it or deal with their grievances himself. The government conciliation service was too slow for the men, and it was necessary to force them back to work by service of a War Labor Board order on the union. The actual problem was not solved until November. Pay rates by this time were considerably higher than six years earlier. By the end of 1944 rates ranged from between $1.44 to $2.00 per hour, and of course in its new contract, the union was calling for yet more, in a range from $2.10 to $2.75 per hour. Most of these strikes and petty disputes, however, reflected not so much discontent with the company and the work, but general war-weariness, fatigue and malaise, which led to a much lower threshold of tolerance and patience. With civilian orders backlogged for years ahead, the end of the war was a relief to both the men and the company. The postwar era was entered with high hopes and improving morale.

Antenna mounts in action somewhere in Italy, 1944.

CHAPTER 22

PEACE HOWEVER DID not bring the immediate improvement in conditions that had confidently been expected. Negotiations on the terms for cancellation of the large defense orders were protracted, decontrol of materials allocation was a long drawn-out process, and critical shortages persisted for many months. But the order books for civilian vehicles were full, with more business coming in daily, and the final abandonment of government controls gave the Car Company the opportunity to purchase the most useful of the government-owned machinery used in wartime manufacture.

After the initial problems of the first few months were overcome, the period 1945-1950 was a time of continued high production, and correspondingly large profits. The company securities were for the first time worth more than their par value, and by the beginning of 1947 there was still a backlog of two years' work on the order books. Reliable material supply, a problem since 1942, now became critical as attempts were made to clear off the backlog, and with the war long over, customers were less patient over delays from this cause. As a result, said Kamman

> . . . we had a meeting at our plant . . . of the large suppliers of equipment and trucks (to try and solve) our problem (in) getting a sufficient amount of equipment to meet a large production schedule . . . (Thus) for the most part (our) orders to the suppliers . . . (now) were based on their being able to meet our requirements for delivery. . . . (By this means) we could build five to six units a day of either streetcars or trolley-coaches, or a mix of the two, which was extremely high production for our plant. . . . Our production was in fact built up to the maximum that we could get from our suppliers.[1]

The artificial nature of the demand for vehicles at this time was not yet fully appreciated by the company or its customers. In the early postwar years, the bulk of the demand was for electric vehicles to be used in urban transit. These included 1945-model PCC cars, and their subsequent modifications, trolleybuses, and a small number of electric interurban cars, the most elaborate of which were built for the Illinois Terminal Railroad. But these orders were being placed at a time when wartime transit riding conditions still persisted. There was a continuing scarcity of automobiles and thousands of worn-out transit vehicles remained in operation, conveying people living in relatively compact and densely populated areas. All car builders did well in those first postwar years but General Motors (and others) did incomparably better selling motor buses. In 1949, when the first slump occurred in the ordering of new streetcars and trolleybuses, the bus manufacturers continued to build in high volume. Moreover, General Motors had what no carbuilder could afford—a research and development department that could help the company better evolve new designs to fit customer needs, and offered financing services to new bus purchasers that car manufacturers could not hope to match. Finally, the newest buses were for the first time in a position to compete on a seat-for-seat basis with the capacity of any electric vehicle then being made. Thus, the streetcar's sole remaining advantage over the bus as a "people-mover" no longer existed in the opinion of most transit operators. General Motors' buses for heavy city work could be ordered in 45 and 50 seat models, and a little later in a 54 seat model. Moreover, by 1949, the full force of the automobile as public transit's most formidable competitor had once again became significant, hence the slump in the ordering of new streetcars and trolleybuses. By stimulating the large-scale rush to build new homes in the suburbs, away from the densely populated central city, the automobile helped to create new areas whose need for public transportation was minimal. Fixed modes of transit could not serve the suburbs economically, and indeed they now could barely be adequately served by bus.

In 1949 (the first year that urban transit began to show marked declines in ridership and use)

The last pre-war style PCC cars were built for Pittsburgh in 1945, although these cars were fitted with the 1945-style dash floodlights.

Louisville #505, a 1945 model PCC with revised front end.

The Louisville cars never ran in that city, owing to a sudden change of policy. They were transferred to Cleveland, in exchange for buses and cash.

1946 PCC car for Kansas City and one of the cars it replaced.

St. Louis Public Service #1745 at University loop in the late 1940s. These cars were built to the St. Louis 1941 pattern. *(A. D. Young collection)*

Chicago #7035 of 1947. Notice the three doorways.

The postwar order back-up was immense, and production was heavy until 1949. Here is a typical day's deliveries awaiting transfer to the shipping tracks sometime during 1947. They include Chicago PCC cars, Detroit PCC cars and Cincinnati trolleybuses.

declines began which have continued up to the present. While the bus market was not greatly affected at first, the market for electric urban transit vehicles, except for replacement subway cars, was utterly destroyed within a short time. After 1951, the company received no more orders for streetcars or trolleybuses; fortunately by then it was no longer dependent upon their continued production to survive.

All this, however, was in the future, when in March, 1946, a major strike was called. The 650 production employees of the company left their jobs as part of a widespread general strike of steel workers in the St. Louis area, and did not return to work for more than four and a half months. At that time a new contract was signed, providing for an increase of 15¢ per hour for those on a flat hourly rate, and similar increases for those on piece rates. In addition, there was a clause in the contract specifying that in six months, or after the construction of 600 streetcars, whichever came first, that there would be a further 3½¢ increase.

The strike could have had serious repercussions but for a major piece of luck, which Bud Meissner later recalled.

> We were on strike, which was a great problem, but so were General Electric and Westinghouse. . . . I'm not sure if both companies were down at the same time, but we couldn't get any motors or controls . . . so that we couldn't have built more cars even if we were working, so as much as it hurt, we probably would have hurt either way. . . .[2]

Unhappily, within weeks of the strike's settlement, another long and costly dispute occurred, this time unofficial. In the middle of August, 1946, a "wildcat" strike of 6,000 area steelworkers was called, once again including St. Louis Car Co. men. This strike had been preceded by a sit-down strike in the sheet metal department, prompted by a dis-

San Francisco trolleybus climbing Union Street in 1947.

In 1948 200 Brooklyn trolley-buses were built; #3000 is shown at Baden and Meissner is standing on the left.

pute over lack of laborers. It was not until the middle of October that the walkout was finally settled, and to avoid any such future incidents, the union appointed an advisory committee to handle all labor-management problems. It was frankly admitted that the unofficial nature of the second strike was puzzling; not even the union leaders had a clear notion of why it had been called. The effect on the company of losing five and a half months of production was, however, devastating. The year 1945 had been one where sales of $4,896,296 were made with a net profit of $870,302. The following year, despite the over-full order books, showed a sales total of only $2,877,274, with a net loss of $32,875. It was exceedingly bad luck that this should have happened, for the 1947 results were far more representative of the prosperity of those years, with over $12 million in sales and a profit of $604,561. An even better year was 1948 with $17 million of sales and nearly $1 million profit. However, 1949 showed a decline with $11,500,000 of sales, and $400,000 of profit. The figures for 1950 were largely similar but by the end of that year the company surplus was over $4½ million.[3]

The somewhat reduced sales figures for 1949 and 1950 were not entirely unexpected. By the end of 1947, the company began better to understand the temporary nature of the postwar boom in electric urban transit vehicle sales, and an active search was commenced for new products. The most promising of these was a new type of light-weight rapid transit car, based on PCC car technology, but designed for subway or elevated railways rather than streetcar systems.

The decision to look for new types of products to manufacture was not taken lightly, and called for a great deal of knowledge and understanding of the company's strengths and weaknesses—knowledge that was not always at hand when needed. To remedy that situation during the summer of 1948, Meissner commissioned an industrial analyst to survey the plant and its operations at a time when the transition was about to begin.[4] The resulting report presented an encouraging picture of the company's overall position and future prospects. Interviews were held with top management and key personnel and no holds were barred. Not only the current efficiencies, but the critical shortcomings were freely discussed.[5]

The study was informal in character as it had been commissioned for

> . . . practical use . . . by an exceptionally intimate executive team, headed by owner-management in direct control and thoroughly familiar with all operational matters. In this respect (the report) differs materially from an

Shortly after entering service #3095 was experimentally fitted with reflective tape.

> industrial audit which might be prepared for the most common "absentee" or Wall Street type of administration.[6]

The report's coverage was comprehensive, encompassing investigation into management, sales engineering, production planning, tooling, parts fabrication, assembly operations, inspection, "key" personnel, qualifications and proposed procedures. While it was found that the company was dynamic in sales and engineering policies "to a degree rarely found in organizations so long since founded," it was felt that plant facilities were below accepted industrial standards.

> The main car building shops were erected around the turn of the century (sic) and most of the subsequent plant additions have been acquired through salvage and reconstruction as opportunities arose. The same is true of most of the mechanical equipment, some items of which were of such early vintage as to be entirely unfamiliar to the writer. . . . (However) the facilities are unusually well suited . . . to the needs of their business. The plant layout, for example, is one that offers the greatest flexibility for line production . . . and the . . . suitability of the mechanical means for parts fabrication is apparent, when one observes that the vast majority of all structural components are fabricated in their own plant, and the completed end products are at least on a par with the best produced in this country today.[7]

The report then began to deal with specific topics. In its investigation of the company's management, it was adamant that the entire company was a reflection of the energy and business acumen of Meissner himself, and his continuing emphasis on aggressive selling. Immediately subordinate to Meissner were the "well unified" executives of the various departments, all of whom had been with the company for many years. The report noted with approval Meissner's policy of developing its executives from the ranks, rather than hiring from the outside.

> This has resulted in the creation and preservation of an exceptionally intimate, well trained and effective organization, that can function with agility and singleness of purpose. . . . Under these conditions, the company has . . . an almost unique ability to adjust itself quickly to changing circumstances, and to take advantage of industrial opportunities that would . . . be passed up by more cumbersome and therefore more conservative managements.[8]

Completed 1948 interurban train set for the Illinois Terminal.

In 1948 a licensing agreement was concluded between the Car Company and Les Ateliers de Constructions Electriques de Charleroi, Belgium. This allowed the latter company to make U.S.-style PCC car bodies, and St. Louis B3 trucks under license. One complete car from Detroit order 1661 was diverted to Belgium in 1947, together with parts for two more cars to be used in Den Haag, Holland. The cars were shipped from New York.

Sales procedures in the transit industry were examined closely. The report felt that the company's successful bid on a Chicago contract for 200 lightweight subway/elevated cars was due entirely to its ability to construct a car which most closely anticipated the customer's basic requirements, and at the same time could be supplied through some modification of a reasonably standard item, in this case, the PCC streetcar. This was felt to apply with equal force to other company products, particularly the trolleybus. Although the company had yet to establish the competitive advantage in trolleybus construction that it already had achieved for itself in PCC car and lightweight subway car construction, it was felt that the large order for "stylish" trolleybuses for Atlanta would help—a predication which unfortunately did not prove to be accurate.

Engineering was considered to be the company's greatest strength, especially as the relationship between the engineering and sales departments was very close in all contacts with customer representatives. However, it was strongly suggested that the company could profitably adopt production engineering techniques

> . . . in parallel with, and not in post-mortem to, design engineering, if the exceptional advantages of interchangeable manufacture are to be satisfactorily adhered to. . . . In this way . . . the product (can) be rendered suitable for efficient assembly line production, and the entire "make ready" planned and scheduled . . . to ensure contractual fulfilment and minimum expenditure of time and money, (as well) as . . . (relieving) shop administration of all distributing and technical responsibilities . . . (thus making it) free for the conduct of all operating routines.[9]

Production planning techniques were next examined, it being found that they were conducted as a "phase of shop administration" in a department which also carried on the dispatching functions of shop control.

> The activity is remarkable for its relative efficiency under catch-as-catch-can conditions. . . . Each contract is separately handled as a separate project and the planning consists of calling out the templates, mock-ups and tools . . . for each new part required by engineering release drawings. . . . Graphic control boards are used to post all data needed to indicate the current status of work under each contract. . . . There are approximately 2,000 separate parts required for the production of a . . .PCC car, and about 1800 for a. . . trolley coach.
>
> The principal asset of the . . . company is the comprehensive industrial know-how of its management team, and if its postwar shop activity is to be brought to a parity with its sales engineering excellence . . . steps will have to be taken to . . alter the current jumble of responsibilities relating to production planning, scheduling and control.[10]

Tool engineering was felt to be one of the company's major weaknesses, and a number of recommendations were made to remedy the situation before the report turned to the related question of parts fabrication, which at the time was done in job lots only sufficient to complete each individual contract. This had one advantage, however, in that such a process reduced set-up time to a minimum.

> Activity begins with the shearing of material, which has been wisely placed under the control of the Stores Department. Material of all thicknesses up to ¾″ can be handled efficiently. From there it passes to one or other of the following shops . . . *Tin shop*: a department which fabricates parts made from thin gauge steel or aluminum alloy sheet stock . . . Operations consist primarily of bench forming, punching, drilling and making up detail assemblies by riveting and/or spot welding. *Punch shop*: . . . the typical pressroom . . . (but) equipment is old and relatively crude . . . Operations consist of die forming sheet and light plate stock, as well as punching of rivet and lightening holes in . . . formed and flat material . . . *Forge shop*: Hot (forms) the heavy structural members required . . . Equipment consists of oil-fired furnaces and conventional steam hammers. Through use of dies, only a nominal amount of hand-hammering is required. *Machine shop*: a department for turning, shaping, drilling, reaming and

Railed vehicles were built to fit many gauges, and the test track had to accommodate them all.

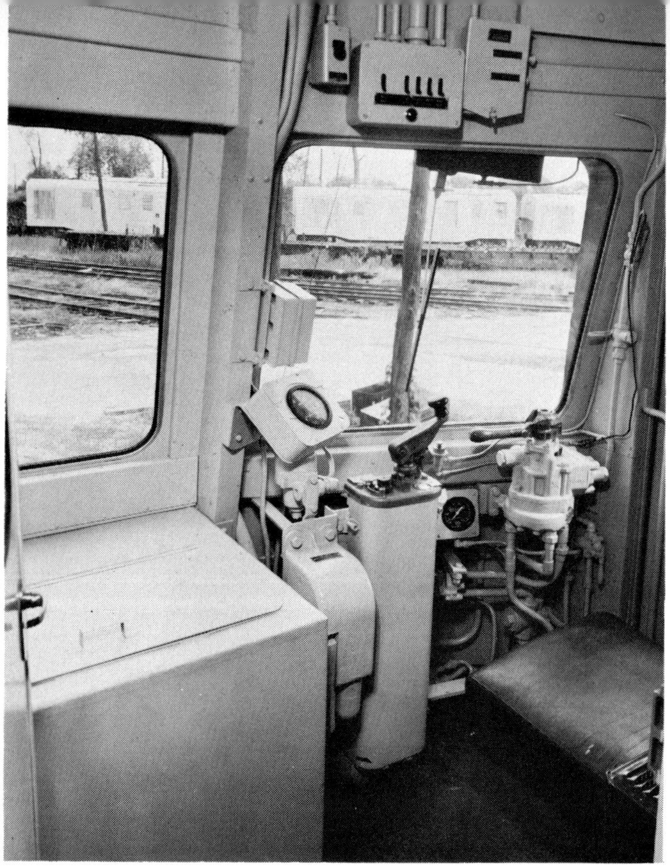

Driver's compartment, Illinois Terminal interurban train set.

Interior of rear passenger car, Illinois Terminal interurban train set.

Pittsburgh's last PCC cars were modified 1945 models with sealed windows and forced air ventilation. Here the body is placed on the truck.

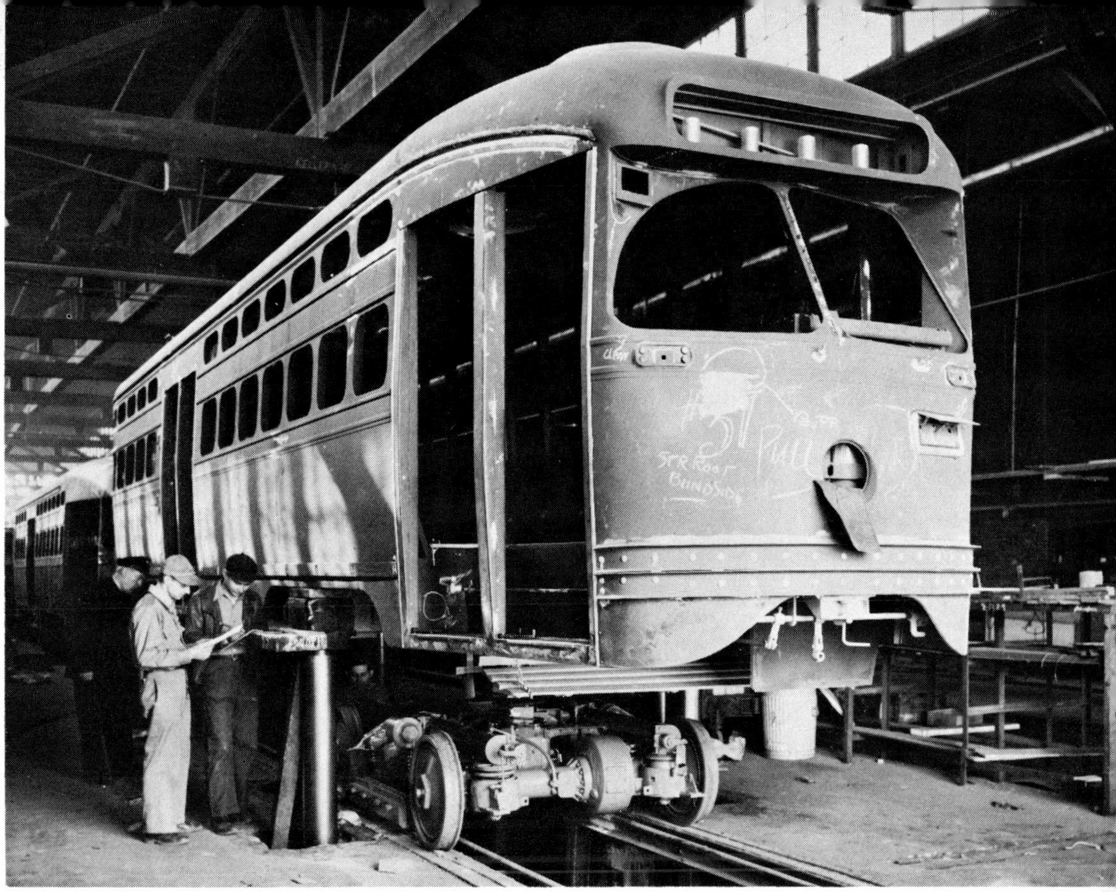

Below car #1709 is being loaded at Baden for shipment to Pittsburgh.

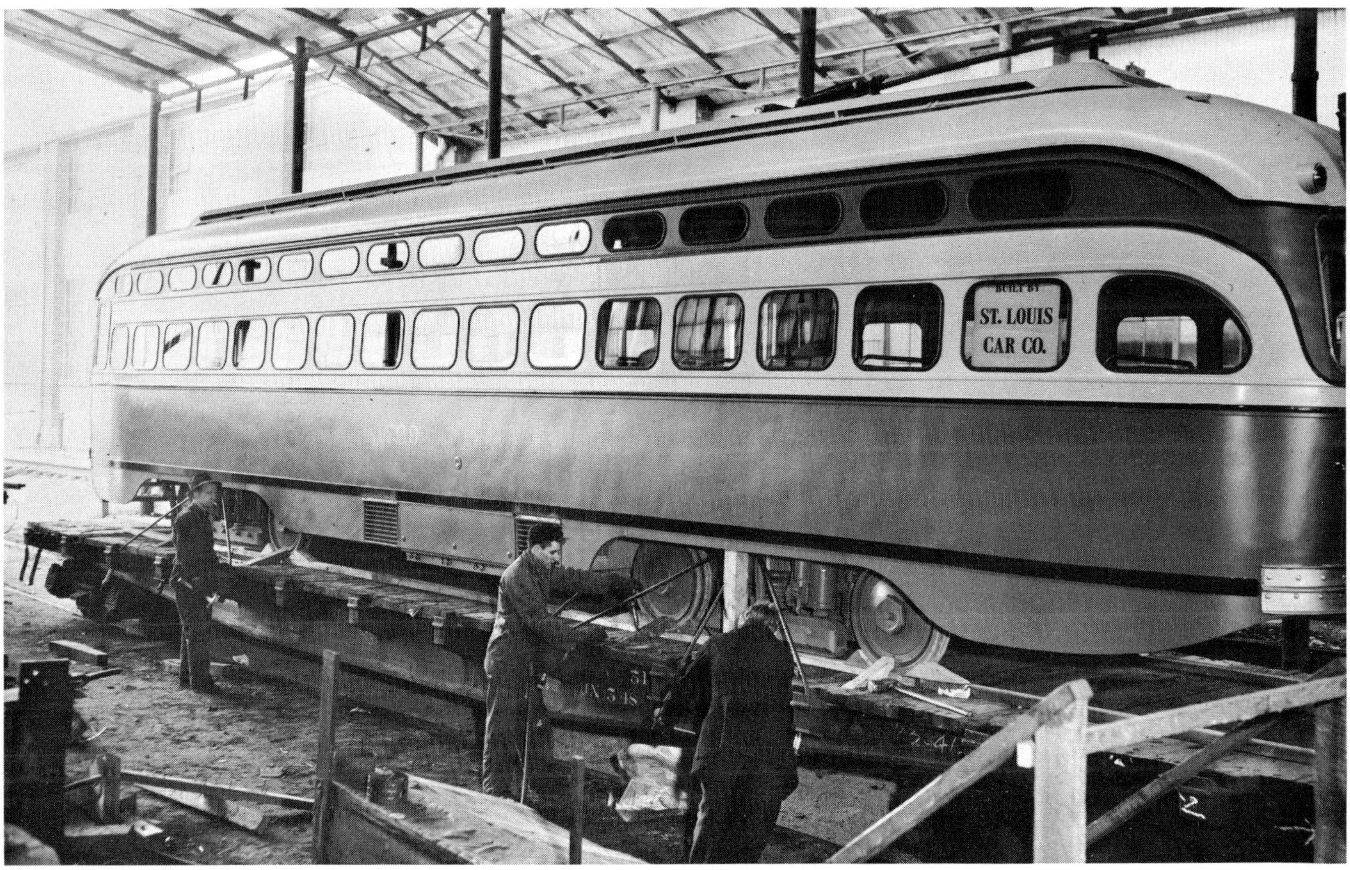

Fitting the rubber window mounts.

boring of precision-made parts. *Wood shop*: . . . fabricates folding doors for trolleybuses, and plywood panels needed for the flooring of all models. [11]

The report felt that apart from the absence of manufacturing pre-planning and some modern machine tools, parts fabrication was reasonably efficient for all purposes.

The next process to be investigated was assembly operations. This commenced with the loading, riveting and welding of the underframe and body assemblies in jigs located in the "lay-down" shops. After removing the completed underframes from the welding jigs, they were then routed through the straightening and sandblasting operations, receiving a "primer" coat of paint before being returned to the "lay-down" shop for erection of the superstructure. When work in that shop was completed, the vehicle was wheeled to the paint shop.

By 1948, every product made by the company was manufactured on assembly lines of the type first set up in 1935 for the PCC car, and each operation performed was priced at piece-work rates which were negotiated separately for each contract, generally not later than the completion of the fifth or sixth vehicle of an order. Separate negotiations for each contract were made necessary by the many new models and design changes made from one contract to the next.

Although the sequencing and balancing of the assembly operations was efficient, the report considered the normal cycle time of four hours on the assembly line as abnormally long and felt the cycle seemed to be fixed by the relatively slow and inefficient methods of structural assembly in the Lay-Down Department.[12]

There were felt to be few operations that did not involve an

> . . . excessive expenditure of highly skilled effort in accomplishing fitting and joinery operations of a handicraft nature . . . Assembly operation consumed . . . four times as much direct labor as did fabrication of parts (with) . . . excess labor hours, (and) higher average wage rates due to . . . greater average skills (needed)in so many of the operations. . . . (Thus) an exceptionally large amount of working capital was naturally tied up by "work-in-progress" which moved through the assembly line sequences at such a rate that the accumulation of vehicles in various stages of assembly was normally equivalent to the

Pittsburgh #1715, one of 25 fitted as interurban cars for use on the Charleroi and Washington lines.

> entire average contract. When one adds to all this the inventory of new materials and purchased components that must be accumulated in anticipation of meeting a promised delivery schedule that is held up by avoidable delays in "make-ready," the sum total of excess capital impounded in 'float' far exceeded any capital investment that might reasonably be needed . . . to thaw . . . most of it out.[13]

Inspection procedures were next investigated, and within their limitations were considered to be excellent. The limitations were imposed by the company, which took the somewhat narrow view, in the opinion of the analyst, that inspection was a function aimed at satisfying only the specifications and the contractual requirements set up by the customer. Quality control inspection was felt to be the company's biggest lack in this area, and the report sketched out a proposal for instituting an inspection operation which it was suggested could be integrated into the proposed Production Engineering functions.

The greatest strength of the company lay elsewhere.

> Assets of . . . greater intrinsic value . . . than all its plant . . . are to be found in the exceptionally long practical experience and know-how of its executive and working organization . . . the result not only of wise selection from among the ranks of the available personnel, but of good faith on the part of top management, which has induced such people to stay and give their best efforts to the company throughout the years. In short, the fair deal always pays off in personnel (sic) relations as well as in everything else . . .[14]

Having made various suggestions for improving procedures by instituting production planning, the report then concluded by describing at length a procedure which it suggested could usefully be adopted by the company to attain that goal, matched to three specific jobs shortly to be started: New York Central electric commuter cars, the first of the Chicago lightweight subway/elevated cars, and the Southern Railway caboose cars. It was not easy to implement all the recommendations made, without major capital investment, and it was at this time that money once again became a major problem, overshadowing many other important projects.

Meissner and Kippenberger in 1946.

(below) Los Angeles #3126 and Car Company staff. Kamman is second from the left, Elmer Wrausmann is on Kamman's right. Meissner is on the extreme right, and his son Bud Meissner is on his right.

Philadelphia Suburban Transport Co. #14 at 69th Street terminal. Philadelphia, in June 1949. The cars were fitted with radio telephones.

CHAPTER 23

By the end of 1948 the company was in as strong a financial position as it had ever been. Orders were coming in at an unprecedented rate, and there was still a two-year backlog of existing orders left to complete. Profits had been substantial since 1941, and with the resumption of normal loan repayments, the company was debt-free by 1948. Meissner, as sole owner, was thus presented with a new tax problem, not contemplated in the days before the debt was finally paid. A tax penalty existed for accumulating an overly large corporate surplus, and in order to legally avoid the payment of such a tax, which could conceivably cripple the company's cash flow at a critical time, it appeared that Meissner would be compelled to pay large dividends to the stockholders rather than plough the money back into the company. Since he was the major stockholder he would thus have equally as great a problem with his personal tax, as his company salary of $48,000 was by itself sufficient to put him in the highest income tax bracket.

In addition, there was the potential hazard of estate taxes. Meissner was no longer a young man, and while in the best of health could not deny his 64 years. He and his family owned 87% of the common stock of the company, which by then had a book value of $5 million. Of the family-owned 87% common stock, the bulk was personally owned by Meissner, representing the majority of his personal assets. The fear was that if he should die, his estate might well have to sell a large block of company stock in order to pay estate taxes, stock which could easily be acquired by a competitor only too willing to shut the plant down—an occurrence the Meissners desperately wanted to avoid.

At this critical juncture, an investment advisor suggested the possibility of selling the entire company at book value to Lafayette College, a small liberal arts school in eastern Pennsylvania. The college would pay for the stock out of the company's profits for a period of years, without having itself to put in any money. The College, being then the owner of the company, could turn over the remainder of the earnings as dividends to the stockholders (themselves) and use the money for whatever purposes they deemed fit. While Meissner would still have to pay capital gains tax on the money obtained from the sale of his company stock, this would represent a considerable saving on his tax liability should he have continued his sole ownership, and would protect the company from the risk of grave financial problems in the event of his death.

For the scheme to work as intended, it was imperative that the Meissners be kept in the company's service—Meissner senior as company president, and Bud Meissner as executive vice-president, to succeed to the presidency in the event of his father's death. This would ensure a continued attention to the affairs of the company by those most skilled in the business, and thus safeguard the College's investment.

The idea was presented to the trustees of Lafayette College and was rejected after some discussion. Although the plan presented the possibility of their eventually obtaining an endowment of over $5 million, the college trustees were skeptical as to its feasibility, being particularly concerned that the tax exemption they possessed as an educational institution made it unfair for them to control a business corporation.

Convinced that the College trustees would accept the proposal if they were better acquainted with its conditions, a meeting was arranged between them and the Meissners. The tax question was clarified when it was explained that the company would continue to pay corporate taxes, but that the after-tax profits would accrue to the college, and probably would be exempt from taxes, just as would dividends paid to the college on other securities already owned by them. This made better sense to the trustees, and the agreement between them and the Meissners, as it was eventually finalized in 1950, provided for the setting up of an independent group (known as the Marquis Foundation) to purchase the Car Company stock. The transaction was completed after some further disagreements, in the spring of 1951. Certain of the trustees remained dubious, however, regarding the company as a "bunch of junk" unable to produce any profits whatever in a market which had unexpectedly contracted in the two years since negotiations had begun. For the present, however, they were prepared to wait on events.[1]

Under the conditions of the agreement, the Marquis Foundation acquired most of the company's 100,000 shares, turning over to Meissner and others $1,200,000 in cash which it had borrowed commercially, and another $4,800,000 in promissory notes. Supervision of the company was left in the hands of the Meissners, and within two years, to the surprise of the skeptics, the college was able to repay its lender the original $1,200,000 loan entirely out of the company's earnings.

The one point in the entire transaction which continued to give the Meissners cause for concern was the possibility that the college might get impatient to realize some quick money, and sell the whole concern to one of the Car Company's competitors, thus putting the Meissners back in the situation they'd hoped to avoid, the risk of being closed down by a competitor. As long as the company produced substantial profits, however, which it did for many years after the consummation of the agreement, this threat was minimal.

The company profits in the years 1950-1954 were as much due to the success of the lightweight rapid transit cars as they were to the final years of PCC streetcar and trolleycoach production. The first order for a lightweight rapid transit vehicle had come from Chicago in 1944, and called for a three-car articulated lightweight unit, constructed of aluminum. Four such sets were required, of which St. Louis Car Co. built two, although wartime delays prevented their being shipped until 1947. The cars were fitted with the company's new B3 PCC truck, especially designed for such applications. Their success prompted Chicago, desperate to replace its nearly 50-year-old fleet, to order large quantities of lightweight vehicles for the elevated and subway lines. The Meissners were very pleased by this development.

> We viewed this as an exciting opportunity. . . . We (were) the dominant PCC streetcar builder in the country, and PCC cars were going . . . out. We saw a dynamic growth potential in rapid transit cars of the lightweight variety . . .[2]

The company worked closely with the Chicago Transit Authority to formulate a design for the new cars, and it was agreed that PCC car technology would be utilized. The design evolved incorporated many of the standard PCC car body features and thus was easily adaptable to existing construction procedures and production lines in the company plant, while being totally new and different in dimension and overall appearance. The use of aluminum was not continued owing to production difficulties.[3]

The successful development of this design, suitable for mass production, led to the placing of large-scale orders from Chicago, beginning in 1949, for non-articulated lightweight PCC rapid transit cars, the first 200 to be on St. Louis Car Co. B3 trucks. Thus was born a new and highly profitable market for the company, which became the major U.S. manufacturer of lightweight subway-elevated cars until 1960.

But lightweight cars of this type still utilized streetcar technology and construction methods, unlike the more conventional heavy subway car used in the eastern cities. Their construction was based on an engineering technology more closely related to that used in mainline railroad construction. These vehicles were heavy and very complex to build. The company was not yet prepared to penetrate that market, dominated as it was by the massive New York Transit Authority, who were an extremely demanding customer, as any manufacturer could ascertain by a glance at the Authority's "red book" of specifications. Although the Car Company had built wooden elevated cars in the past for Boston, and trailer cars for the IRT subway as recently as 1938, the "red book" had been a source of considerable apprehension to the staff for some years. It was felt that the fact that a special book had to be issued, automatically implied that an exceedingly complex subway car was required, far beyond their building expertise. Certainly the cars required by New York were more difficult and complex to construct than the vehicles the Car Company had previously made, at least on

One of two three-car sets of aluminum bodied PCC subway/ elevated cars for Chicago. These vehicles were first proposed in 1940, when car design for the new State Street subway was under discussion. Because of the war, the subway opened with old rolling stock providing service, and these cars were not delivered until 1947. They were fitted with resilient wheels and B3 trucks.

Articulation led to operating problems, and aluminum was difficult to work with. Consequently, the production models for Chicago were more orthodox single unit steel vehicles.

Completed Chicago subway/ elevated body shell in 1949.

a mass production basis. As it turned out, they were much less complex than another type of car which the company had eagerly sought to build—commuter cars for the electrified portion of the New York Central Railroad's suburban lines.

Meissner had first heard of the possibility of such cars being needed in 1948, and sensing an opportunity to break into yet another new market at the precise time when there appeared to be a decline in orders for streetcars and trolleybuses, he was exceedingly eager to build these cars, and took a calculated gamble when he entered the bidding. Initially the New York Central had made it known that only ten cars were definitely required, and probably no more than thirty overall. Kamman, in various informal contacts with New York Central personnel, managed to find out that the railroad company would eventually need 100 cars for the commuter services, and might be prepared to order them at one and the same time if the price were right. Armed with this information, Meissner bid a price based on the unit cost of manufacturing one hundred vehicles, rather than ten. He was understandably nervous when he left for New York, for despite long experience in making transit bids, he was not used to dealing with one of the country's largest railroads.

> I remember my father left St. Louis with a certain price, and when he got to New York . . . he got cold feet, and the night before the bid, he reduced the bid . . . a few thousand dollars per car, because he wanted that order real bad. . . . The next day they opened the bids and . . . we were about ten to fifteen thousand dollars a car lower, and he was kicking himself all over the lot! . . . One of our competitors, in a snide way, turned to him and said, "What's the matter, Ed, did you forget to put the trucks in your bid?" . . . But . . . despite the fact that the price was too low, and we left a lot of money on the table, we built those cars . . . well (and) they were on time . . .[4]

The cars were shipped during 1950 and 1951, and the experience gained with the successful execution of so complicated a design reopened the question of participating in New York subway car construction. The consensus finally arrived at was that if they could build the New York Central cars without difficulty, the New York subway cars could hardly be any more difficult to construct. It was decided to make a bid on the new R17 contract which was in the process of being drafted.

At this time the New York contracts were dominated by ACF and Pullman-Standard, and the delivery times quoted in the "red book" reflected the familiarity that these firms had in the setting up of a production line for this type of vehicle. The contract for the R17 specified that within 210 days of the signing, a sample car should be ready, and within 240 days, the first ten cars be ready for delivery. This, of course, was a very short time for St. Louis Car Co., who had yet to prepare the shop drawings and designs for the car. It was not so short for their competitors, who had already built similar cars and had shop designs and drawings for them. Preparation of shop drawings thus promised to be a major job for the Car Company's engineering department. In effect, they were starting with a blank sheet of paper, even though the New York Transit Authority had provided certain general arrangement drawings covering the basic specifications. It was obvious that there were not enough people available in the engineering department to get the job done in sufficient time to be within contracted delivery dates, and when the company was, to its surprise, awarded the R17 contract, for the first time in its history it became necessary to look for outside engineering help.

Every firm in the St. Louis, Chicago, Cleveland, and New York areas that purported to have engineering or drafting experience was consulted, and it became generally known that the company was in the market for such help. The most promising reply, however, came from a firm in Philadelphia, completely unknown to the Car Company. Because it did seem so promising it was decided to inspect this firm more closely before coming to a decision. What was seen was very impressive. The Yoh Company of Philadelphia had done some car building under sub-contract from both the Canadian Car Co. and the Budd Co. It was thus not new to the type of work St. Louis Car Co. required—a great advantage. Moreover, the jobbing work that had been done for Budd had been done

Chicago subway/elevated car #6201.

PCC subway elevated car for Boston. Car #0548 is undergoing a waterproofing test.

New York Central commuter car #4501 of 1951.

in Philadelphia, where the Budd Co. was also located. Consequently, the Yoh Company had on their list of available personnel, people who had worked for Budd in the past or on Budd car building contracts, and were completely familiar with the type of work required by the St. Louis Car Co. The Yoh Co. was prepared to assemble a team of such men and carry out the project under the supervision of St. Louis Car Co.'s chief draughtsman and his assistant. Under those terms it was decided to hire the Yoh Co. to prepare the necessary drawings for the R17 contract. As a result, the drawings were completed considerably faster than the four or five months that it probably would have taken the company's engineering department working on its own, and the cars were delivered on time.[5]

The R17 contract was signed in January, 1954, and came at an opportune moment for the company. While the lightweight PCC subway cars were selling well to Chicago and Cleveland, no orders for streetcars or trolleybuses had been received since 1951, and the large military orders which had provided continuing full-time work for the plant during the Korean war were no longer available in great quantities.

Postwar military work had commenced in 1949, with the conversion of mobile power stations (built under job 1742 in 1946) from 50 to 60 cycles AC. These units were to have been delivered to Russia as had the previous vehicles, but the beginning of the "Cold War" stopped deliveries and the cars had been stored until a new use had been found for them. The major work, however, was in the building of more amphibious Tracked Landing Vehicles, and the production of large numbers of ambulance and kitchen railroad cars for the army.

This last project had no direct connection with the Korean war. World War II hospital cars, while providing reasonable service, were not as sophisticated as those required for the proper care of patients being moved over long distances. The Army Medical Corps in 1950 had designed a new type of ambulance car for construction and use only when existing equipment had worn out. But the outbreak of the Korean war in mid-1950 made it necessary to ship to Korea every ambulance car

The last PCC cars to be built new in the USA. San Francisco #1018 in 1951.

San Francisco trolleybus #881 in 1951.

stored within the U.S.A., and the project for constructing the new type of ambulance car was given top priority. Designed by the Transportation Corps Research and Developing Station in conjunction with the Office of the Surgeon General, the new ambulance cars conformed to standards set for interchange service in the U.S.A., Canada, and Mexico. Sixty-three of these cars were ordered to replace the entire 63-car ambulance fleet which had been shipped to Korea, and which it was expected would not return. A further order for 89 kitchen cars was also received at this time.

Military production did not completely dominate the company's work during the Korean war as it had during World War II. Most of the work done between 1951 and 1954 was for main-line railroad companies, or for the Chicago Transit Authority. The main-line railway vehicles were largely caboose cars of a design which had been built for many years. The Chicago vehicles were the lightweight PCC subway/elevated cars which had been successfully introduced in 1949, but the contracts for the subsequent Chicago vehicles were somewhat different. Chicago had bought many hundreds of PCC streetcars between 1946 and 1948, from both St. Louis Car Co. and the Pullman-Standard Co. By 1951 it had decided gradually to replace its streetcar fleet with propane-fueled buses—thereby gaining the advantages of cheapness in operation that a bus could offer, as well as a pollution-free exhaust.

The Chicago Transit Authority was understandably reluctant to write off the millions of dollars already invested in their almost-new PCC car fleet, and it was decided experimentally to rebuild two of their PCC streetcars into a subway car of the general type delivered since 1949. Cars intended for conversion arrived at the St. Louis Car Co. and Pullman-Standard plants respectively, being experimentally rebuilt during 1952. St. Louis Car Co., however, received the contract for the complete job, and from 1953 to 1958 purchased practically all of Chicago's surviving PCC streetcars, salvaging trucks and electrical equipment. The streetcar bodies were scrapped and the salvaged material was incorporated in the new subway car bodies. Chicago Transit Authority officials had estimated that the converted vehicles cost them $20,000 a car less than a totally new car, enabling them to buy a new bus to replace the streetcar which had been so converted.

By 1954, the company had thus made the successful transition from a builder of streetcars and trolleybuses to an all-purpose rail-traction builder, largely specializing in electric vehicles. It had done so without incurring losses, and in most years had maintained the high level of profits which had characterized the artificial boom of the first few postwar years.

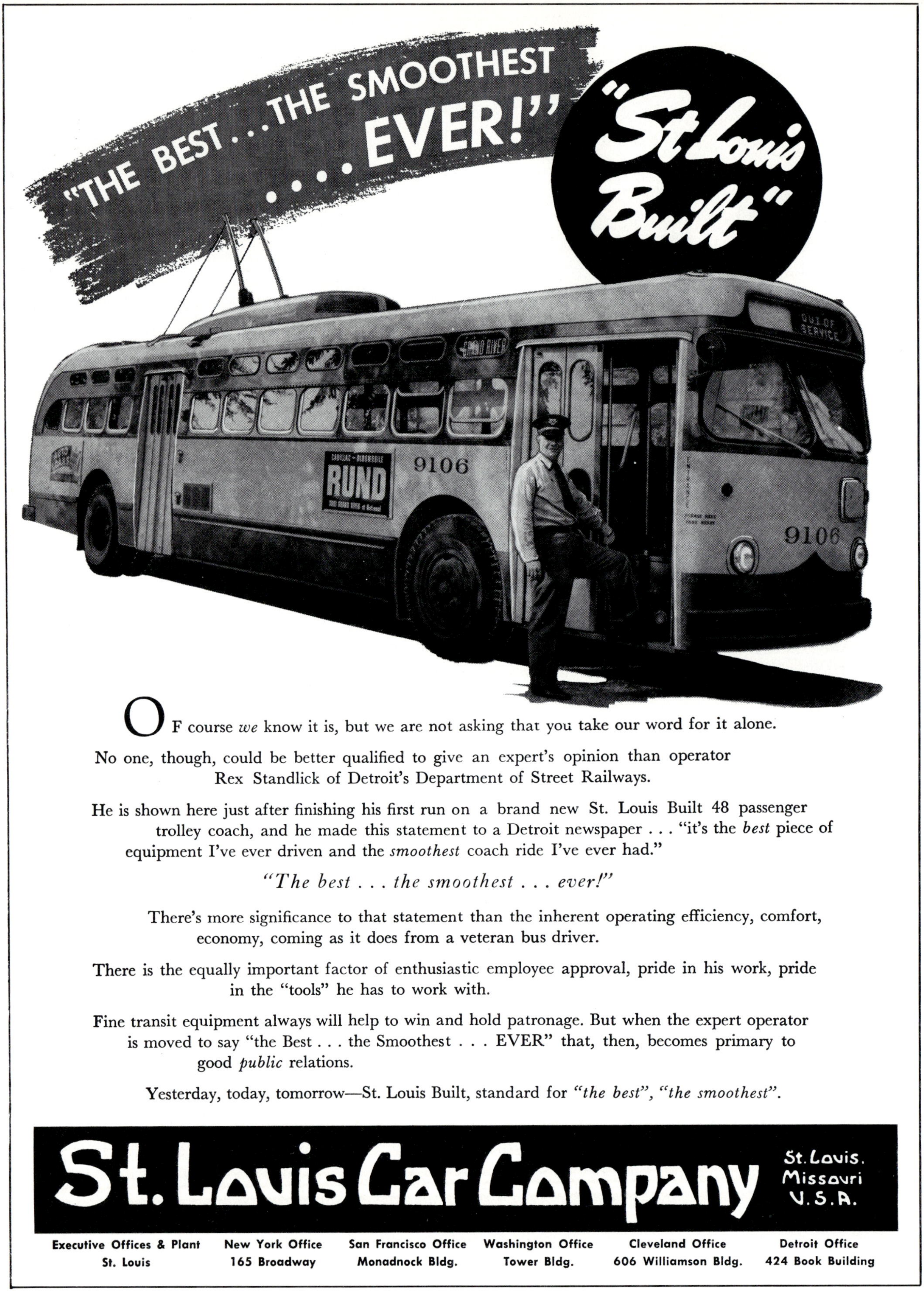

Advertisement for 48-seat trolleybuses, the largest ever built by the St. Louis Car Co. Eighty of these vehicles were sold to Detroit in 1950 on order 1765.

CHAPTER 24

A SIGNIFICANT YEAR for the Car Company was 1954. The first of the New York subway cars were finally under construction with prospects for other large orders in sight. An important order for lightweight PCC subway cars was in progress for the new Cleveland subway, and many hundreds of lightweight subway-elevated cars continued to be built for Chicago by "conversion" of PCC streetcars.

The transition from urban transit vehicle production to the building of subway and mainline railroad cars was made at a time when urban mass transit was well into its postwar decline, as commuting by private automobile to suburbs away from existing transit lines grew to be the dominant form of urban transportation. One of the results of this decline was the marked reduction in the number of new orders received at the Car Company. These orders were largely confined to subway, railway and military vehicles. But the size of the orders and their complexity more than compensated for the contraction of the market. Individual orders frequently were for quantities in excess of 200 units at a time, and while the company would be tooling up for production in the six to nine months that generally elapsed between the signing of a contract and the roll-out of the first completed vehicle, more orders for similar vehicles would be received.

This enabled the Car Company for the first time fully to take advantage of the production line facilities which it had possessed since 1936. In the fifties, the lines were constantly working with large numbers of standardized cars, something that the company had not been able to achieve in the best days of PCC car production. Even the placing of only three new orders in a year, as occurred in 1955, was sufficient guarantee of enough full-time work for a further year.

Not only were new orders more complex to build than in the past, but the time taken to develop new designs to production stage also began to increase during this period.

Elmer Wrausmann, Vice President of Sales, had for many years delivered papers to the various Transit Industry Associations on the subject of developing new car designs. On April 19, 1955, he delivered to a meeting of the Car Department Association of St. Louis one such paper dealing with new passenger car development at St. Louis Car Co. during the mid-1950s. In this paper he used as an example an order of double-deck passenger cars for the Chicago and North Western Railroad, just completed by the Car Company.

> Among the objectives was one to secure the utmost seating capacity without sacrificing comfort . . . and without lengthening the car beyond 85′ (to) have wide center door openings . . . and at the same time provide toilet room and ample space for luggage, parcels, coats and hats. The result is a car having the greatest passenger capacity of any railroad car in the country—169 passengers seated. But to do this, it was necessary to brush aside many previous practices . . .[1]

Mock-ups of the car were built, sample seats were constructed, and studies were made to check dimensions, clearances and appearance. Changes were made in the mock-ups and re-examined until finally the finished design evolved. This was a time-consuming process.

> These goals were accomplished co-operatively through . . . conferences with the railroad's mechanical officials, equipment and specialty suppliers' representatives . . . and evaluation of previous experience with similar projects. Layouts and calculations were made, studied, discussed and revised. . . . Skilled shop personnel (were) . . . consulted. What seemed to be good ideas were sometimes, as a result of these procedures, judged to be found wanting and discarded, or considerably revised.[2]

As each order became more complex, so design evolution became a long drawn out cooperative process between the company and the customer, and the length of time which the process took continued to further increase over the next few years.

> Conditions are entirely different in various parts of our vast country . . . and we have different classes of service—suburban and commuter service, comparatively short runs between major cities, service for the industrial and commercial sections of the nation, and cross-country travel, where comfort and scenic views are an important attraction, all of which makes it necessary . . . to design and develop equipment tailored for the particular service for which it is intended.[3]

This had always been St. Louis Car Co.'s particular strength, its ability to function as a quality manufacturer of custom-built rail passenger vehicles. In the past, however, its design skills had been limited to the electric urban transit vehicle. Now it seemed as if a new era was about to open with this successful large-scale entry into the main-line railroad passenger equipment market.

Unfortunately, now that the control of the company's finances was out of Meissner's hands, there was no guarantee that the Lafayette College deal would not go sour, whether the company was profitable or not. In dealing with the College trustees and the officials of the Marquis Foundation, there was always the chance that personnel changes or political upheaval among those who constituted or controlled those bodies might upset the arrangement, even though financially the college would lose.

In 1955, this did start to happen, and the scheme began to founder. The original plan had been that after thirteen years, the College would have paid off its loan on the purchase price for the Meissner shares, and then would be able to enjoy sole control of the company profits. Since 1948 these had been averaging in excess of $400,000 a year. The college, however, became impatient to realize a more immediate profit, and the Meissners became very worried.

> Some of these guys got the bright idea that they could cash in on their great investment and one of them got a deal going through a New York broker called Kauffman (for a customer) to buy the company from the college. The way the numbers worked out, the college would have about $2 million. This was kind of a dumb deal because we had enough orders on the books, and profits in hand or in sight that we'd have made $2 million that year which the college would have received in earnings.[4]

The customer the College had in mind was one with a reputation as a company liquidator, and naturally the Meissners were not prepared to see the company closed down for no good reason. They managed over a long period of time to talk the College out of the transaction, and made a further arrangement with the College that in the future there would be no negotiating for sale without the company's knowledge. If the College were inclined to sell at some point in the future, they should talk to the Meissners first, on the assumption that they, as managers, working with the College as owners, could make a better deal than any one of them working alone. In addition, the Marquis trustees were reminded that the original agreement provided that if the college received an offer that it was inclined to accept, the Meissners would have a 30 day period in which to meet it. After that time, the Marquis Foundation's directors would be free to proceed. With that, the matter was settled for the time being.

Unfortunately, these dealings on the part of the Marquis Foundation were probably a contributing factor in the sudden decline of Meissner's health. Now aged 71, it was hardly surprising, though no less tragic, that this new, and from the Meissners' point of view, totally unnecessary threat to the company's continued existence, should have taken its toll on him. There is no doubt that whatever the medical cause of the decline in his health in 1956, it was greatly aggravated by the stress and worry caused by the action of the Lafayette trustees. The old cliché suggests there is no room for sentiment in business, and while in this instance it is obvious the Lafayette action was not sound, their fundamental attitude to the company was indeed businesslike and unsentimental: it was a tool to get them badly needed money for new facilities, and as a tool could be discarded once that object had been achieved. To Meissner the company was more than a tool with which to earn money. It was not simply that the continued ownership and control of the company gave him a powerful financial and social springboard inside and outside his community. His son years later went to the heart of the matter.

> I was born and raised in an era where the concept of a father building up a business and passing it on from son to son was still the desire of most . . . people who owned their own businesses. That was their main goal in life, to be able to create something and pass it on to the next generation . . .[5]

That is exactly what Meissner had done, and thus the struggle with Lafayette over the continued existence of the company was more than just a simple wrangle over an unnecessary sale and potential liquidation. It was the clash of two incompatible business philosophies, two irreconcilable attitudes as to the real purpose of the company. More than that, for Meissner it was akin to a judgment on his life in business, which a collection of strangers apparently was prepared to dismiss as meaningless. The struggle to justify a philosophy which had motivated him since at least 1911, undertaken at an age when most men can afford to sit back and review their lives in tranquility and satisfaction, was not one calculated to aid an individual already declining in health. Though the sale was averted, and Meissner continued to work as before, travelling around the country in his usual fashion, it was not long before he became ill and was taken to a hospital. Cancer was found, and though he fought valiantly to get back to his desk at the company, he died on September 9, 1956 within a few weeks of the diagnosis.

The late 1950s were exceedingly busy years, and the engineering department staff was constantly at work.

Gallery commuter car for the Chicago & Northwestern Railroad under construction in 1954.

CHAPTER 25

While the loss of the company's driving force was a major calamity, the company was fortunate that no crucial problems needed attention during the critical period of readjustment. Though Meissner's physical presence was badly missed, there was little outward change in the company's organization or business philosophy, and Bud Meissner quietly took his father's place.

Little new business was done for a period. The uncertainty of the last year together with Meissner's subsequent illness and death had meant that few orders had been actively solicited. While the company was as busy as ever, substantial new orders were for a time sadly lacking; indeed, not since the Depression had so few been forthcoming. Fortunately the three orders received in 1955 and the two received in 1956 were extremely large, in a couple of instances being repeat orders of vehicles previously ordered but only now being constructed. Thus volume remained high, while tooling and production costs were relatively low.

This continued to be the pattern of the business throughout the remainder of the 1950s. Huge and complex orders were received from New York, many hundreds of lightweight subway/elevated cars continued to be required by Chicago, and smaller orders were received from many mainline railroad companies. There was also the occasional substantial military order. Production problems and delays, while not crippling, ensured that some orders, placed in 1953, were not totally completed until 1957, so that finding new work was not as great a matter of urgency as it had been in the days when it took only three months between the ordering and delivery of a streetcar contract.

By 1957 more New York and Chicago cars were required, together with smaller quantities for Cleveland, and the Car Company, for whom these were repeat orders was naturally the lowest bidder. Further lightweight cars were required for Boston, but though the company made a bid, that job went to Pullman.

In 1957, Kamman was sent on an extensive European trip. It was felt that transit vehicle development had ceased in the U.S.A. while the Europeans were continuing to evolve new designs and building techniques. He saw all-aluminum cars in London and rubber-tired subway cars in Paris, where he also talked with a car manufacturer to start preliminary negotiations for a U.S. building license. He went to Linkoping in Sweden to inspect a modern car building plant, and to Germany to see the Wuppertal and Alweg monorails. On the basis of his findings and recommendations, it was hoped the company would find new designs and manufacturing techniques with which to augment its existing range of products.

But just as the company was ready to make a concerted effort to find more new business, the Lafayette issue once more became a problem. In October of 1957, the question of sale was once again raised.

> I went to a board meeting in October . . . 1957 . . . at the Astor Hotel in New York. . . . I could tell they weren't very much interested in my report and finally we got to the end of the session and they asked me if I'd ever heard of Henry Crown. . . . They said he'd made an offer to buy St. Louis Car Co. which they were inclined to accept, and I subsequently found out that under this deal, we'd paid off enough of the loans, and the price was up somewhat (so that this time) they would have netted not just \$2 million but \$6 million.[1]

Henry Crown was the head of Material Services Corporation, a large company with interests in Puerto Rican sugar and other enterprises. Bud Meissner decided to see him. The interview, while pleasant enough, did not quell his unease. Although Crown praised the working of the St. Louis Car Co., he continually mentioned the names of many men known to be financially involved with St. Louis Car Co.'s competitors and Meissner began to gain the impression that Crown was being used by those competitors to purchase the company from the College, only to resell to others, or

R17 car #6771 at Grand Central Station, 1954.

New York subway cars had a severely functional interior.

New subway cars for the Hudson-Manhattan tubes, New York in 1959.

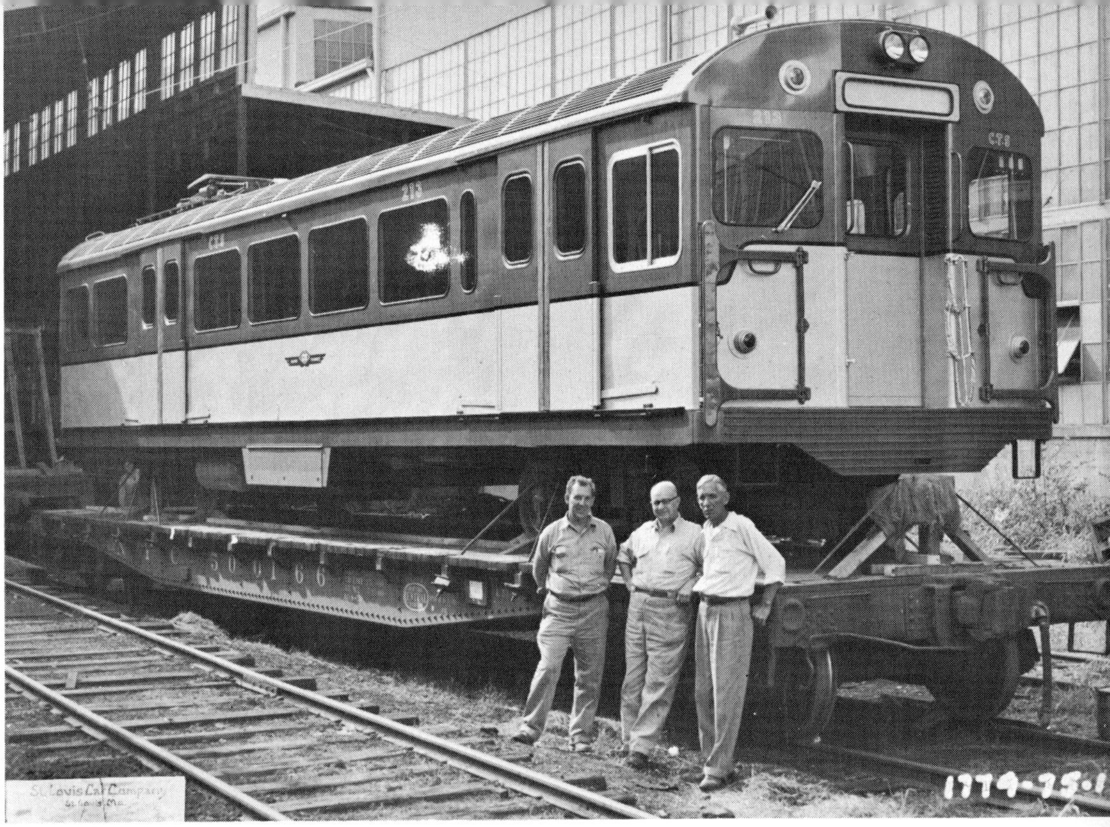

Lightweight subway car for Cleveland, 1954.

The transfer of used PCC cars to othe systems was very common in th 1950s, and as a result, the Car Com pany was deprived of much useful extra revenue which should have arisen from continued new PCC car construction. Here is Detroit #197 of 1949, after a rebuild and repaint job in Detroit. It is seen as Mexico City #2197 in Detroit, just prior to its sale from that city to Mexico City, on May 25, 1956. *(Richard F. Glaze)*

The last Chicago lightweight PCC subway/elevated cars were built in 1960. Car #2 is one of four experimental high-speed cars, painted in a special livery.

An early train of Wolfwagons for Mobil Oil Corp. in 1959.

Ten Wolfwagons under construction in 1960.

A complete Wolfwagon for Swift in 1961.

liquidate it himself at a handsome profit. This would put the Car Company in the very situation it had been hoping to avoid when the Lafayette deal was first considered.

While the suggestion has never been proven, nor indeed is it known if there is any truth to it, it was a sufficiently worrisome possibility to persuade Bud Meissner to exercise his option to purchase the company back from the College within 30 days. Unfortunately, to buy back the company would re-open the question of Meissner's estate taxes, and in any event, the money was not available from within the Meissner family to do such a thing. The next month therefore was spent in a frantic search to find a possible purchaser. These were busy days, involving many negotiations with potential buyers. One deal was finalized, but the buyers then defaulted before closing. However by the beginning of 1958, another interested buyer was found. Clint Murchison was an oldtime Texas oil man, looking for new investments. He was willing to buy the company from the College, and Bud Meissner assigned his buying rights to him. On January 31st, 1958, an agreement was signed, purchasing the Marquis Foundation's stock for $5,600,000 in cash, and $3 million in interest-bearing notes. Although liquidation was thereby avoided, it was not a great improvement for Murchison played havoc with the Car Company's balance sheet. Meissner recalled how "Shorty" Burch, one of Murchison's associates:

> called me up one day and wanted to know how much surplus cash we had. . . . I said I thought we had $1½ million we could spare (but) I reminded him . . . to be prepared to put this back because . . . (there was) another New York job coming up and we needed it for working capital. (But) after receiving my call (he) declared a $6 million dividend and (thus) pulled $6 million right out of the company. (He) did other things . . . we invested in oil and gas leases out in the west . . . and owned gold bullion in some place . . . and guaranteed other companies' obligations, but when we got ready for the next New York order we didn't have any money to run it on and I wasn't going to sign that bid until I knew how we were going to finance it. . . . (He) said, "Don't worry, the banks will take care of it," except that the banks didn't choose to at that point. . . . I was running around banks (in Texas and in Chicago) trying to get a loan to run the company on and about that time Charlie Whitehead, President of General Steel Castings Corporation . . . called me in and asked me if I thought (Murchison) would sell . . . (the Car Company) . . . to GSC.[2]

In this way the St. Louis Car Co. became a division of General Steel Castings Corporation in June of 1960.

Head end of a New York subway car.

New passenger cars for the Union Pacific, built in 1959.

Rail post office car for the Spokane, Portland & Seattle, built in 1960.

CHAPTER 26

General Steel Castings Corporation was an old established St. Louis area company. It was a major producer of steel castings and for many years had supplied cast steel trucks to St. Louis Car Co. In the 1930s it had acquired the Commonwealth Steel Castings plant of Granite City, Illinois, another major producer of trucks for electric railway and streetcar manufacturers. From every point of view, it made considerable sense that at this juncture some kind of merger between the two companies should occur. Practically all of St. Louis Car Co.'s truck production had for years been sub-contracted to GSC for casting, and while St. Louis Car Co. was one of GSC's better customers, GSC had immediate access to greater funds than had the Car Company. In addition, there was considerable advantage in having effective financial control of the company return to the St. Louis area.

For the first few years little overt change occurred in the Car Company as a result of the merger. Bud Meissner, while appointed a vice-president and director of General Steel, remained in full charge of the Car Company, and his staff and the operating policies of the company (now technically known as the St. Louis Car Division of General Steel Industries) were largely unchanged. Those changes that were made were of a subtle nature.

> I was born and raised to buy nothing but second-hand machinery, but they quickly let me know that at General Steel, they didn't buy second-hand machinery, (and therefore) . . . I should go out, spend money and buy new machinery. So we did. We had money to spend that we (never had) before . . .[1]

One of the greatest advantages of the merger from the Car Company's point of view, was that of having immediate access to a number of experienced younger men, through transfer from GSI into the Car Division. This meant that the maintenance of long term senior staff continuity, the element so highly praised in the 1948 report, could continue largely as before and thus give the division the best chance of operating as effectively as it had done in the past. In addition, the new money available as a result of the merger meant that for the first time in its existence, St. Louis Car Co. could afford the services of an industrial design firm. The company selected was the Michigan firm of Sundberg-Ferar.

The new approach was best expressed in a speech used throughout the mid-1960s by St. Louis Car Co. executives at design presentations:

> We believe in a team approach, combining the manufacturing experience and capabilities of St. Louis Car, with the artistic qualifications and practical design skills of one of the nation's industrial design firms. . . . Affiliation with General Steel has added great strength and breadth to St. Louis Car's resources. Our physical facilities have been greatly improved, engineering capability . . . is at a new high and one of the country's most modern metallurgical and physical laboratories is used extensively by the St. Louis Car Division.[2]

Some of the improvements made as a result of the merger were long overdue.

> We had no pension plan at St. Louis Car until GSI acquired us (even though) we as a group were getting older. We went down the list of (our) executives, and only three of us (qualified) under the plan, because (that's all who were) under 60. . . . Every other top executive was too old and would have to be pensioned separately.[3]

Orders now began to increase as new railroad customers began to re-equip their passenger and mail coach fleets. St. Louis Car Co. in the period 1960-1964 built nearly 200 full-size passenger coaches, messenger express cars and postal cars, as well as over 1700 New York subway cars under contracts R 27, R 29, R 30, R 30A, R 33, and R 36. Other orders from this period included cars to completely re-equip the Hudson-Manhattan subway of the Pennsylvania Railroad; fifty cars had been delivered as recently as 1959, but with the

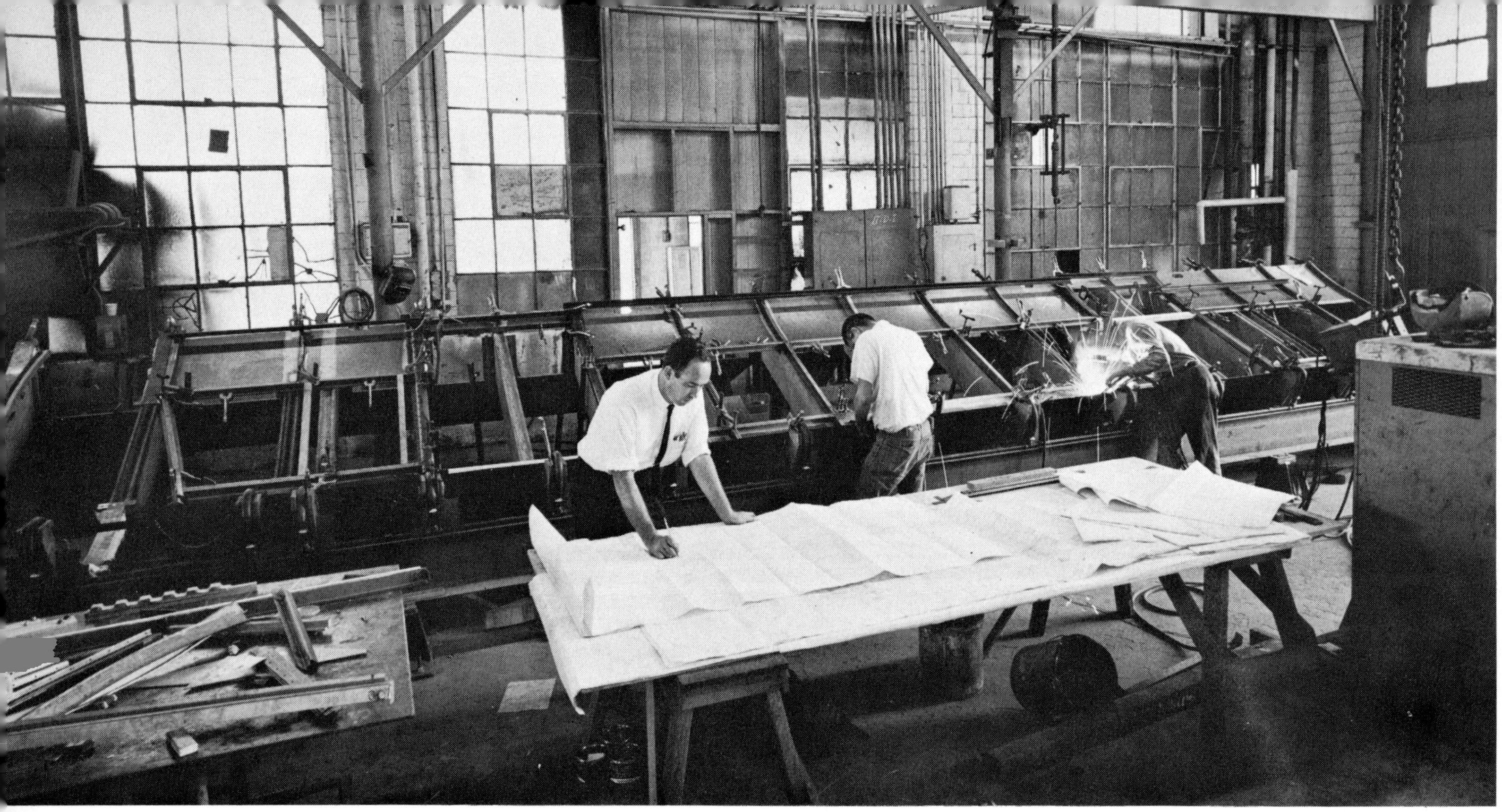

Constructing the underframe of a monorail car, 1963.

Monorail cars in service at the New York World's Fair in 1964.

Union Pacific box car, built in 1964.

Bud Meissner and PATH's director of rail transportation at a formal car handover ceremony, March 29, 1965. The two men are standing on the platform of a 1909 car. The new cars are on the right. *(PATH)*

Westinghouse skybus car in Grant Park, Pittsburgh in 1965.

takeover of the tubes by the Port Authority of New York's Trans-Hudson division (PATH) new rolling stock was immediately required, and the Car Company eventually received an order for 162 cars and a repeat order for another 44 cars.

New projects began to be investigated once again. One of the more interesting was the Wolfwagon concept. This had its origins in 1957 when Bud Meissner had been put in touch with a Texas designer who had an idea for the operation of heavy trucks. The idea was to operate these trucks in coupled trains along the new interstate highways then being built. Each train of trucks would be controlled by one driver. At the point where the trucks would split to go to their separate destinations, the train of trucks would be broken up, and individual drivers would take over their own truck. It was an idea which had promise, and the St. Louis Car Co. took it up. In four years over 50 of the vehicles were sold to a number of customers, but while the idea was good, and the vehicles of high quality, the savings available by running the vehicles in trains were exceeded by the costs of keeping extra drivers at the transfer points. Moreover, most shippers had less than truckload consignments and this could also lead to difficulties. However, the project was modestly profitable.

The company also started building mainline railway freight cars in quantity for customers such as Union Pacific and the Illinois Terminal Railroad. This was not always good for the company's production standards, particularly when doing the rough work considered adequate in building freight cars. There were always problems of quality control when a run of freight cars had been completed and the shop staff switched back to building passenger vehicles.

Perhaps the company's most exotic venture was the building of monorail cars. To the end of its life the company could claim to be the only commercial manufacturer of monorail cars in the United States. Some time after the end of the war an attempt was made to get a bill through the California State Legislature that would create a California monorail authority, primarily to construct monorails in the Los Angeles area.

> (My father) . . . was . . . a real pioneer . . . He wanted to build the first of everything . . . and we worked very closely with Ralph Merritt (the promoter of the LA monorail) on the expectation that if he succeeded we would be the car builder . . . or at least compete for the business. . . . We did a lot of work . . . Bill Kamman went to Europe to look at Wuppertal, and we loaned Bill Wheeler to an engineering firm and he went over to see the Alweg. . . . These were the only two places in the world where you could see a monorail, and we were really pointing to the Los Angeles order.[4]

Monorails were not new to America, although their use had been limited primarily to industrial and exhibition purposes. Patents can be found as far back as the 1860s. Actual examples included the passenger monorail built in 1876 by General Roy Stone for the Philadelphia Centennial Exposition, and a passenger monorail, opened in 1880 between Brooklyn and Coney Island. But by 1959 when the design and plans for the Seattle World Fair were beginning to take shape, the monorail was considered to be an outlandish new form of transport, and the proposal to build one for Seattle was seriously taken up only by St. Louis Car Co., Lockheed and Alweg, a German company. Many trips were made to Seattle by Bud Meissner, Bill Kamman and Bill Wheeler. A proposal was made by the company to Seattle, based on the knowledge that the Seattle transit system had a surplus of some $5 million with which it intended to pay for the cars. A design was worked out, based on the successful Wuppertal monorail which had been operating since 1901. The proposed design was to be a suspended monorail. This type of design gives added stability and eliminates the problem of having guide rails or gyroscopes to maintain the balance of the car. The only disadvantage is that it makes passenger exit and entry slightly more difficult. The proposed Seattle design was for a 6 car unit capable of carrying 15,000 passengers per hour, of aluminum construction and with four 100hp electric motors to move each 20-ton car. PCC technology was to be borrowed for the control mechanisms and the resilient steel wheels.

This was an installation whose basic premise was that Seattle had a need for such transportation facilities after the fair closed. Using materials and technology already widely applied in urban transport, it was an entirely feasible concept.

> . . . (But) then (Seattle) got the bright idea that this was going to be a great privilege for the manufacturer to build these cars and that instead of getting paid for them, we should build them . . . install them and get paid . . . on a . . . percentage of what people paid to go to the fair, regardless of whether they rode the monorail or not. . . . They had two estimates . . . widely separated as to how many millions of visitors they were going to get at the fair . . . (but) I figured there just weren't going to be that many people. . . . I was 100% wrong because it was one of the most successful fairs they ever had . . . But I couldn't see us building $4.8 million (of equipment) because . . . we didn't have the money . . . and if we had been able to finance it, I didn't see how you could do that on the basis of 25¢ a head. . . . Lockheed was announced as the successful bidder . . . and then they backed out and Alweg finally took the order on the terms we were unwilling to accept. Another provision of the contract was that after the fair was over (one) had to dismantle it and I remember we had $½ million in costs in (an estimate) for taking the thing away. . . .Alweg . . . got all their money back, and then got out from under the dismantling costs by donating it to the city. . . . Alweg had spent over $15,000,000 of their own money (up to that time) trying to develop a monorail, and had absolutely nothing to show for it except a test track. . . . So for them to put another $4 or $5 million in it to get something to show the world, made a better investment for them than for us . . .[5]

Despite their failure at Seattle, the company successfully contracted to build the cars for the AMF Co.'s monorail at the 1964-1965 New York World's Fair. The $3 million unit conformed closely to St. Louis Car Co.'s Seattle design and was supported on columns at a height of 45 feet. There were fourteen cars, and it was considered at the time to be the safest mass transit system in the U.S.A. Originally AMF was considering other ideas for their World's Fair exhibit, but had not worked them out sufficiently well. On the spur of the moment (or so it seemed to the Car Company) AMF proposed a monorail, and the Car Company had jumped at the chance to build it. Regrettably no further monorail orders were received, and the AMF monorail remained a curiosity.

Another new transit system with potential was being developed at this time by the Westinghouse Co., and St. Louis Car Co. was very willing to be involved with it. The concept of the system was that of a "people-moving" device, designed to meet the needs of large metropolitan areas that did not have the massive passenger flows of the very largest of cities. A subway train of between 8 and 10 cars could move between 30 and 40 thousand passengers an hour, but a bus only between 8 and 10 thousand an hour. Westinghouse was trying to find something other than the trolley or light rail rapid transit that would be suitable for metropolitan areas where perhaps 15 to 20 thousand people an hour had to be moved. An experimental line was erected in Grant Park, Pittsburgh, in 1965 and the Car Company received an order for three car bodies to run on rubber tires on a supported concrete track. A further order was received in 1969 for cars to be used on a system at Tampa airport.

Another interesting design project to come out of the late 1960s was the Vert-A-Pac freight car. The Vert-A-Pac was a method of carrying automobiles inside a covered freight car in a vertical position, thus protecting the automobiles from the vagaries of wind and weather to which they would be exposed in a normal rail transporter. The order was received on sub-contract from ACF industries. Unfortunately the rail vehicle produced was of excessive height, and as the cars they were to carry were the sub-compact Ford Pinto, it was obvious that the project would not be wholly successful in carrying full-size, or even compact automobiles. Moreover, although the actual vehicles performed very well, the additional expense of these freight cars over the normal rail transporter was considerable, and thus only a little more than 180 Vert-A-Pac cars were built by the St. Louis Car Division.

The company was always eager to follow customer trends. Lightweight stainless steel cars became fashionable in the 1960s, and GSI together with the Car Company decided to enter the market. New, specially designed fabrication and assembly equipment for stainless steel cars was installed at the Baden plant, but though some orders were received, the company lost a considerable amount of money on the project owing to lack of expertise and heavy tooling costs. The market was not as great as had been hoped, and it soon proved impossible to compete with other manufacturers.

The biggest and initially the most exciting of the trends in the 1960s was the promise of renewed large scale urban transit vehicle buying. This came about as a result of the establishment of a scheme for federal funding of mass transportation projects. Under the Urban Mass Transportation Act of 1964, Federal funds were for the first time made available to purchase capital equipment and facilities used in urban mass transit service. In most cases, the Federal share of the grant was two-thirds, and local matching funds accounted for the remaining one-third. The old system of purchasing new equipment out of revenue, or by means of a bond issue, or through commercial loans, was no longer available as most transit companies after World War II were regarded as commercially risky. Yet it was felt that the age and the inefficiency of existing transit equipment was a negative factor in the cities in which they ran; one more element in the complexity of factors which accounted for an urban decline whose inexorable progression had become clear by the 1960s. The new pattern of city development, as it was evolving, was of a declining hard-core compact center region and a thin wave of population in widely dispersed municipally independent suburbs. Not even bus transportation could effectively serve such a population distribution and the automobile became the only conceivable practical transport mode for the suburbs. Transit had declined in quality of service, equipment purchase became minimal as more companies became uncreditworthy, and those who continued to rely exclusively on public transport were the poor, the elderly and the disabled, thus further adding to the decline in public transit's image. In the meantime, vast sums were being spent on highway construction to enable those with automobiles better to reach the city center, or the newer suburbs. While most city centers continued to function normally, an ever-increasing number of cities were suffering from chronic urban blight in their inner suburbs. As property declined in value, so city tax bases eroded, and the visual and noise problems new highway construction brought to these already derelict areas was one more element in the inevitable process of decay. Inner suburbs had to be re-established if the city was not to be totally deserted, and it was felt that the most effective way of stemming the decline, and re-establishing those suburbs was to provide better public transit systems and facilities. As it was obviously impossible to justify such investment on purely commercial grounds, and as it was equally obvious that the continuation of public transit was vital if total city collapse were to be avoided, the system of federal funding was devised.

Much experimental work was done in the 1960s in the devising of new transit modes, from "people moving" concepts such as Westinghouse's "skybus" (in which the Car Company was deeply involved) to "dial-a-bus" and "personal rapid transit." Of more immediate concern was the funding of existing systems to permit them to be modernized and expanded, and the provision of money for new high quality, high speed big city subway systems to divert the automobile commuters off the roads, eliminating the need to build more costly highways and tearing up more suburbs. This has not yet been proven a successful strategy. Of the four new subway systems funded in this way (two of which were already planned and building before the Act was passed) only BART of San Francisco, and WMATA of Washington D.C. had opened their systems by July 1977, and then on only a fraction of the lines originally planned with service intensity far less than anticipated. Neither system came in time to prevent highway building in the cities they serve, nor do they appear to offer the once hoped for alternative to highway commuting.

This was recognized at the beginning of the 1970s when an attempt was made to revive the streetcar as a transit mode, a mode which may yet prove to be the least costly high speed rail alternative to commuting by automoble. Private rights of way and tunnels of course will have to

Cable-hauled capsules for the Planet Corp., used in the St. Louis Gateway Arch's transportation system. The units were installed during 1966 and 1967.

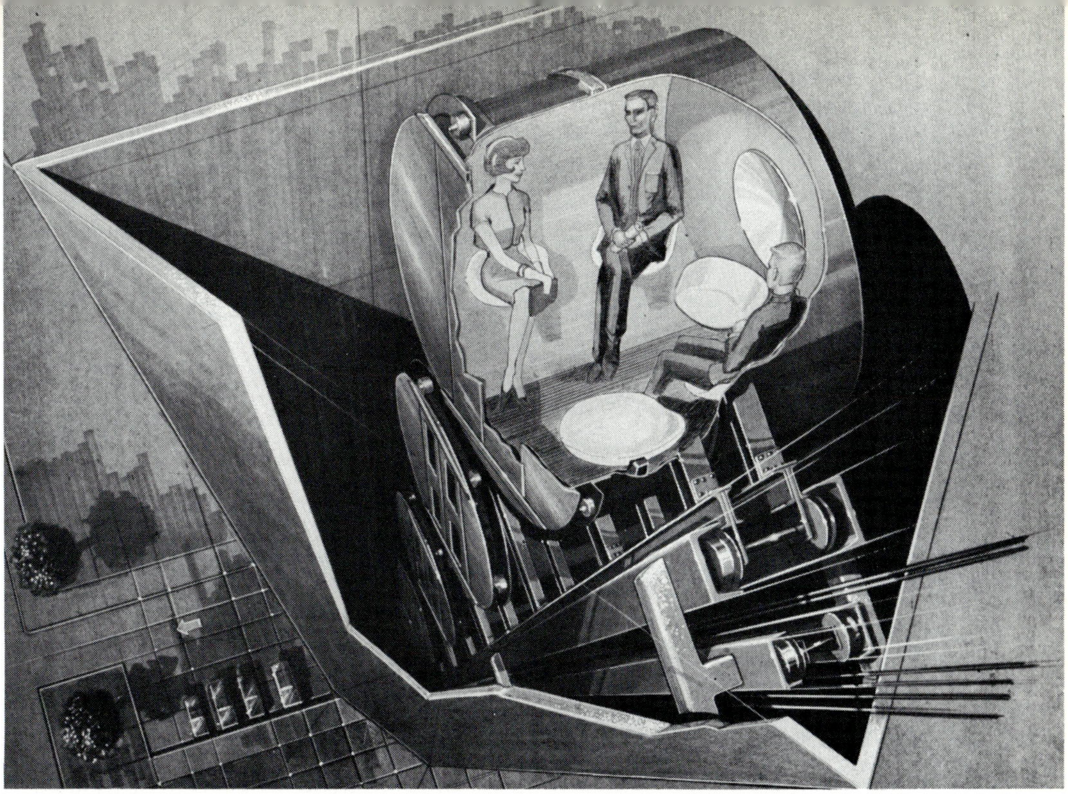

be constructed, and it is all the more ironic that so many of the streetcar systems abandoned in the 1950s and 1960s had exactly those features. Those that survive also possess them, and indeed these features largely account for their continued survival.

Another city problem was the lack of overall municipal taxing power in the fragmented suburban areas. With the decline of the city, the continued municipal independence of the suburbs became highly valued. Typically, each suburb feared that if any metropolitan-wide plan for traffic management or construction were introduced, it would have to pay more than it would receive in benefits, and as all these plans were to help the central city rather than the suburbs, such authorities would typically take the position that the city should look after its own problems and "not bother" them. This unwillingness to take effective concerted local action was yet another reason for Federal involvement at a time when in fact there was no overall Federal transport policy, except that expressed in the Act itself. Essentially the Act was expected to help revitalize the cities, and restore property values (thus making cities self-supporting from their own tax bases) by the provision of long-term Federal aid to urban regions to be spent in modernizing and expanding mass transit systems rather than highways.

Almost immediately after passage of the Act, money became available to mass transit operators, and new vehicles were once again a possibility on urban systems. At the same time, as noted previously, the prospect of Federal financing stimulated the birth or revival of many subway transit schemes for cities previously minus such facilities.

The provision of Federal money thus had a twofold impact on the potential market for new transit vehicles. Existing operators had, for the first time in years, money to make new purchases, while the Federal money at the same time encouraged the creation of new Regional Transit Authorities with sweeping powers to rationalize and coordinate all modes of transit in their area. Unfortunately, the majority of transit operators were by this time committed to transit modes in which the Car Company had no commercial interest, and therefore the Act had limited impact on their sales. Some contracts were of course placed with the help of money provided by the Act, but they were relatively few in number. Thus when BART found itself with money to spend, and a desire to advance the state of the rapid transit art in the designs for its new subway cars, the Car Company was eager to participate in the preliminary design work, in co-operation with Sundberg-Ferar, the industrial design firm retained by the Car Company. The passing of the Act, and BART's

Models used by the Car Company and Sundberg-Ferar in the BART proposals.

BART mock-up, 1965.

eagerness to buy many hundreds of subway cars, created a climate that seemingly promised a subway car market far greater in size than ever before, and the Car Company courted the new authority assiduously.

The development of the PATH car in the early 1960s had been a useful foretaste of what was hoped could be expected from these new bodies in encouraging originality of design. The designing of the PATH car had been organized as a public competition, and it was in this kind of situation that the new strengths the merger with GSI had made available to the Car Company showed to greatest advantage. Being able now to hire design consultants, real innovations in subway vehicle body design and styling could be initiated by the company, rather than by the company's customers, an important extra "edge" in this highly competitive but still restricted market.

> We are very much aware of the fact that the success or failure of rail rapid transit and commuter service will largely depend on their acceptance and use by the public. Our experience in passenger-oriented design proves to us that aesthetic excellence and emphasis on passenger comfort are of the first order of magnitude in establishing successful rail transportation . . . With Sundberg-Ferar's assistance, we have made many . . . design studies . . . for rapid transit equipment . . .(and) for railroad commuter equipment. The experience thus gained in working together culminated . . . in the award to St. Louis Car of a contract for 162 transit cars for the Port Authority of New York's Trans-Hudson lines. . . . In competition against three other car builders, including a foreign builder, each invited to make an original proposal, we were challenged to provide aesthetically satisfying equipment, pleasing and comfortable to the passenger, economical and practical to operate. . . . The Port Authority retained outside consultants, and even undertook computer studies to evaluate as objectively as possible the four proposals made, so we feel it is an outstanding recognition to have been placed first.[6]

A similar, but more protracted process, occurred with the new BART proposals. BART had received money from a local bond issue some time before the passage of the Act in order to study possible subway vehicle design and Richard Ashby, GSI's West Coast manufacturer's representative already engaged in looking after the western interests of three of GSI's divisions, was asked to take on the car division, in order to try and stimulate a transit market in California.

> I agreed, and went to the Car Company in St. Louis for a time to familiarize myself with its operations. . . . In the meantime, BART became very active and we began, along with our competitors, to assist BART formulate some preliminary specifications for their cars. . . . To my knowledge, for the first time in the history of transit, an operational authority went to outside engineering and construction consultants to look at and perhaps introduce . . . technology which had been learned in other industry.[7]

Eventually, outside "joint venture engineering consultants" were hired by BART and the resulting consortium of Parsons, Brinckerhoff, Tudor, Bechtel was employed as BART's consulting engineer throughout all phases of the project. Parsons, Brinckerhoff, Quade and Douglas were experts in subway and tube construction, Tudor Engineering were aerial structures and lightweight construction methods specialists and Bechtel Corp. dealt with electrical and electronics work. This consortium, acting as joint venture engineers, then requested Budd, Pullman-Standard and St. Louis Car Co. to join in discussions for a car design, and subsequently to offer a proposal for a design of car. A similar means was used to induce firms concerned with controls and motors to join the project.

> When the time came for the presentation of the preliminary designs to BART our competitors brought in small models to show those interested. The Car Company and Sundberg-Ferar on the other hand . . . made a sophisticated presentation. We selected a ballroom in the St. Francis Hotel, San Francisco, and invited the board of directors, the BART district staff, and leading Bay Area citizens who had assisted in the creation of the district.[8]

Completed R38 car in stainless steel, 1966.

The presentation was staged by an outside organization specializing in the management of such affairs, and the existence of several mock-ups, as well as three alternate designs, made for an exceedingly fine display. But,

> We went further than any of the other suppliers by bringing in . . . ½ scale actual mock-ups . . . rather than miniature models . . . shipped in by air from Michigan.[9]

The mock-ups had been built for this presentation by a Michigan sub-contractor to Sundberg-Ferar. This company did an exceedingly fine job. On the basis of their presentation and the mock-ups displayed, the Car Company was selected to build a ⅝ size mock-up of the BART design car. Although billed as job 1837 in the company's normal job order number sequence, the mock-up was in fact built at the same Michigan location as the ½ scale mock-ups built previously, and never went to St. Louis at all. The finished mock-up was built on a Freuhauf trailer to give it easy mobility. A mirror was installed inside at the back of the car to give the illusion of a full-size model, and the whole ensemble was shipped by rail to BART's Concord test track, eventually to be displayed at all major Bay Area shopping centers to be served by the new BART subway. Later it was loaned to other cities contemplating new subway systems, including Seattle, Los Angeles, Atlanta, and Washington, D.C.

Until the publication of the final bids in 1967, the spirit of co-operation shown by the car industry in the BART project was remarkable. Nothing like it had been seen since the days of the PCC more than 35 years before.

> This in fact was the car industry's opportunity to express their recommendations, as opposed to what the customer insisted on. . . . Exchanges and reviews would take place and then PBTB would make the final decisions as to the direction the final design should proceed. . . . All were as objective as possible (although attempting) . . . to express their engineering expertise, knowing that in the end a competitive bid would result. At the same time, we knew that this was the opportunity for the great breakthrough in U.S. rapid transit, and almost all gave unselfishly. No one manufacturer ever hoped to recover all the design input costs; it was rather an effort on behalf of the rapid transit manufacturers to expand the market. . . . There was certainly very little money available for research and development in the industry.[10]

A similar type of "courting" operation was mounted in Washington by the Car Company once WMATA had been formed, although this was but a continuation of that undertaken in respect of WMATA's predecessor. For some years the Car Company's Washington representative had kept a

New York R40 car under construction in 1967.

watch on WMATA and its ancestors, and each week kept top executives of St. Louis Car Co. and GSI informed as to the latest developments in Washington. Again, technological innovation was called for in this installation, and many years of preliminary design work and transit supply industry cooperation was involved.

Despite the passage of the 1964 act, remaining streetcar operators seemed reluctant to use the money to upgrade their fleets. A good proportion of the trolleys still in use required extensive rebuilding to keep them in working order during the time needed to design and market new streetcars. Pittsburgh was a good example of a city where streetcars existed in considerable quantity, but bad condition, yet the transit system operators preferred to use their money to buy new buses and replace the cars and tracks in the worst of condition. Even though it was planned to retain at least 100 vehicles, the Car Company could not persuade them to rebuild the vehicles. On one occasion, Bud Meissner offered to ship his own men out to Pittsburgh to do the job there, and thus save $800 per car in shipping charges, but they still could not be convinced. Ironically, when such customers were ready to do the job, St. Louis Car Co. was no longer in business.

By 1967 the average age of a PCC car varied between 15 and 25 years, and no matter how well they might have been rebuilt, if streetcars were to be retained, new types of car were vital. With the Federal money, and encouragement of existing rail systems suddenly fashionable, the Car Company once again began to interest itself in the possibility of constructing new streetcars

> In 1966 or 1967, I made a thorough study of the potential for streetcars, trying to decide whether . . . to update the PCC car or . . . go to a European design . . . We'd quit streetcar development in this country after the last order, whereas in Europe, they'd kept on . . . Duwag was one (company) . . . and we had a great deal of correspondence with them, and I think I even had the draft of a license agreement. Then I left St. Louis Car, and my successor . . . sent the Chief Engineer over there. We knew there was a potential for some cars . . . but the potential in our judgment indicated . . . 600 cars. If you were realistic, it might be . . . less than that . . . It wasn't really attractive to go through a whole new design and tooling, and the trick would be to get the order and spend as little money as possible on it. What we had in mind . . . was importing trucks and maybe the motors and controls and . . . probably build the bodies here. This took a long time to develop. I . . . stimulated the first meetings (San Francisco and Boston) ever had trying to get a standard design . . . By the time (cars were ordered) we were

A 1963 design proposal for a Los Angeles subway car.

Proposed stainless steel *Silverliner* car for the City of Philadelphia, to be operated by the Pennsylvania Railroad.

really out of the business, and Boeing was looking for a way to get in it and thus they bought themselves this first order . . . They may build more, but I don't think the volume is there to justify a complete new design . . . for any long pull. If they build 600 cars . . . I think they will have saturated the streetcar market in this country again."[11]

The older Car Company staff were not now as dominant in the concern as once they had been, and the period 1964-1968 saw the resignation and retirement of practically all Meissner's old executive team, after more than 30 years in the company's top jobs. The men who replaced them did not work as a team in quite the fashion that those who had grown old with Meissner had done. Though Bud Meissner remained in charge of the Division until the end of 1967, troubles with new senior staff developed. Meissner was however determined to deal with these problems himself, while preserving as much as possible the integrity of the company staff team. Consequently, when, during his absence in December 1967, one of his associates on General Steel's executive team replaced a key Car Company man without his knowledge or approval, Bud Meissner offered his resignation. A compromise was reached, and instead of resigning completely, he moved to GSI corporate headquarters as senior vice president of GSI, leaving the day-to-day running of the St. Louis Car Division to others.

CHAPTER 27

It was at this point that the fortunes of the company began to change, as the totally different management styles and techniques of the new men began to be felt. Working as a team under the Meissners, weaknesses in one individual in certain areas of expertise could be minimized with the aid of other individuals in the team. But in the new setup, efficiency was the keynote, and every man who had a job of responsibility was supposed to be a specialist, hired for his competence. Personnel were moved between jobs more frequently and dismissed when they did not work out as well as had been anticipated. To replace them, more new men were brought in, not always from within the ranks of the Car Company, and therefore not always in possession of practical experience in car building. Gradually, the feeling of corporate stability and contentment, so long a feature of working life at the Car Company, began to dissipate and with the increase in tension, production problems, already aggravated by the terms of some of the latest union contracts, became serious. Some of these problems had begun to appear before Bud Meissner's resignation; indeed 1967, his final year with the company, was financially disastrous, owing to the large losses sustained by the stainless steel car plant, and the personnel problems. Volume of business dropped from $50 million in 1966 to $20 million in 1967.

> This constant juggling (of) people . . . was expensive (and) caused plenty of problems in quality and delivery . . . Costs went out of control, and they started losing so much money that it damn near broke General Steel. I'd had some losses too . . . but when you haven't got the business, and you have to take the stuff on a break-even basis . . . you're going to have to take some bummers once in a while[1] . . .

However, the management problems of the late 1960s were not the worst, nor even the major aspect of the problem. The character and kind of customer with whom the company dealt was changing radically, and with it, their style of doing business. Until the 1960s, the typical customer had been a transit company, which in financial structure and corporate hierarchy was essentially an ordinary business corporation, where generally one man was given the sole responsibility for making final decisions on design changes, price and the signing of the contract. Kamman briefly reviewed typical procedure with such a customer.

> The company would learn that someone was interested in a piece of equipment . . . I, and the man in charge of sales, would call on him and see what he was thinking about. Sometime after that, we may get an enquiry. I would get the papers . . . go through (them) and work up a bunch of questions . . .go back and see them . . . and talk . . . Maybe there was some better way to do (it) . . . My people would do what was necessary if some drawings had to be made, or weight estimates. We would furnish the shop with what they needed to know to figure their labor (as well as) the estimating department . . . and the purchasing department . . . All this was brought together in the final estimate . . . and when the estimate was finished, it would go to the sales department. At that time, I would go over there, call the estimator . . . and start questioning his estimates . . .When I was satisfied it was all right then the man in charge of sales supervised the proposals . . . then he and I and . . . Fitzgerald . . . would go to the boss' office and the price would be fixed.[2]

In many cases Meissner (as president) and his chief engineer would then meet with their opposite numbers on a one-to-one basis, to hammer out problems as the work proceeded, and decisions were easy to obtain when action needed to be taken. But during the 1960s, the typical customer was increasingly a publicly-funded Authority or Agency, whose power to make decisions on any given topic was, through no fault of its own, subject to the authority of a governing committee,

Aerial view of the St. Louis Car Co.'s Baden plant, June 11, 1966. *(William J. Clouser collection)*

W. J. Kamman, W. J. Clouser, Bud Meissner and F. P. Beardsley, November 2, 1965. This group is examining a model of a 1941 St. Louis Public Service PCC car built by Clouser, prior to its placement in the Smithsonian Institution's Transportation collection. Notice the ornately carved mantelpiece behind them, which Meissner Senior had installed in his office years before. *(William J. Clouser collection)*

with all the attendant delays and misunderstandings that decision by committee can create. Moreover, as these agencies were handling public money to pay for their new vehicles, they felt an obligation to ensure that the vehicles they received embodied some definite improvement over those previously delivered. Specifications thus ceased to be specific, becoming instead more closely akin to policy statements. This in turn led to increased chances of misinterpretation, and a correspondingly longer period before such mistakes could be put right; a difficult enough situation when dealing with cars of conventional design, but one that could be impossible to live with when constructing cars of new and untried design. Bud Meissner cited as a typical example of such a change, their experience with New York.

> All during the time . . . we were building New York subway cars, if we had any problems, it wasn't too difficult to get the thing settled. Bill Kamman and I could go down there and we'd get a hold of Charlie Patterson . . . the chairman, and Reg Welch . . . the engineer of car equipment, and between the four of us we could settle darn near anything in a couple of hours. We had mutual respect for each other . . . Well, Patterson went out and in effect three guys took his place, and Welch left and (another) bunch of guys . . . came in, and it got to the point where you couldn't even settle the size of the stripe, or (its) color . . . without building a model and having committee meetings, and it would take weeks and weeks and weeks . . . everybody . . . scared of his own shadow, and (with) the people who were supposed to give the answers . . . being incompetent to make a decision, you got no decision.[3]

This was particularly unfortunate for the Car Company. The car builders have traditionally been expected to finance building operations out of their own funds, receiving no money from the customer until the first car of the order is delivered and passes the customer's inspection. This creates tremendous cash-flow problems, and at times it was not unusual for the company to take out short-term commercial loans to finance the construction of a large number of cars. Until the merger with GSI, the company had no access to sizeable financial reserves, and thus was entirely dependent upon the willingness of banks to loan them money—an uncomfortable situation. It had been hoped that the merger with GSI would eliminate this problem.

Unfortunately during the 1960s, financial inflation, and the great slowdown between first intimation of an order, and the final delivery of a car quickly proved even GSI's resources to be less than adequate to finance work. In Kobusch's day, cars had been paid for in cash, or funded through equipment trusts, and at most had been built within three to six months of the order being placed. In contrast, serious work on the BART project went on for over five years before even the bids were called for, and on the WMATA Washington subway project, nearly eight years elapsed before contracts were let.

Another problem occurred when diversification was undertaken, after the increase of work expected once Federal money became available did not materialize. The diversification spread the company's technical resources beyond their limits. Building railroad freight cars, and sophisticated subway passenger equipment in the same plant caused problems enough, and they were all rail vehicles, being built in a rail vehicle manufacturing plant. The Skydock however, was not a rail vehicle; it was an airport jetway.

> I can't claim (said Bud Meissner) that while I was there everything was profitable . . . , but the losses I did have turned out to be very small in comparison to the losses (of my successor) . . . The loading bridge project (the Skydock) is a perfect example of that . . . (We) started building these as sub-contractor for some guy who had bad credit and . . . (we) got into (the project) . . . for about $800,000 . . . (It was suggested) that we take over the company, and some of us were against it, even in writing . . . but . . . (it was done) and we lost more money on that project than the total sales volume . . . (Those) kinds of losses are really what did the company in . . .[4]

The Skydock problem was not crucial to the eventual demise of the Car Company, but it was a symptomatic problem. Ashby commented that:

Proposed car for the Lindenwold line of the Delaware River Port Authority, 1967. St. Louis Car Co. did not get the order.

Proposed subway/elevated car for the Chicago Transit Authority, 1967. Once again, the order did not go to the St. Louis Car Co.

Proposed car for the North-East corridor project, 1967.

> After all, there is a tremendous conflict between the techniques to be used in the same plant for constructing airport bridges and . . . (subway) cars at the same time. (In my opinion) the problem in the last few years was not so much a lack of quality, but financial problems (and) the manufacture of totally (dissimilar) . . . products, which could not be (satisfactorily) accommodated.[5]

Not even the hitherto unfailing subway work was automatically available to the Car Company after 1968. Between 1969 and 1972, New York, Boston, Cleveland and Chicago, all old established customers, asked for bids on large quantities of cars, but the Car Company could not bid low enough to get more than a little of the work. What was much worse was the distressing news that the long-awaited BART and WMATA contracts had gone to Rohr Industries; a consortium based on the corporate structure of a California aerospace industry supplier. The Car Company had been second-lowest bidder on both contracts—a galling situation, made even more unpleasant by the fact that Rohr had never previously built a subway car, and had almost certainly "bought" themselves the chance to do so at such a low price.[6]

Perhaps the final ignominy occurred in September 1972, with the loss of the immense New York R46 contract for 745 (later 752) cars practically identical in design to the New York R44 cars which the Car Company was by then manufacturing. There had been major production problems with the R44 which had inflicted losses on the company through cost over-runs, which it was not permitted to recoup by increasing the already agreed price.

The losses had been serious; $2.8 million in 1970 and over $8.7 million in 1971 for GSI.[7] Over $6 million of GSI's 1971 loss was attributed to the Car Company alone. As a result, GSI had completely reorganized the Car Company's top management early in 1972 and at the same time introduced stringent new financial and budgetary controls. It was hoped that the use of modern cost estimating procedures would assure that future Car Company bids would be based on realistic cost estimates, which in turn would produce satisfactory profits.

At the time, the new approach seemed to make sense, and throughout the summer, the plant showed preliminary signs of pulling out of its seemingly chronic depression. It is also true that 1970 and 1971 had been exceptionally poor years for business. The only substantial work done in those two years had been the completion of work on New York's R40 and R42 contracts, the Vert-A-Pac subcontract, the building of 130 electric double deck lightweight commuter coaches (the HiLiners) for the Illinois Central Railroad's Chicago services, and New York's R44. But in mid-1972, substantial new orders seemed possible. The R46 proposal was already the subject of a bid, at least 15 more HiLiners would be required and new commuter cars for the Chicago South Shore and South Bend line were being considered. In addition, Cleveland was considering the replacement of its original fleet of subway cars, and the Chicago Transit Authority would shortly need at least 550 new cars to replace the Car Company-built subway-elevated lightweight cars, most of which would be over 20 years old by the time replacement vehicles could be delivered.

Some of the new development projects with which St. Louis Car Co. was involved might also have been expected to produce more work eventually. In 1972, two projects were under way. A design study was being undertaken jointly with General Electric, for a gas turbine-electric commuter car, and through a sub-contract from the Boeing-Vertol company, two State-of-the-Art subway cars were being built, and were delivered on August 31, 1972. These cars were little different in overall appearance from the R44 cars, except for their front end, but their electrical and control equipment was more advanced. The then Secretary of Transportation, John Volpe, thought highly of them.

> Despite incremental improvements over the years, the transit systems represent . . . the technology of the past. Our challenge in building these State-of-the-Art cars was to include every new change we could think of and then go out and think of a few more. These cars demonstrate the optimum in current technology in rail rapid vehicle development. Vertol was chosen as systems man-

ager for the UMTA Urban rapid rail vehicle and systems program . . . The development of the State-of-the-Art car is a comprehensive effort, drawing on the resources of many . . . Vertol has brought aerospace systems and management techniques to the program. (The) cars (were) built by the St. Louis Car Co., and, the industrial design was by Sundberg-Ferar. This combination of traditional car builder and aerospace know-how, is exactly what we are looking for to take advantage of the best of both worlds.[8]

In any case, these cars were the last new design turned out of the Car Company plant. The R44 cars, at a selling price of $210,000 each, had been one of the most expensive vehicles ever constructed by the Car Company, and still a loss had been made. Pullman-Standard's 1972 low bid for 200 essentially similar cars on the first proposal for the R46 contract, was $299,700 per car, with a reduction to $273,000 per car on an order exceeding 900 cars.[8] This was an impossible situation. With the R46 contract in the Car Company's possession, there would have been a guarantee of work for at least four years, and a chance to recover the losses made on the R44, by "running-on" the R46 to the existing R44 lines. But without a substantial new contract in their possession, GSI could not possibly continue financing the Car Company losses, without seriously affecting its own financial viability. There seemed no alternative but to cut loose from the financial millstone that the St. Louis Car Co. had become to GSI, and close it down, together with the GSI castings division, which had built all the Car Company's trucks for many years.

The decision to close was made at the beginning of December 1972 when, three months after the award of the R46 contract to Pullman-Standard, no further orders of any size had been received. Almost immediately, Bud Meissner was asked by GSI to supervise the liquidation. Although until then his career at GSI corporate headquarters had proved more palatable than he first imagined it would be, he had mixed feelings about the assignment.

> I didn't really think I'd stay very long (at GSI) corporate headquarters. I didn't think I'd like it. But . . . it wasn't so bad after all . . . and I found out that . . . not having a plant to worry about and unions to fight with . . . was really a (luxury) . . . So I stayed with GSI for longer than I thought I would . . . I'd sworn to myself (though), I'd even put it in writing, that I'd never have anything to do with the liquidation of St. Louis Car . . . but after (all) . . . five years had passed, and there was nobody else around to do it. I felt I could do it as well or better than anyone else . . I never came back into active management of the Car Company. I was merely the corporate officer in charge of supervising the liquidation. We sold millions of dollars worth of stuff ourselves, then we had auctions . . . I finally got the buyers, and worked out contracts to sell the buildings . . .[9]

The plant continued its commercial existence for some months in order to complete the work in hand and deal with warranty problems on the R44, of which regrettably there were many. The bulk of the work had been shipped when in mid-1973, the entire Baden plant was auctioned. Much of the machinery was sold to the Boeing-Vertol Co., and the plant buildings, now emptied of their contents, were turned into an industrial park by their new owners. The engineering office, of all places surely the heart of the company, was not closed until 1974. Even then, the Car Company maintained a ghost-like existence for more than a year, to deal with the continuing R44 warranty problems. But by the spring of 1976, except for the buildings, nothing remained of the company, which for nearly ninety years had been the "Quality Shops" of the American transit industry.

Demonstration of the Verta-Pac freight car concept in 1970.

(below) Car for the Tampa airport expressway system, 1969. This vehicle was an updated "skybus" car.

Airport jetways under construction in 1970.

Inspection of progress on the Hi-liner construction project by Illinois Central officials during 1972.

Completed Hi-liner car ready for delivery in 1972.

FOOTNOTES

Introduction

1. *Street Railway Journal,* July 6, 1901, p. 45
2. *Ibid.*

Chapter 1

1. Articles of Association of the St. Louis Car Co., April 4, 1887. Contained in file 3379, Missouri Secretary of State, company registration office, Jefferson City, Mo.
2. *Street Railway Journal,* July, 1887, p. 601
3. *Ibid,* p. 661.
4. Statement of capital increase, filed August 12, 1887. Contained in file 3379, *op. cit.*
5. *Street Railway Journal,* October, 1887, p. 868
6. *Ibid.*
7. *Ibid.*
8. *Ibid,* February, 1888, p. 58
9. *Ibid,* May, 1888, p. 135
10. *Ibid,* January, 1889, p. 23
11. *Ibid,* September, 1889, p. 280
12. *Ibid,* February, 1890, p. 69

Chapter 2

1. *Street Railway Journal,* April, 1890, p. 205
2. *Ibid,* July, 1891, p. 385
3. *Ibid,* October, 1891, p. 555
4. *Ibid,* November, 1892, p. 697
5. *Ibid,* December, 1892, p. 757
6. *Ibid,* February, 1893, p. 123
7. *Ibid,* 778
8. *Ibid,* July, 1892, p. 443
9. *Ibid.*
10. *Ibid,* June, 1894, p. 405
11. *Ibid,* February, 1894, p. 140
12. *Ibid,* March, 1894, p. 190
13. *Ibid,* June, 1894, p. 404
14. *Ibid,* March, 1894, p. 206
15. In demanding this high standard of finish and elegance to their cars, the street railway operators were following the example set by George Pullman 20 years previously, of providing sumptuously fitted cars, incorporating rare and costly woods, and other luxuries, for a traveling public unused to such elegance. It was felt that the sheer beauty of the car would attract passengers independently of the service the car could offer.
16. *Street Railway Journal,* June, 1893, p. 400
17. *Ibid,* May, 1895, p. 343
18. *Ibid.*
19. Statement of capital increase, filed April 9, 1894. In file 3379, *op. cit.*
20. *Street Railway Journal,* November, 1894, p. 715, lists George J. Kobusch among those attending the Atlanta convention of the American Street Railway Assoc., as a representative of the Kalamazoo Co.

Chapter 3

1. *Street Railway Journal,* October, 1896, p. 638
2. *Ibid.*
3. No records, save for a handful of drawings, exist from the North Broadway period, and it is believed they had already been destroyed by 1911.
4. *Street Railway Journal,* March, 1899, p. 191. The layout of the new plant was as unlike the old as could be. The North Broadway factory had been in essence a specialized type of carriage-building plant. The new Baden plant was essentially a modern railroad car manufacturing plant, similar in many respects to Pullman's Chicago plant.
5. *Ibid.*
6. *Ibid.* It would be fair to say that the cabinet shop, and the men who worked in it, represented the heart of St. Louis Car Co.'s manufacturing capabilities at this time.
7. Statement of capital increase, filed May 18, 1903. In file 3379, *op. cit.*
8. *Street Railway Journal,* May 30, 1903, pp. 812, 813
9. William Marion Reedy, *The Makers of St. Louis* (St. Louis: The Mirror, 1906), p. 66
10. For a detailed history of this transaction, see A. Murphy, *The Consolidation of Street Railways in St. Louis,* unpublished Master's thesis, St. Louis University, 1964.
11. St. Louis *Post-Dispatch,* February 8, 1902, p.1
12. *Ibid,* February 10, 1902, p. 2
13. The St. Louis newspapers published full accounts of the trial for many weeks. Snyder made no attempt to deny Kobusch's testimony, but sought instead as a Kansas City, Missouri resident, to rely on the Missouri Statute of Limitations, which specified a three-year limit to the period in which Missouri residents accused of crimes of this nature were liable to prosecution. As the bribe had occurred four years previously, no one except Snyder was now liable for prosecution, for they had all clearly maintained their Missouri residence. As Snyder's sole answer to the charge was his reliance on the Statute; he made no attempt to deny the prosecution's evidence of his involvement with the bribery. Thus his failure to prove Missouri residence led to his being found guilty of bribery. He was sentenced to five years in jail although he only served 18 months. For a complete contemporary account of the affair see the chapter entitled "Tweed days in St. Louis," pp. 29-59, included in Lincoln Steffens, *The Shame of the Cities* (New York: McClure, Phillips and Co.), 1904.

Chapter 4

1. From an unpublished address to the Birney Club (c) 1920 by a J. G. Brill staff member, presently in the personal research collection of Andrew D. Young.

2. Reedy, *op. cit.*
3. *Street Railway Journal,* May 30, 1903, p. 813
4. Mark Bennitt and Frank Parker Stockbridge (editors): *History of the Louisiana Purchase Exposition* (Universal Exposition Publishing Co., St. Louis, 1905), p. 587
5. *Street Railway Journal,* July 11, 1903, p. 70

Chapter 5

1. The American Car Co. was by 1901 building more than $1 million worth of cars per year, and was by that time St. Louis Car Co.'s principal local competitor. But their financial difficulties persisted throughout 1901 and 1902, and American Car Co.'s final sale to Brill was completed by September 12, 1902.
2. *Street Railway Journal,* October, 1896, p. 631
3. *Ibid.* Laclede Car Co. advertising supplement, pp. 13-18
4. *Ibid,* April 15, 1903, p. 641
5. It was not generally known that the purchase also provided Kobusch with a substantial amount of ready cash, made available by the simple expedient of reducing Laclede Car Co.'s $80,000 of capital to a mere $2,000.
6. *Street Railway Journal,* September 19, 1904, p. 555

Chapter 6

1. *Louisiana and the Fair,* J. W. Buel (editor), (St. Louis: World's Progress Publishing Co., 1905), p. 3169
2. *St. Louis Car Co. at the Universal Exposition.* (St. Louis: St. Louis Car Co., 1904), p. 1
3. *Ibid.*
4. The Car Company began to manufacture these accessories in the early 1890s as part of its continuing diversification process. They opened their own iron foundry on January 1, 1901 *(Street Railway Journal,* July 6, 1901, p. 45) and continued to manufacture these items of ancillary equipment until the Great Depression.
5. *Street Railway Journal,* October 22, 1904, p. 763
6. *Ibid,* December 17, 1904, p. 1092. Nothing is known of the London office, now when it was closed. So far as is known, this was the company's only foreign office. The rest of its extensive foreign business was conducted on its behalf by agents, principally H. H. Böker in the early 1900s. On occasion, there was direct contact between Kobusch, or other top company executives, and representatives of foreign governments.
7. *Ibid,* March 12, 1905, p. 498
8. Letter from E. I. Robinson to E. T. Robinson dated January 25, 1905. All the letters written by Robinson to his son cited in this chapter are included in the St. Louis Car Co. collection, Washington U. Archives, St. Louis.
9. *Ibid,* February 7, 1905
10. *Ibid,* February 19, 1905
11. *Ibid.*
12. *Street Railway Journal,* October 29, 1904, p. 810

Chapter 7

1. Statement of capital increase, filed March 15, 1904. In file 3379, *op. cit.*
2. Robinson's 1905 cruise had eventually taken him to France, where he made contact with the Mors syndicate and initiated the detailed negotiations between the Car Company and Mors. Subsequently, Kobusch established the "Kobusch Automobile Company" to construct automobiles under the Mors franchise. Some prototype vehicles were built by the company, but he quickly felt it advisable to have the greater financial strength of the Car Company behind him and in August 1906, the Mors franchise was taken over by the Car Company.
3. *Motor Age,* August 30, 1906 (no page number) noted that George C. Johns was in the process of making a demonstration run in the American Mors from Chicago to New York, stopping in all of the major cities en route in order to place agencies. See also *Motor Age,* September 20, 1906 (no page number).
4. *Street Railway Journal.* December 8, 1906, p. 1099
5. *Automobile,* December, 1906, p. 394.
6. St. Louis *Post-Dispatch,* February 14, 1909, Automobile supplement p. 2. This article, reviewing American Mors production to January 1909, suggested 875 cars had been sold between September 1906 and January 1909. It is not known how accurate those figures are. American Mors production did not cease until either April or May, 1909.
7. *Railway Age,* April 4, 1905, p. 153
8. Statement of capital increase, filed April 16, 1906. In file 3379, *op. cit.*
9. The preceding discussion is based in part on an analysis made by Ronald DeGraw in *The Red Arrow* (Haverford, Pa.: Haverford Press Inc., 1972), pp. 202-207.
10. *Street Railway Journal,* December 8, 1906, p. 1106. Also see statement of capital increase, filed December 14, 1900, contained in file 3379, *op. cit.*
11. The line itself, after making one small branch-line extension to Norristown, Pa., settled down to an uneventful existence as a high-speed electric interurban and commuter line, still in operation today.
12. *The Horseless Age,* September 18, 1907, p. 773.
13. For a legal view of this extraordinary transaction, see letter of Lehmann and Lehmann to John I. Sullivan, Missouri Secretary of State, quoted in Chapter 12 of this book.
14. *Street Railway Journal* in its 1907 editorials provides excellent examples of the industry's new perception of itself and its obligations.

Chapter 8

1. *Motor Age,* December 27, 1906, p. 4. As this was the same month that the 4-cylinder American Mors was first exhibited commercially, it is almost certain that this 6-cylinder car must have been under development at the time the franchise arrangements were being made with the St. Louis Car Company. It is therefore all the more surprising that Kobusch decided to stay with the 4-cylinder car exclusively.

2. *Ibid,* March 14, 1907, p. 35
3. *Ibid,* May 30, 1907, p. 25
4. *Automobile Age,* October 24, 1907, p. 557 and October 30, 1907, p. 641
5. *Horseless Age,* November 6, 1907, p. 703 has a photograph of a 6-cylinder American Mors fitted with a touring body. So far as is known, this is the only photograph of a 6-cylinder American Mors fitted with a body.
6. *Ibid,* November 18, 1908, p. 687
7. This story was related to the authors by Richard Kobusch, George J. Kobusch's grandson, in an interview conducted on July 31, 1975.
8. St. Louis *Post-Dispatch,* September 3, 1908, p. 2
9. *Ibid,* December 30, 1908, p. 4
10. *Ibid,* May 6, 1910, p. 9

Chapter 9

1. St. Louis *Post-Dispatch,* September 11, 1908, p. 5
2. *Ibid.*
3. *Street Railway Journal,* October 19, 1907, pp. 806-8
4. St. Louis *Post-Dispatch,* August 21, 1910, p. 10
5. *Ibid.* The reason for Beggs' long-term interest in this particular company was never satisfactorily explained. It is true that for many years, Beggs' companies had been good customers of St. Louis Car Co. It is possible that Beggs was maneuvering to establish on his own account in St. Louis, the monopoly on utilities he already had in Milwaukee through the North American Co. He quite probably feared that if he did nothing about the St. Louis Car Co. on his own behalf, North American would.
   On Beggs' relationship with the North American Company generally, see Forest McDonald, *Let There be Light* (Madison: American History Research Center, 1957).
6. *Ibid,* August 16, 1910, p. 1
7. *Ibid,* p. 10
8. *Ibid,* p. 11
9. *Ibid,* August 21, 1910, p. 10
10. *Ibid,* August 27, 1910, p. 2
11. *Ibid,* September 22, 1910, p. 4
12. *Ibid.*
13. *Ibid,* September 20, 1910, p. 5
14. *Ibid,* September 22, 1910, p. 4
15. *Ibid,* October 25, 1910, p. 2
16. Circular letter dated October 31, 1910, quoted in *Electric Railway Journal,* November 5, 1910, p. 960
17. *Electric Railway Journal,* February 18, 1911, p. 307
18. *Ibid,* March 4, 1911, p. 399
19. St. Louis *Post-Dispatch,* May 19, 1911, p. 2
20. *Ibid.*
21. *Ibid,* June 13, 1911, p. 1
22. *Ibid,* June 22, 1911, p. 7
23. *Ibid,* October 16, 1912, p. 6
24. *Ibid,* July 15, 1913, p. 6
25. *Ibid,* May 1, 1914, p. 18

Chapter 10

1. *Street Railway Journal,* June 2, 1906, p. 891
2. Neither the Laclede plant, nor the automobile factory, were ever put back into regular production and (except in wartime) they were leased, thus providing a small source of extra revenue until they were finally sold in the 1950s.
3. *Electric Railway Journal,* October 12, 1912, p. 866
4. Interview with Mrs. Edwin B. Meissner, conducted August 20, 1974. St. Louis Car Co. collection, Washington U. Archives, St. Louis.
5. Other streetcar manufacturers, most notably the J. G. Brill Co., were at this time experimenting with the construction of airframes.
6. Regrettably, he did not take the precaution of contacting the British purchasing authorities to confirm his belief, an omission which was fatal to the outcome of his negotiations in England.
7. On Benoist, see Eugene F. Provenzo, Jr., *Thomas W. Benoist—Early Pioneer St. Louis Aviator 1874-1917. The Bulletin,* Missouri Historical Society, Volume XXXI, No. 2, January, 1975, pp. 101-112
8. The report is included in the corporate records files of the St. Louis Car Co. collection, Washington U. Archives, St. Louis.
9. *Ibid,* p. 2
10. *Ibid.*
11. *Ibid,* p. 3
12. *Ibid.*
13. *Ibid.*
14. *Ibid.*
15. *Ibid,* p. 4
16. *Ibid,* p. 6

Chapter 11

1. *Street Railway Journal,* November 5, 1904, p. 852
2. A review of the developments in steel car design can be seen in *Electric Railway Journal,* January 2, 1915, pp. 3, 4
3. *Ibid.*
4. A useful discussion on the origins of the lightweight one-man safety car, and its design philosophy can be found in the introductory text of Harold E. Cox, *The Birney Car* (Forty Fort, Pa.: Published by the author, 1966).
5. The jitney was a private automobile which operated for hire over the streetcar routes. They were unregulated, and had no major expenses of the type the streetcar companies had to endure. In the years immediately preceding the First World War, jitney competition hurt the streetcar operators badly, since the jitneys' passengers were obtained from the crowds which waited at street corners for the streetcar.

Chapter 12

1. Undated, untitled manuscript on the history of the St. Louis Car Co. by Curtis K. Stadfeldt, written between 1963 and 1965 at the Car Company's plant, Chapter 3, p. 48. The original letter from which this quotation is taken has since been lost, and the authors have not been able to authenticate its text; however, the style of the letter is consistent with other examples of Beggs' writing that have been verified. A copy of the Stadtfeldt manuscript

is in the St. Louis Car Co. collection, Washington U. Archives, St. Louis.

2. Letter from Lehmann and Lehmann to John I. Sullivan, Missouri Secretary of State, dated December 15, 1917. In file 3397, *op. cit.*
3. *Ibid,* pp. 1, 2
4. *Ibid,* pp. 2, 3
5. Interview with Mrs. Edwin B. Meissner *op. cit.*

Chapter 13

1. *Glenn Curtis,* C. R. Roseberry (New York: Doubleday & Co., 1972).
2. *American Heritage History of Flight,* Alvin M. Josephy, Jr. (editor), New York: American Heritage, 1962), p. 164
3. *Jenny Was No Lady,* Jackie R. Lincke (New York: W. W. Norton & Co., 1970), pp. 16, 17
4. Interview with William Fitzgerald, conducted July 3, 1974. St. Louis Car Co. collection, Washington U. Archives, St. Louis.
5. *Ibid.*
6. Interview with Severin Merz, conducted January 30, 1975. St. Louis Car Co. collection, Washington U. Archives, St. Louis.
7. *Electric Railway Journal,* May 23, 1918, p. 1037
8. *Ibid,* May 11, 1918, p. 943
9. Interview with William Fitzgerald, *op. cit.*
10. *Electric Railway Journal,* October 27, 1920, p. 903
11. *Ibid.*
12. Introduction to Skelton catalogue. St. Louis Car Co. collection, Washington U. Archives, St. Louis.
13. Interview with William Fitzgerald, *op. cit.*
14. *Ibid.*
15. Interview with William Fitzgerald, *op. cit.*
16. Interview with Mrs. Edwin B. Meissner, *op. cit.*
17. For details concerning Beggs' return to power at North American see Forest McDonald's *Let There be Light, op. cit.*

Chapter 14

1. An informal, but very useful history of the Electro-Motive Co., and its relationship with the St. Louis Car Co. can be found in *On Time,* Franklin M. Peck (Electro-Motive Division of General Motors Corp., 1948), particularly pp. 24-49.
2. Letter from unknown correspondent to Edwin B. Meissner, February 8, 1924. St. Louis Car Co. collection, Washington U. Archives, St. Louis.
3. Undated letter from E. B. Meissner to J. M. Bosenbury, probably written in February 1924. St. Louis Car Co. collection, Washington U. Archives, St. Louis.

Chapter 15

1. We have been unable to find any documentary proof for this crucial episode. It was used without citation in the Stadtfeldt manuscript on the basis of his interviews with the Meissner family. Mrs. Meissner verbally confirmed the accuracy of the story to the authors in an interview already cited.
2. Letter from Gus Koch, St. Louis Car Co.'s West Coast agent, to E. B. Meissner, November 6, 1925. St. Louis Car Co. collection, Washington U. Archives, St. Louis.
3. Letter from E. B. Meissner to Gus Koch, November 11, 1925. St. Louis Car Co. collection, Washington U. Archives, St. Louis.
4. Articles of Association and Amended Articles of Association of the Liquidating Car Co., 1925. In file 3379, *op. cit.*
5. These statistics were cited in the St. Louis Car Co.'s privately circulated 1925 commemorative brochure. St. Louis Car Co. collection, Washington U. Archives, St. Louis.
6. Letter from Lehmann and Lehmann to E. B. Meissner, June 1927. St. Louis Car Co. collection, Washington U. Archives, St. Louis.
7. *Ibid.*
8. Letter from E. B. Meissner to Lehmann and Lehmann, January 21, 1928. St. Louis Car Co. collection, Washington U. Archives, St. Louis.

Chapter 16

1. Interview with Severin Merz. *op. cit.*
2. Interview with Severin Merz, *op. cit.*
3. *Ibid.*
4. *Ibid.*
5. Interview with William F. Kamman, conducted July 28, 1975. St. Louis Car Co. collection, Washington U. Archives, St. Louis.
6. *Ibid.*
7. *Ibid.*

Chapter 17

1. *Electric Railway Journal,* June 13, 1925, p. 938
2. *Electric Railway Review,* March 6, 1926, p. 428
3. *Ibid.*
4. *Ibid,* p. 427
5. *Ibid.*
6. *Electric Railway Journal,* October 9, 1926, p. 644
7. East St. Louis *Daily Journal,* November 23, 1927, p. 8

Chapter 18

1. *Electric Railway Journal,* January, 1930, pp. 1-26
2. This was the last substantial order to be filled by the company until 1935, and the last on which a sizeable profit was made until the Second World War.
3. St. Louis *Post-Dispatch,* June 1, 1930, p. 8
4. *Ibid.*
5. *Ibid.*
6. St. Louis *Globe-Democrat,* June 6, 1930, p. 5
7. Microfilm of Annual Reports (1925-1969) of the St. Louis Car Co. St. Louis Car Co. collection, Washington U. Archives, St. Louis.
8. Circular letter from E. B. Meissner to the company bondholders, April 11, 1933. St. Louis Car Co. collection, Washington U. Archives, St. Louis.
9. Microfilm of Annual Reports *op. cit.*
10. *Ibid.*
11. *Ibid.*
12. Letters relating to the Scruggs affair are contained in the corporate records files of the St. Louis Car

Co. collection, Washington U. Archives, St. Louis.

13. Orders were so few, that the company became a credit risk, and for a time, the St. Louis banks refused to loan Meissner more money, Kamman recalled that Meissner thus:

    "went across the river to the stockyards, to bank (in Illinois) and they were willing to loan him money . . . His connection with the stockyards resulted in someone over there giving him one or more sheep and at the time this happened . . . we received an order . . . We were all but broke, and he kind of thought this was good luck, and so he went on breeding these sheep through the years, and he . . . raised quite a (flock)."

    Interview with William F. Kamman *op. cit.*

Chapter 19

1. The New Birney was a startling departure from accepted practice. It borrowed heavily from automotive technology, being fitted with propellor shafts for transmitting the drive, universal joints, and internal expanding brakes.
2. Ironically, those properties which did possess research and development facilities, such as those at Louisville, Kentucky, or the Brooklyn and Queen's Co., New York, did not subscribe to the transit industry's erroneous view as to the merits of new car design. These properties felt, and their research departments confirmed their feelings, that only overall modernization of transit properties would help combat competition.
3. See, for example, the editorial in *Electric Railway Journal,* August, 1929, p. 755, which, although written after the first of the regional conferences had concluded, was in fact typical of this attitude.
4. *Electric Railway Journal,* January 1930, pp. 1-25
5. The now-obsolete Birney safety car, because of its small size, light weight and technical simplicity, had been manufactured in relatively standardized form by many companies without difficulty.
6. The body of this car was one of those from the three 1928 experimental cars built by Twin Coach.
7. *Transit Journal,* October, 1933
8. *Ibid,* November, 1933, p. 403
9. *Ibid,* July, 1934, p. 213
10. The AERA had become the ATA during 1932.
11. Interview with William F. Kamman, *op. cit.*
12. *Ibid.*
13. *Ibid.*
14. *Ibid.*
15. After Brill left the PCC project, they designed and marketed their own version of a modern streetcar, known as the "Brilliner." The car borrowed heavily from PCC car technology, capitalizing on the Transit Research Corp.'s reluctance to patent anything except the rubber suspension, and portions of the truck. The Brill-designed truck, which did not use any TRC-patented systems, was the car's principal weakness.
16. Interview with William F. Kamman, *op. cit.*
17. *Ibid.*

Chapter 20

1. Interview with William F. Kamman, *op. cit.*
2. *Ibid.*
3. *Ibid.*
4. Microfilm of Annual Reports, *op. cit.*
5. Interview with Edwin B. Meissner, Jr., conducted August 30, 1974. St. Louis Car Co. collection, Washington U. Archives, St. Louis.
6. *Ibid.*

Chapter 21

1. Interview with Edwin B. Meissner, Jr., *op. cit.*
2. Interview with William F. Kamman, *op. cit.*
3. Stadfeldt manuscript on the history of the St. Louis Car Co. p. 78. Confirmation of this story was given by Severin Merz in an interview conducted on January 30, 1975.
4. *Ibid.*
5. Microfilm of Annual Reports *op. cit.*
6. Meissner, though an exceedingly hardworking businessman, was exceptionally active in community affairs. He was president of Temple Sha'are Emeth for 19 years. He was a St. Louis Police Commissioner, and at the same time was prominent on the St. Louis Race Relations Council, a body which pioneered in the desegregation of public places in St. Louis. In 1949, he was a founder-member of the St. Louis Crime Commission, and was a trustee of the St. Louis Conference of Christians and Jews. In addition, he was a board member of the St. Louis Urban League and was well-known for his custom of accepting parolees from prison, and giving them work in the plant. These represent only a few of his many community activities.

Chapter 22

1. Interview with William F. Kamman, *op. cit.*
2. Interview with Edwin B. Meissner, Jr., *op. cit.*
3. Microfilm of Annual Reports. *op. cit.*
4. Leland Bryant, the industrial analyst, visited the plant during the week of August 16, 1948.
5. *Analytical Study of St. Louis Car Co. With Subsequent Technical Recommendations,* September 7, 1948. The pages of this report are unnumbered. St. Louis Car Co. collection, Washington U. Archives, St. Louis.
6. *Ibid.*
7. *Ibid.*
8. *Ibid.*
9. *Ibid.*
10. *Ibid.*
11. *Ibid.*
12. *Ibid.*
13. *Ibid.*
14. *Ibid.*

Chapter 23

1. Interview with Edwin B. Meissner, Jr., *op. cit.*
2. *Ibid.*
3. Interview with William F. Kamman, *op. cit.*
4. Interview with Edwin B. Meissner, Jr., *op. cit.*

5. *Ibid.* Kamman earlier noted that the price bid by the Car Company was based on turning out two cars per day, in the knowledge that their competitors had bid on a price based on one car per day. Interview with William F. Kamman, *op. cit.*

Chapter 24

1. Elmer C. Wraussmann, *Development of New Passenger Cars.* Paper delivered to the Car Department Assoc. of St. Louis, April 19, 1955, p. 4. St. Louis Car Co. collection, Washington U. Archives, St. Louis.
2. *Ibid,* p. 5
3. *Ibid,* p. 12
4. Interview with Edwin B. Meissner, Jr., *op. cit.*
5. *Ibid.*

Chapter 25

1. Interview with Edwin B. Meissner, Jr., *op. cit.*
2. *Ibid.*

Chapter 26

1. Interview with Edwin B. Meissner, Jr., *op. cit.*
2. *The Qualifications of St. Louis Car Division, General Steel Industries Inc.* p. 4. St. Louis Car Co. collection, Washington U. Archives, St. Louis. This was a Car Company presentation, first used on January 19, 1966.
3. Interview with Edwin B. Meissner, Jr., *op. cit.*
4. *Ibid.*
5. *Ibid.*
6. *The Qualifications* etc. *op. cit.* It is interesting that in the nearly 80 years of the company's existence, the new Transit Authorities were the first customers consistently to ask the Car Company (and the other car builders) to submit its own designs to them.
7. Interview with Richard Ashby, conducted June 16, 1975. St. Louis Car Co. collection, Washington U. Archives, St. Louis.
8. *Ibid.*
9. *Ibid.*
10. *Ibid.*
11. Interview with Edwin B. Meissner, Jr., *op. cit.*

Chapter 27

1. Interview with Edwin B. Meissner, Jr., *op. cit.*
2. Interview with William F. Kamman, *op. cit.*
3. Interview with Edwin B. Meissner, Jr., *op. cit.*
4. *Ibid.*
5. Interview with Richard Ashby, *op. cit.*
6. BART's problems with the cars have been with the control systems, which Rohr had no part in manufacturing. But having encountered tremendous delays and losses in building the cars, and those for Washington, Rohr has now left the car building industry.
7. *Metropolitan,* May/June, 1972, p. 4
8. *Railway Age,* November 13, 1972, p. 13
9. Interview with Edwin B. Meissner, Jr., *op. cit.*

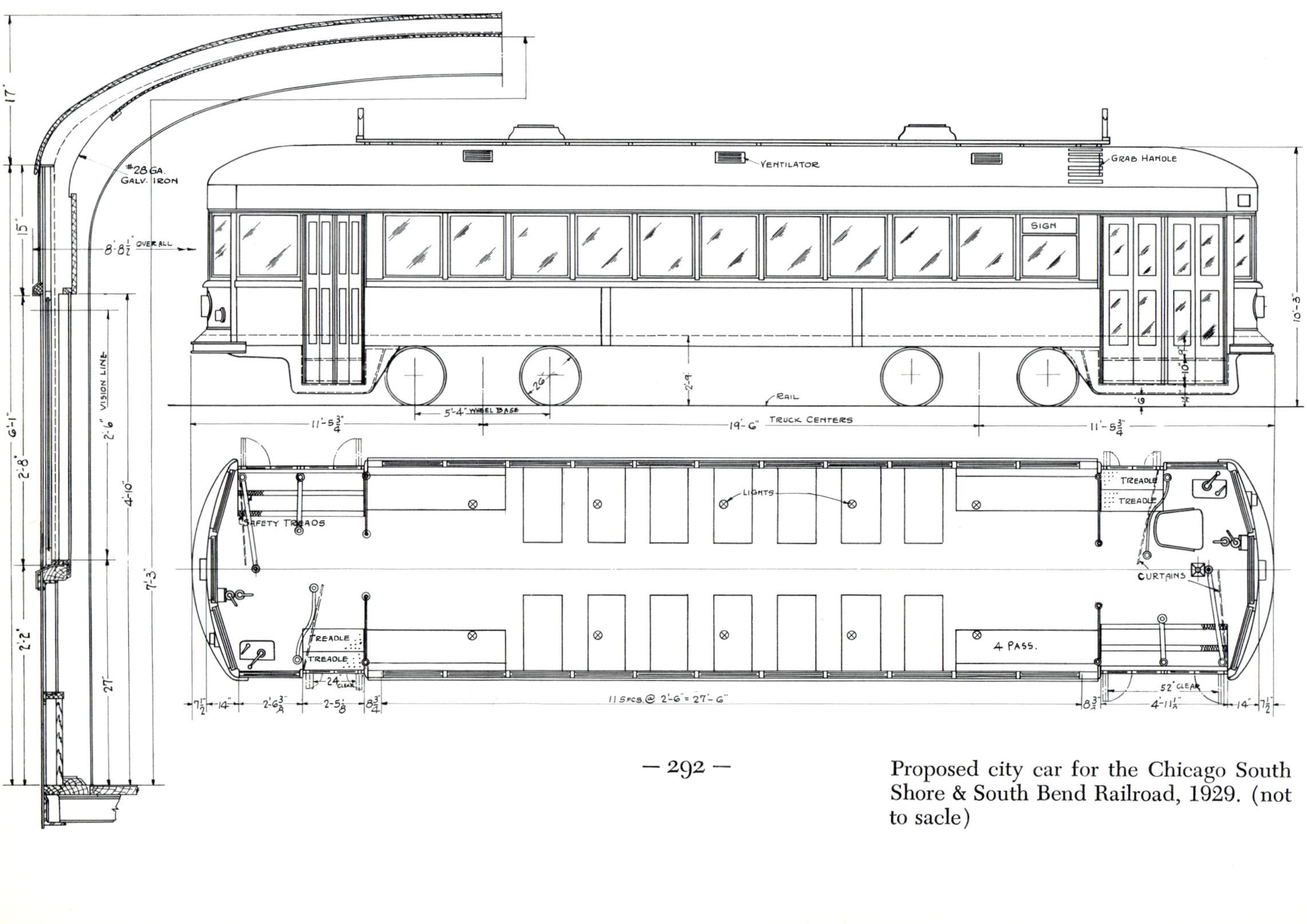

Proposed city car for the Chicago South Shore & South Bend Railroad, 1929. (not to sacle)

Appendix

ST. LOUIS CAR COMPANY

PATENTS

PATENT NO.	PATENTEE	SUBJECT	DATE
689,611	Hagemeier, August H.	Body Bolster	12/24, 1901
687,354	Weber, Moritz	Car-brake	11/26, 1901
689,629	Weber, Moritz	Folding car-step	12/24, 1901
670,190	Witte, Hubert	Car-seat	3/19, 1901
676,169	Witte, Hubert	Car-seat	6/11, 1901
676,170	Witte, Hubert	Car-seat	6/11, 1901
714,979	Weber, Moritz	Locking device for car-seats	12/ 2, 1902
704,227	Witte, Hubert	Ratchet-brake for cars	7/ 8, 1902
709,249	Vogel, Henry F. & M. Weber	Platform-car	9/16, 1902
725,393	Baggerman, Peter C.	Ratchet-handle for car-brakes	4/14, 1903
730,853	Kohout, Ferdinand	Reversible car-seat	6/ 9, 1903
736,639	Scott, John F.	Door-check	8/18, 1903
744,983	Smith, George J.	Car-truck	11/24, 1903
729,980	Vordemfelde, Wm.	Sliding-door fastener	6/ 2, 1903
743,210	Witte, Herbert	Car-seat	11/ 3, 1903
809,620	Meinhard, Theo, P.	Steering Mechanism for motor-vehicles	1/ 9, 1906
812,664	Meinhard, Theo, P.	Transmission gear for motor-vehicles	2/13, 1906
835,917	Roediger, Jacob	Sand Delivery Box for Railway-Cars	11/13, 1906
822,639	Vogel, Henry F.	Railway-car	6/ 5, 1906
824,393	Vogel, Henry F.	Passenger-car	6/26, 1906
809,596	Witte, Hubert	Revolving and Reclining chair	1/ 9, 1906
878,899	Robinson, E. T.	Convertible-car	2/11, 1908
897,017	Robinson, E. T.	Fire-extinguisher	6/25, 1908
878,745	Robinson, E. T.	Auto door-hinge	2/11, 1908
878,828	Robinson, E. T.	Semi-convertible car	2/11, 1908
896,463	Robinson, E. T.	Fireproof support for electrical wires of railway-cars	8/18, 1908
896,464	Robinson, E. T.	Combined sash-holder and sash life	8/18, 1908
897,663	Robinson, E. T.	Convertible automobile body	9/ 1, 1908

ST. LOUIS CAR COMPANY

PATENTS
(Continued)

PATENT NO.	PATENTEE	SUBJECT	DATE
897,664	Robinson, E. T.	Disappearing luggage-carrier for automobiles	9/ 1, 1908
899,763	Robinson, E. T.	Railway-car	9/29, 1908
904,150	Robinson, E. T.	Garment, umbrella, and cane rack for automobiles	11/17, 1908
904,151	Robinson, E. T.	Hood for automobile	11/17, 1908
905,001	Robinson, E. T.	Canopy for automobiles	11/24, 1908
878,830	Sisson, A. H.	Metal window-sash	2/11, 1908
918,185	Miller, W. S.	Draft-rigging	4/13,1909
926,279	Miller, W. S.	Draft-rigging	6/29, 1909
914,751	Robinson, E. T.	Passenger-car	3/ 9, 1909
917,361	Robinson, E. T.	Railway-car	4/ 6, 1909
917,362	Robinson, E. T.	Disappearing luggage-carrier for automobiles	4/ 6, 1909
925,133	Robinson, E. T.	Semi-convertible car	6/15, 1909
926,356	Robinson, E. T.	Door hanger and guide	6/29, 1909
926,309	Witte, H.	Extensible leg-rest for car-seats	6/29, 1909
934,121	Witte, H.	Car-seat	9/14, 1909
935,242	Witte, H.	Car-seat	9/28, 1909
925,066	Witte & Schuermann	Car-seat	6/15, 1909
976,601	Robinson, Edward T.	Passenger-car	11/22, 1910
1,123,777	W. S. Miller	Truck	1/ 5, 1915
1,254,604	Keil, Lewis E.	Journal-box	1/22, 1918
1,303,069	Keil, Lewis E.	Brake-hanger	5/ 6, 1919
1,331,529	Seelar, Luther F.	Spring mounting for car-trucks	2/24, 1920
1,431,050	Seelar, Luther F. & Neal	Driving-horn	10/ 3, 1922
No listing	Neal, Franklin G.	(See Seelar, L. F., and Neal)	
1,557,648	Blair, Joseph H.	Splicing cane ends	10/20, 1925
1,554,135	Seelar, Luther F.	Window post	9/15, 1925
1,619,039	Richards, Leslie W.	Brake	3/ 1, 1927
2,114,743	Lohrman, Robt, F.	Sliding Door	4/10, 1938

PETER M. KLING PATENTS

1887 - 1900 Inclusive

Patent No.	Date	Title
384,530	6/12/1888	Dust Guard for Car-Axle-Boxes
394,774	12/18/1888	Sliding Door for Street-Cars
404,288	5/28/1889	Car Pedestal
404,289	5/28/1889	Track Brake for Street-Railway Cars
417,647	12/17/1889	Street-car-window sash
450,941	4/21/1891	Car Truck
464,100	12/1/1891	Brake Handle
*466,539	1/5/1892	Car Truck for Electric Railway Cars
485,548	11/1/1892	Ratchet Brake for Cars
492,727	2/8/1893	Car Truck
516,934	3/20/1894	Street Car
516,935	3/20/1894	Railway Car
550,757	12/3/1895	Car Truck
614,397	12/15/1898	Transom Sign
612,825	3/28/1899	Car Seat
612,826	3/28/1899	Car Truck
658,949	10/2/1900	Car Seat
658,950	10/2/1900	Car Seat
658,951	10/2/1900	Seat
658,952	10/2/1900	Lacing Attachment
660,902	10/30/1900	Turnstile
660,903	10/30/1900	Buffer for Street-cars
660,904	10/30/1900	Car Seat

*Assigned 1/2 interest to E. Verstraete

PETER M. KLING DESIGN PATENTS

1887 - 1900 Inclusive

Patent Design No.	Date	Title
31,314	8/1/1899	Hand-rail for Car Seats
32,705	5/22/1900	Truck Frame

1887 - 1900 INCLUSIVE

PATENTS ASSIGNED TO PETER M. KLING

Patent No.	Date	Inventor	Title
443,074	12/16/1890	Otis J. Depp and S.J. Munn	Electric Signaling Device for Moving Vehicles
(1/4 interest to P.M. Kling)			
454,532	6/23/1891	Edmond Verstraete	Trolley for Railway Car
457,016	8/4/1891	Edmond Verstraete	Electric Car Brake
465,034	12/15/1891	Edmond Verstraete	Electric Car Brake
(1/2 interest to P.M. Kling)			
467,259	1/19/1892	Edmond Verstraete	Electric Railway Brake
471,639	3/29/1892	Friedrich W. Horstmannshoff	Combined Sled and Roller Coaster
(1/2 interest to P.M. Kling)			

PATENTS ASSIGNED TO P.M. KLING AND G. J. KOBUSCH

Patent No.	Date	Inventor	Title
435,872	9/2/1890	Edmund Verstraete	Pole for Electric Wires, etc.
438,036	10/7/1890	Edmund Verstraete	Pole for Electric Wires, etc.
440,780	11/18/1890	Edmund Verstraete	Underground Conductor
440,781	11/18/1890	Edmund Verstraete	Trolley or Plow for Electric Railways
441,043	11/18/1890	Edmund Verstraete	Underground Wire System
(1/2 interest to P.M. Kling and G. J. Kobusch)			

1887 - 1900 INCLUSIVE

PATENTS ASSIGNED TO G. J. KOBUSCH

Patent No.	Date	Inventor	Title
459,101	9/8/91	Moritz Weber	Ratchet handle for car brakes
463,738	11/29/91	Moritz Weber	Car Truck

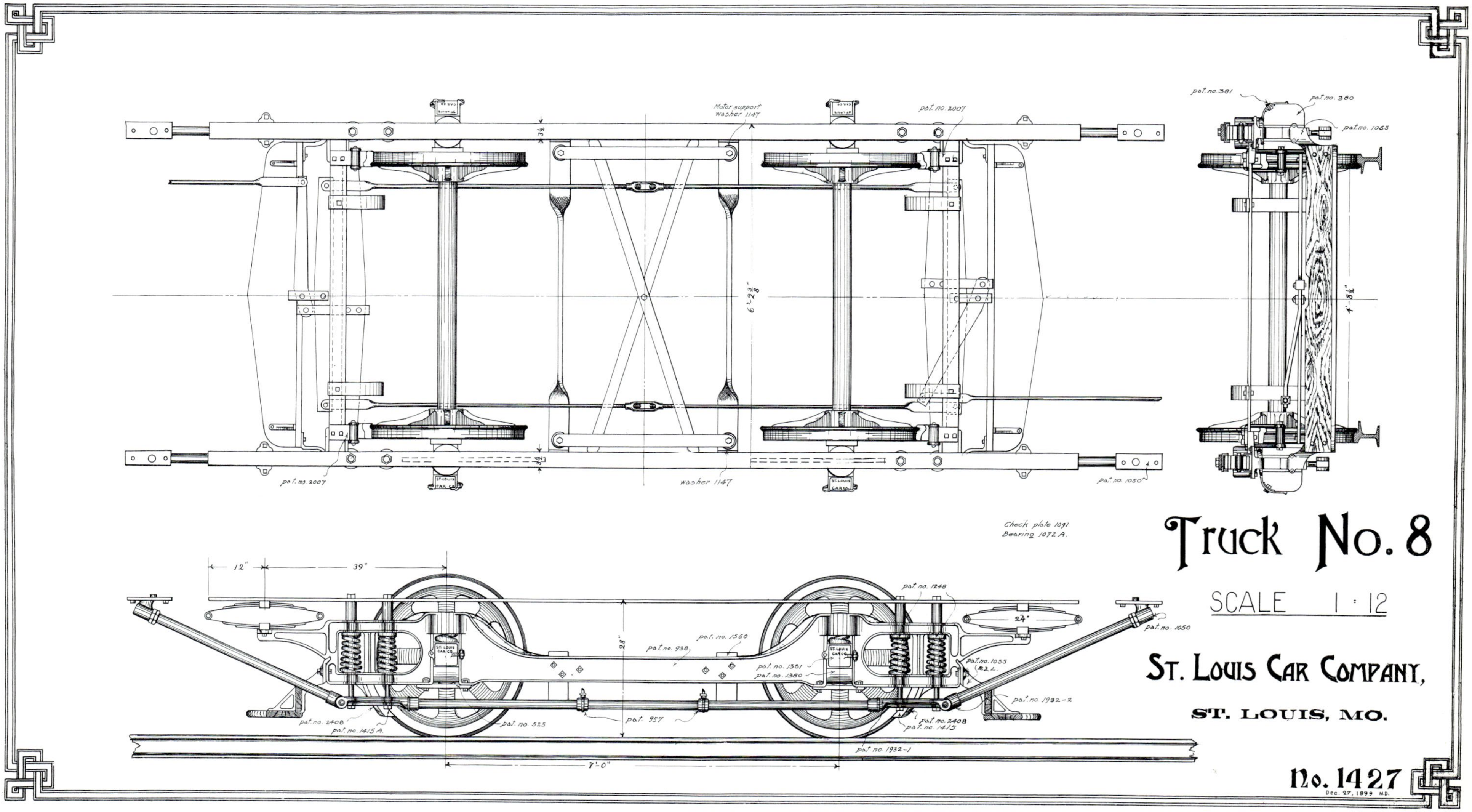

Working drawing for an
early truck. Not to scale.

Index

*Denotes picture reference

— T —

— U —

— V —

— W —

The Spirit of ST. LOUIS

A partial list of the cities where St. Louis Car Company Modern Cars are operating:

Aurora, Illinois
Brooklyn, New York
Chicago, Illinois
Coral Gables, Florida
Dallas, Texas
Detroit, Michigan
East St. Louis, Illinois
Fort Wayne, Indiana
Grand Rapids, Michigan
Jamestown, New York
Johnstown, Pennsylvania
Los Angeles, California
Memphis, Tennessee
Milwaukee, Wisconsin
Muskegon, Michigan
New Orleans, Louisiana
San Antonio, Texas
San Francisco, California
Springfield, Ohio
St. Louis, Missouri
South Jacksonville, Florida

Courage
Vision
Effort
Achievement

First in Baseball!

First in the Air!

First in the building of Modern Electric Railway Cars which are operating successfully in many cities!

Let us assist you with your railway problems

St. Louis
St.
"The Birthplace

Reprint from ELECTRI